1

Corner House Publishers

SOCIAL SCIENCE REPRINTS

General Editor MAURICE FILLER

THE PILGRIMS AND THEIR HISTORY

MANOR HOUSE AT SCROOBY

THE
PILGRIMS
AND THEIR
HISTORY.

BY

ROLAND G. USHER, PH. D.

Professor of History, WASHINGTON UNIVERSITY, ST. LOUIS.

Author of the RECONSTRUCTION OF THE ENGLISH
CHURCH, PAN-GERMANISM, *Etc.*

CORNER HOUSE PUBLISHERS
WILLIAMSTOWN, MASSACHUSETTS 01267
1984

COPYRIGHT, 1918
By THE MACMILLAN COMPANY

REPRINTED 1977

BY

CORNER HOUSE PUBLISHERS

ISBN 0-87928-082-4

SECOND PRINTING 1984

Printed in the United States of America

TO HER
WHOSE STEADFAST AFFECTION
HAS STRENGTHENED AND INSPIRED ME
WHOSE HIGH IDEALS HAVE
UPLIFTED AND GUIDED ME
MY MOTHER

PREFACE

I have attempted a new study of the Pilgrims and their history from the sources. While I was unable to find much new evidence of prime importance, I have perhaps been able to exclude from further consideration the possibility of ascertaining information about the Pilgrims from the evidence concerning the Puritan Movement in England from 1580 to 1610, and from that regarding the history of the Established Church for the same period. But I have been able to place the older material about the Pilgrims in its relation to the more recent evidence concerning English church history, and have as well utilized for the first time the Plymouth First Church records and many Plymouth wills, which contain much of great value on economic and social history. No further accession of evidence is now probable and it is therefore an important fact, though due to no merit of mine, that the narrative presented in these pages possesses a certain aspect of finality. A new study of old evidence and the use of some new material has made possible certain differences in interpretation, in emphasis, and in judgment, the importance of which must not be unduly exaggerated. I have felt it possible to show that the Pilgrims were not subject to active persecution in England from Church or State; that Robinson's Congregation at Leyden was considerably smaller than most students have estimated; and that the really significant achievement was not the emigration itself, but the economic success of the years 1621 to 1627. Indeed, the Plymouth wills make it now possible to claim that the colony was an economic success in the literal sense of the word and that poverty and hardship did not continue at Plymouth as long as has not infrequently been implied. It has also been possible to define rather more exactly the relation of the Pilgrim Church to the Puritans in England and to other Protestant Sects in New England.

At the same time, perhaps the chief excuse for this volume lies in the lack hitherto of a consistent attempt to present the story as a whole, with serious attention to proportion, emphasis, and perspective. Such valuable books as those of Dexter, Arber, or Ames have emphasized only one period or one aspect of the story, while in other books the genealogical information has fairly dwarfed the narrative. I have therefore sought to treat each section of the narrative adequately, and in particular to devote considerable space to the period after 1627, partly because the heritage of most importance to us seems to be that of this particular period, and partly because comparatively little attention has hitherto been paid to it. While our genealogical information about the Pilgrims' immediate descendants is vast in bulk and frequently entertaining and vital, I have felt it important to emphasize the political narrative and to subordinate all genealogical detail.

The conclusions of most importance are frequently to be reached only by elaborate inference and deduction from indirect evidence and are sometimes in the end no better than presumptions and probabilities resting upon a lengthy process of conjecture. To attempt to give, even in important instances, the whole train of logic and the evidence on which it is based, is to create a critical apparatus of quotations, references, and speculations wearisome and vexatious to the general reader and not really necessary for critical students. In such a mass of inference, the Pilgrims and their history have sometimes been lost to sight. It has become increasingly common in books on the Pilgrims to reproduce as many of the old abbreviations and contractions as can be provided in modern type with the result that a familiar and simple idea is presented to the reader in such strange guise that he fails to recognize it. Nor does such meticulous accuracy serve any real purpose. I am not aware of any passage the meaning of which is in doubt or from which additional information can thus be extracted. Frequently, too, such reproductions raise in the minds of readers unskilled in research a presumption of a critical judgment and of an extent of information in the author which are not always realized. I have preferred to subordinate the critical apparatus to the narrative proper and to reproduce in citations what Bradford or others would have had printed rather than exactly what they wrote.

This is the fifth in a series of related monographs which I am attempting to write on the constitutional and administrative history of the Tudor and Stuart periods in England. This particular volume, though not without relation to my previous books, the *Reconstruction of the English Church* and the *High Commission*, is primarily a part of the treatment of the period between 1610 and 1640, upon which my studies have already been prosecuted at considerable length, but on which as yet nothing has been published, partly because the war has temporarily suspended access to the English archives, and partly because it has also made difficult the publication of technical books which appeal only to a very limited number of readers. I am venturing thus to call attention to my continued interest in Stuart history because the character of the research itself, aside from fortuitous interference, may require some years of work still before the more important volumes can be finished.

I have already made repeated acknowledgments in my previous books of my indebtedness to many foreign scholars and archivists, but I cannot close this preface without acknowledging once more, in this of all books, the influence upon me as a student of Edward Channing. To no single man, out of many in Europe or America to whom my indebtedness is great, do I owe so much.

ROLAND G. USHER.

Washington University,
    Easter, 1918.

CONTENTS

LIST OF ILLUSTRATIONS

THE PILGRIMS AND THEIR HISTORY

THE PILGRIMS AND THEIR HISTORY

CHAPTER I

SCROOBY AND AUSTERFIELD

In the autumn of 1606, about fifty or sixty men and women began to gather weekly for devotional exercises in the chapel of an old Manor House at Scrooby, in northern England, about forty-five miles south of the city of York. They thanked God that they had been vouchsafed a glimpse of the true Light and walked no longer in darkness; that they were separated from that abomination of Anti-Christ, the Church of England. They assured each other of their ability and willingness to bear with all fortitude the persecution and travail sure to be entailed by this obedience to "the Ordinances of God." There were among them none of wealth, birth, or learning as those words were then or are now used; they professed religious ideas maintained by a few hundreds at most in the British Isles, if not in the world; they lived in a part of England not then considered important; they were simple farmers, tilling the open fields of an old hunting park, between moors and fens alive with game. Their little assembly was too insignificant to attract the attention of the Puritans in southern England or to rouse the officials of the Established Church to more than a spasmodic and perfunctory hostility. But they took courage from the words in Ecclesiastes: "the race is not to the swift, nor the battle to the strong, neither yet bread to the wise, nor yet riches to men of understanding, nor yet favor to men of skill; but time and chance happeneth to them all." And they were right. Among them were the leaders of a mighty movement— the emigration of Englishmen to the New World in search of homes. They were the true progenitors of the westward march of the Anglo-Saxon race, a group of men and women worthy of becoming the ancestors of a virile nation of one hundred millions of souls.

The spiritual origin of the Pilgrim movement [1] lay in the impulse toward freedom of thought which was itself the root of the Protestant Reformation. The historical and literary study of antiquity, the new knowledge of the classic languages, the new texts of the Scriptures proved to Lutherans and Calvinists that the Papacy of 1521, its hierarchy and usages, was not warranted by the Scriptures. Christianity had been defiled, its pristine purity sullied by the introduction through the agency of the Popes of pagan ritual and ceremony. The task of the reformers was clear: to reject the innovations of the Pope, to abjure him as

---

[1] "As applied specifically to the early settlers at Plymouth, Pilgrim first appeared in 1798 and Pilgrim Fathers in 1799." Bradford and others had used the word pilgrim, but not as a generic historical designation. From about 1800 till the middle of the nineteenth century, the term was applied indiscriminately to all early New England settlers, but was then by more critical students limited to Plymouth colonists. This usage of the term Pilgrim has been consistent for not more than forty years. See interesting information on this point collected by Albert Matthews in *Publications of the Colonial Society of Mass.*, XVII, 293–392.

the Man of Wrath, and to establish once more on earth in all its pristine purity the primitive Church of Christ. In convincing their own followers of the verity of this great discovery, they found the most cogent evidence in the Scriptures themselves. Read the Bible, they besought the men of their own time. Read and see that there is nowhere mention of Pope or hierarchy, of this ceremony or that practice, of copes or indulgences. Read and see that we are right and that the Pope is wrong and a usurper, the untrustworthy servant in the vineyard of the Lord, who shall be thrown out by the servants when the Lord shall come.

It became, however, speedily necessary that the reformers themselves should define with some precision what form of discipline and doctrine Christ had instituted. Once this definition had been promulgated, once Calvin, Luther, and Zwingli, Knox, Cranmer, and Whitgift had made up their minds, they became one and all convinced that the Scriptures could be understood only by those to whom God had vouchsafed the truth. Accordingly, the new reformed organizations insisted upon a conformity with their own particular practice and belief no less rigid than that against which they protested, and each expelled from its ranks without mercy or hesitation those who ventured to differ from it in the interpretation of primitive Christianity. In England the peculiar circumstances under which the Reformation was begun, the character of Henry VIII and of his daughter, Elizabeth, the peculiar temperament of the English people, resulted in a compromise between the old forms and the new platform. After a good deal of hesitation, a few sweeping changes in doctrine and discipline were affirmed, but, while many of the observances of the Roman

Catholic Church were definitively abandoned, in outward appearance the old service and the old discipline still predominated in the observances of the Established Church of Elizabeth. The Pope was expelled but the hierarchy remained.

The little group of people, who separated from the Established Church with such consecration and seriousness in the autumn of 1606, had thoroughly grasped the injunction of the reformers to read the Scriptures for themselves. Their strong and practical minds quickly appreciated the inconsistency of a liberty of thought and expression which permitted the laity to find in the Scriptures only the material they were told was there, and which denominated all further examination into the truth as "unholy prying." They opened their eyes and saw in the Bible proof that the Church was not yet purified, that the reformers were no more infallible in their interpretation of Scripture, no more consistent in practice, nor more liberal in attitude than the "Bishop of Rome" whom they rejected with such determination. The Reformation had not been thorough, the Pope himself had been abjured but not his "detestable enormities." They found in the Scripture no more warrant for the bishops and deans of the English Established Church than for the Pope and his cardinals. They saw no more proof in the New Testament of the validity of a prayer-book and canons than they found for the mass and indulgences.

Scrooby was hardly a favorable environment for so radical a Protestant movement. Situated about forty-five miles south of the city of York and about fifty miles north of Lincoln, along the great highway leading from London to Edinburgh, within easy ride of the old Sherwood Forest long connected by legend with Robin Hood, there lay to the north and west of Scrooby great districts in which the Roman Catholics were at the time of Elizabeth's death in the overwhelming majority. In the immediate vicinity of Scrooby were powerful Catholic families. From this district had come the Pilgrimage of Grace and the Rising of the North. From it the leaders of the Bye Plot had confidently expected support and it was not yet certain in 1605 that the fears of a Catholic rising were entirely groundless. Indeed, the Protestants in the North of all descriptions had commonly preferred to bury their own differences and present a determined front to the Catholic majority who had not yet accepted the fact of the Reformation.

About Scrooby we know a great deal, thanks to its location upon the great highway between London and Edinburgh.[1] The officials who collected the information for Domesday Book recorded its existence as a part of the property of the Archbishopric of York, but it was not in 1606 and indeed never had been since the Norman Conquest an agricultural or industrial district in any proper sense of the word. It was in fact a hunting lodge, located upon a tongue of fenny land, thrown out in the midst of the moors, broad lakes, and swamps of the lower Trent valley. It was also a sort of halfway-house used by official travelers, north and south, and an occasional residence of the Archbishop of York or his officials when occupied with affairs in the southern part of the Province. A good many notables, first and last, slept there from the Conquest down to the time when Margaret Tudor paused overnight on her journey north to marry James IV, from which marriage was to spring the union of England

[1] See the notes at the end of the Chapter.

and Scotland. In the early sixteenth century there was a good deal of hunting at Scrooby. Wolsey himself spent a whole month in the house. The custom had been for the Archbishop to travel with his servants, furniture, linen, and plate and set up for a time his establishment in the great Manor House, and, when His Grace pleased, he departed bag and baggage and left the empty house and its outbuildings in the care of a Receiver or Bailiff.

The population at Scrooby consisted therefore of the small tenant farmers and their laborers, connected more or less immediately with this estate of the archbishops, and living around the Manor House, subject in civil as well as in economic matters to the authority of the Archiepiscopal Receiver or Bailiff. There was of course no leisured class; men of any education at all were few; and the little district boasted no residents of wealth, birth, or station. For all that it was a place of some consequence and of considerable size. Leland, the official historian of Henry VIII, found at Scrooby a great house of two courts, built of timber and brick, standing on a plot of some six or seven acres, the whole surrounded by a deep moat. As the years elapsed, the Manor House fell into decay, perhaps because the game became less abundant and the House less used; toward the middle of the century the number of buildings were certainly fewer; and, when James I on his progress to London in 1603 noted it as a useful hunting lodge, he also remarked upon its "exceeding decay."

There is today little left at Scrooby to tell of these times. Except for the slender gray spire of St. Wilfred's Church and a few parts of the present stone farmhouse, there is nothing left which the eyes of Brewster or Bradford might have seen of the great estate on which Wolsey

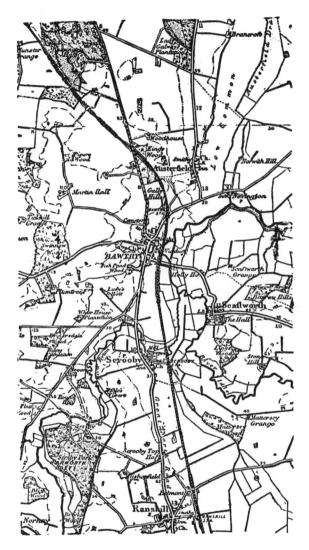

MAP OF THE SCROOBY REGION

amused himself and which Elizabeth and James I coveted. The very earth is different. The moors and fens have been drained and ploughed; the game has departed, leaving only the lark and the cuckoo behind; the tangled thickets are now waving fields of grain, dotted by scarlet poppies and fringed with hawthorn, wild roses, and honeysuckle. Here and there only is an untamed spot, where the brilliant yellow of the gorse against the dark green of its own foliage gives us a suggestion of the sort of landscape the first Pilgrims left behind them.

In this town of Scrooby, there had come to live about 1571 a certain William Brewster and his wife, with a small son some five years old. About him we know nothing prior to his appointment by Archbishop Grindal in 1575 to the office of Receiver and Bailiff of the Manor of Scrooby and "all liberties of the same in the County of Nottingham." He became not only the Archbishop's agent in the management of his farms and in the collection of rents, but also the civil authority, for this particular district was legally and administratively exempt from the County of Nottingham. He must also have exercised such ecclesiastical jurisdiction as there was when the Archbishop and his commissaries were not themselves present. Some seventeen little groups of people in villages lived on the large domain and of them his position made him practical ruler. Although Grindal agreed to pay him only £3 6s. 8d. in money a year, the position was calculated to be worth not less than £170 a year, the equivalent today of about $4000. In 1588, this William Brewster was appointed Postmaster under the Crown; Scrooby was made a posthouse on the road to York and it became his duty to provide horses for the Queen's messengers, and such privileged travellers as rode post, and to keep an inn where they might remain until it became convenient to pursue their journey.

It is obvious therefore that the father of the famous William Brewster was a man of some substance and position, easily the most prominent individual in the little village and its immediate environment. The boy tasted somewhat of this modest affluence, was prepared somehow or other for the University, and matriculated at the college of Peterhouse at Cambridge in December, 1580. He began residence at the great Puritan University of England, although not at its most radical college nor under the instruction of the most erudite and magnetic of Puritan teachers. But its atmosphere was electric at just this time with radical tendencies. Peter Baro, eminent as a Calvinist, was Professor of Divinity; William Perkins, whose books Brewster later owned, was lecturing at this time; and at least four notable Puritans and Separatists were in residence—Udall, Penry, Greenwood, and George Johnson. There is no record that Brewster ever received a degree and it is indeed not clear whether he remained at the University two years or only a few months. We do know from Bradford [1] that he achieved there a firm knowledge of Latin and "some insight into Greek," that he there became inoculated with radical religious ideas, and was "first seasoned with the seeds of grace and vertue." This probably denotes Brewster's own belief that his radical views originated in Cambridge. The autumn of 1583, however, saw him in London as a member of the household of William Davison, at this time a man of some consequence at Court, serving in various administrative and diplomatic capacities. How Brewster became connected with him,

[1] See the note at the end of the chapter on the Bradford *History*.

exactly in what capacity he "served" him, we do not know. Bradford is our only informant, and, while he makes it clear that the relationship was close, he does not show good reason to suppose that Brewster was anything more than a sort of confidential attendant, something better than a valet but a good deal less important than a secretary, a position which, if not menial, could hardly be called official. Certainly, he won Davison's confidence and demonstrated a certain ability. How closely he followed his patron in his many expeditions and journeys we have no means of knowing.

He must have seen a good deal of England and Scotland, something of court life, much of London, and certainly accompanied Davison on one or more of his important diplomatic missions to the Netherlands in 1584 and 1585–86. Bradford alludes in an account written half a century later to a long ride across the Eastern Counties on the way back from Holland, when Davison placed around Brewster's neck the great gold chain presented to the Ambassador by the States General, and bade him wear it as they fared on towards London. Undoubtedly, this was one of the few incidents of that time which stuck clearly in Brewster's own memory, and which he told and retold in those long evenings of quiet and amiable conversation at Plymouth. In 1587, on the disgrace of Davison after the execution of Mary Stuart, Brewster remained with him for some little time—perhaps attending him while he was in the Tower—and then returned to Scrooby, urged apparently by the illness of William Brewster, Senior. At any rate he was acting as his father's deputy in January, 1588–89, and at his father's death in 1590 continued to discharge the functions of Master of the Post and of Re-

ceiver and Bailiff. After some little misunderstanding
and difficulty, he was confirmed in the position of Master
of the Post, which he retained until 1608. He married in
1591 or 1592 and had three children before the exodus to
Holland, the first, born about 1593, named Jonathan, a
Biblical name not then common as a Christian name; a
second child, born about 1600, called Patience; and a
third, who seems to have been born just before the
flight to Holland, named Fear. Both girls lived to reach
Plymouth. About this time Brewster's mother, Pru-
dence, died. Other relatives he does not seem to have
had.

There is little reason to doubt that Brewster was the
leading spirit in gathering the little group of people which
was afterwards organized as a Church and which finally
took up its permanent abode at Plymouth. Exactly how
and when it was organized we do not know. The usual
form of Puritan growth in southern England was the
gathering of a classis of ministers who then proceeded
to convert the laity and to draw them together into
churches. In many cases some wealthy man or woman of
rank appointed to benefices, of which they owned the
advowson, Puritan clergymen whose energy and magnetism soon converted the laity. Possibly the influence
of two radical ministers was responsible for the group at
Scrooby. Richard Clifton was minister at Babworth,
some seven or eight miles south of Scrooby, and had
developed as early as 1595 pronouncedly radical ideas.
About ten miles east of Scrooby, at Gainsborough, was
located John Smyth, once Fellow of a Cambridge College,
who professed even more radical notions about government and doctrine.[1] Members of the later Scrooby group

[1] Much information about Clifton and Smyth will be found in

certainly worshipped from time to time with these groups in the ten years following 1595; probably both ministers officiated occasionally in the Manor House at Scrooby, but the nucleus of the famous Plymouth Church was a little group of laymen gathered together by the magnetism and high personal example of Brewster himself.

They did not at first renounce the Established Church nor refuse to attend its services, and had for the first years or months no minister, teacher, creed, or organization of any sort. Apparently they met at first with the utmost informality on Sunday afternoons or during the week. Later meetings were begun on Sunday forenoon, but such Puritan preachers as happened to be travelling through Scrooby or whom they could induce to come to them for a time from a little distance were their utmost reliance, and the expense was borne, Bradford hints, very largely by Brewster himself. Not until the autumn of 1606 did they conclude to separate from the Established Church and organize a Church of their own. Bradford explicitly declares that the Plymouth Church was created at Scrooby,[1] but in the light of its later history at Leyden it is hardly likely that they had reached any more definite conclusion than that the Established Church was not warranted by Scripture and that they must separate from it forthwith. Indeed, a phrase from their Church Covenant of Leyden days quoted by Winslow reveals a decided fluidity of opinion about organization and discipline. "We promise and covenant with God and one with another to receive whatsoever light

Mr. Champlin Burrage's useful, if discursive, *Early English Dissenters*, two volumes, Cambridge, 1912.

[1] *History*, 14.

or truth shall be made known to us from his written Word." Of the personnel of the group at this time we know only too little.[1] It comprised only a minority of the people actually living at Scrooby, with an indeterminate number from nearby villages—certainly by 1607 Clifton himself and some of his group from Babworth, and less probably some of Smyth's congregation at Gainsborough, the majority of which (with perhaps some of Clifton's Church) had already migrated to Amsterdam.

One extremely important recruit now came to them, who had been converted to Puritanism by Clifton, William Bradford, a young lad, not over eighteen years old at this time, and perhaps not more than sixteen.[2] His father, then dead, had been a substantial farmer in the neighboring village of Austerfield, was one of the two residents who were assessed for subsidy, and apparently therefore owned some considerable property in land and goods. The boy's uncles and cousins were all honest farmers of more or less property and had cordial relations on an evident equality with the best families of the hamlet of Austerfield and the surrounding villages.

---

[1] Most elaborate researches by Dr. Hunter and by Rev. H. M. Dexter and his son, Morton, have identified as residents at Scrooby or Austerfield only Brewster, Bradford, and "a bare possibility," one George Morton.

[2] The date of birth we do not know. Mr. Dexter, after correctly quoting the date of Bradford's baptism from the register—"the XIXth day of March, Anno dm. 1589."—unaccountably transposes it into New Style as March 19–29, 1588–89. It should be of course March 19–29, 1589–90. Dexter, *England and Holland of the Pilgrims*, 389. Dates of the month in this volume have been kept Old Style; those of the year however, in accordance with common historical usage, have been changed to New Style.

While still a child, young Bradford was intended by his uncles, who became his guardians after the father's death, for "affairs of husbandry" upon attaining his majority and receiving his inheritance, but, as he tells us, being somewhat weak in body, his thoughts turned elsewhere and his study of the Bible combined with the magnetism of Clifton converted him to Separatism and made him a member of the Scrooby group.

About this time there came to them a young man of about thirty, possessed of two Cambridge degrees, who had also been Fellow of Corpus Christi College—John Robinson. His earlier career is in many ways still obscure.[1] He seems to have remained at Cambridge until about 1603, and then to have been presented to a benefice in the Established Church in or near Norwich, where he came into contact with one of the strongest bodies of radical Protestants then in England. Perhaps he was suspended for non-conformity, but was at any rate chosen in 1603 preaching Elder of St. Andrews, Norwich, and stayed there till 1606 or 1607, tormented with doubts and spiritual misgivings. For a while he may even have made some effort to meet the technical requirements of the Established Church. He paid a visit to Cambridge and there heard two sermons about the Light and the Darkness "between which God hath separated" and "the Godly hereby are endangered to be leavened with the others wickedness." He determined to leave the Established Church and drifted somehow from Cambridge back to Norwich and thence to Lincolnshire and Scrooby. There he joined this little congregation of men and women who "shooke of this yoake of antichristian bondage and as the Lords free people,

[1] C. Burrage, *A Tercentenary Memorial*, Oxford, 1910.

joyned them selves (by a covenant of the Lord) into a
church estate in the felowship of the gospell to walke in
all his wayes, made known, or to be made known unto
them, according to their best endeavours, whatsoever it
should cost them, the Lord assisting them.   And that it
cost them something this ensewing historie will declare." [1]

BIBLIOGRAPHICAL NOTES

Until the middle of the nineteenth century nothing was
known of the origin of the Pilgrims in England.   Bradford's
History of Plimouth Plantation had been used by Nathaniel
Morton in his *New England's Memorial*, 1669, and by Prince,
the author of the well known *Annals*, but Bradford gave
neither names nor details about their English residence.
Nor did any of the Pilgrims leave behind in writing or oral
tradition any clue.   In 1842, Mr. Savage, editor of the papers
of John Winthrop, Governor of Massachusetts Bay, interested in this problem the Rev. Joseph Hunter, the noted
antiquarian and student of the history of northern England.
In 1849, Dr. Hunter was able to announce that the

[1] Bradford, *History*, 13.   The reproduction of the abbreviations and typographical peculiarities of the manuscripts and older
printed books has not been carried in this volume as in some of
those recently published about the Pilgrims to a point of meticulous
accuracy.   If we are to write u for v, vv for w, ye for the, yt for
that, we must also decline to expand the common contractions.
The truth is that we cannot with modern type reproduce the
manuscripts and books with exactitude and it therefore has seemed
better to follow the practice of scholars in general and print what
the author meant to write.   Spelling and punctuation have been
scrupulously followed but all the abbreviations and contractions
have been consistently expanded.   It should be more generally
known that the y in ye is an old diphthong for th, and in quoting
Bradford I have so rendered his text, on the ground that the and
not ye was what Bradford thought he was writing.

main facts were established, substantially as related in this chapter.

To make definitely sure nothing had been missed, Dr. H. M. Dexter, a wealthy Congregationalist minister of New Haven, Conn., devoted most of his life to untiring researches upon the Pilgrim history previous to the migration to America. Archives in England and Holland, public and private; church registers without number; all repositories of any sort within a wide range of Scrooby or Leyden; all American collections; the vast pamphlet literature of the period, directly and indirectly concerned with non-conformist history, all were tirelessly ransacked. Not less than thirty years of work is represented by the volume, finished and published by the son after the father's death, *The England and Holland of the Pilgrims*, Boston, 1905, xiv, 673. The volume contains not merely all definitely ascertained facts about the Pilgrims, but also the entire residuum of this extensive research in facts about them possibly relevant, about places they may have visited, men they may have known, books they might have read, and such information about the events of English and Dutch history as in any degree of probability they might have learned.

The present author felt that the records of the more general Puritan movement between 1600 and 1610 must contain something of importance with reference to the Pilgrims, and that the history of the English Church at large would shed extensive light at least upon the charge, so universally believed, that the Pilgrims were persecuted and "harried from the land" by Archbishop Bancroft and James I. To his surprise, elaborate researches in the manuscript and printed literature only established more and more firmly the negative but excessively significant fact, that the authorities at London can not be shown to have known even of the existence of the Church at Scrooby. There seems now to be no collection of material in England, Holland, or America, even remotely relevant, that has not been thoroughly ransacked for Pilgrim material. Something like finality may therefore be assumed for the main features of the narrative as given in this volume.

The Bradford History. The only title used by Bradford was *Of Plimoth Plantation.* It was written at Plymouth in 1630 and subsequent years from his own notes and recollections as well as from letters and from oral testimony. Used in manuscript in the seventeenth century by Morton and in the eighteenth century by Prince, the manuscript disappeared, carried off perhaps during the Revolution by some American Tory refugee or by some British soldier, and was finally discovered in 1854 in the Library of the Bishop of London at Fulham Palace. The manuscript is now in the State House at Boston. The full text was published in 1856 with notes by Charles Deane by the Massachusetts Historical Society. A photographic facsimile edition appeared in 1896. The State of Massachusetts published in 1898 a careful reprint, which contains a number of corrections of Deane's transcript and adds some sixteen lines omitted. While Deane's notes are invaluable, his edition is long since out of print and is accessible only in the larger libraries. References in the footnotes of this book are therefore to the official edition of 1898. So much of the narrative depends solely on Bradford's authority and the date is generally so direct a guide to the passage referred to, that page references to Bradford have been given only for particularly important or elusive facts. A reprint of the text of the official edition of 1898, with notes by W. T. Davis, was published in New York in 1908 in the series *Original Narratives of Early American History.* The most recent edition, with elaborate notes by W. C. Ford, sumptuous letter press and illustrations, was printed by the Massachusetts Historical Society in 1912 in two volumes.

CHAPTER II

THE EXODUS FROM ENGLAND

No sooner was the little congregation "gathered" than persecution began. Not indeed by Church and State; the orthodox majority at Scrooby and the nearby villages, the friends and relatives of the Separatists, raised vehement objection to the new Church. Numerous too they were compared to the new congregation, for we can be quite sure that prior to this time there was no trace of Puritanism or Separatism in the district, and that after the migration of the little church the population was orthodox enough.[1] Behind this opposition was something akin to indignation that any Protestants should turn traitor to the great cause in the face of the Catholic majority in Northern England, and so cherish their own particular angle of thought as to decline to coöperate against that common enemy, the Scarlet Woman. But there was also behind it much honest dislike that these relatives and neighbors should presume to stand apart in Pharisaical attitudes as holier and wiser than the rest.

Was not the Church which their fathers had accepted good enough for these? Was this William Brewster, to whom they had so long paid their rents, and whose

[1] Cotton Mather in his life of Bradford in the *Magnalia* no doubt accurately represents the oral tradition at Plymouth about those left behind at Scrooby. "The people were as unacquainted with the Bible as the Jews seem to have been with part of it in the days of Isaiah; a most ignorant and licentious people."

orders they had so long accepted, who had grown up
among them from a child, to be rated then as a prophet
and wiser than the learned in London, Oxford, and Cambridge?   Was this pale and puny youngster, William
Bradford, who in truth declared himself too weak and
too proud to hold the plow, like his honest father and
grandfather, now to stand forth as instructor and leader
in the deepest experiences men can have?   Their hostility was outspoken and frank; the scoffing and jeering
frequent and biting.   All made a deep impression on
Bradford.   He could scarcely credit the testimony of his
eyes and ears.   A great light had shone upon him,
clarifying his mind and uplifting his soul, and now his
relatives and friends made this most sacred of experiences the subject of derision, made religion itself a
"byword, a moking-stock, and a matter of reproach."
He could neither excuse nor entirely forgive it.   It was
too unwarranted, too unjust.   He resented the prying,
spying, watching which became its constant expression.
The importance of this hostility of the little community
must not be underestimated, if we are to grasp one of the
really significant reasons why the Pilgrims concluded
life in England to be unbearable.   Such daily nagging,
scoffing, and deriding was to them the most difficult of
persecutions to endure.

From the authorities at London and from the ecclesiastics at York had thus far come neither reproaches
nor interference.[1]   The Archbishop of York, for the

---

[1] There is absolutely no evidence in the records, civil or ecclesiastical, that the existence of the Scrooby group was known
at Whitehall or at Lambeth, before the attempt to flee in 1607 led
to the report by the Magistrates of Boston to the Privy Council.
Nor was importance attached to their existence then.

previous decade, Matthew Hutton, was one of the most tolerant of Anglican clergy and too much in sympathy with Puritan objections to the established order, to interfere with so peaceable a congregation, located in so out of the way a place. Like most of the Northern clergy, he felt that the profession of the essentials of Protestant faith was all that should be expected or exacted in the face of the Catholic majority. The definite judgment had long been maintained at London, that, so far as the laity was concerned, no interference with conduct, belief, or practice was to be attempted by the constituted authorities, except for breaches of the peace or opposition to the temporal authority of the Crown. As a little body of laymen, who had until 1605 or 1606 openly attended the services of the Established Church, who were moreover residents of a tiny district exempt both from the county of Nottingham and from the jurisdiction of the regular ecclesiastical courts at York, ruled only by the personal authority of the Archbishop as Lord of the Manor, the Scrooby congregation had attracted no attention and had certainly not been molested by the authorities.

Now however in 1607, the ecclesiastical authorities at York instituted proceedings of inquiry into the reports and complaints which the hostile majority of the Scrooby district disseminated.[1] Hutton was dead and a new prel-

[1] This is a point of much interest and importance. We have no positive information other than inferences from Bradford and the meagre court records at York, and what we know about the routine work of the High Commission, as shown by material utilized in Usher's *Rise and Fall of the High Commission*, pp. 380, Oxford, 1913. The entries in these cases are entirely formal; prosecution *ex officio* was commonly assumed by the court in such cases because informants refused to prosecute; the failure to utilize the full

ate that knew not Joseph ruled in his stead; at Canterbury and at London the new dispensation of Bancroft had determined to put pressure upon the non-conformists, in order to force them either to accept the Church or to leave it. The orders had therefore gone forth to investigate promptly and thoroughly all complaints of divergence from the Prayer Book and Canons of 1604. We accordingly find at least five members of the new Church summoned before the Ecclesiastical Commissioners of the Province of York—Gervase Neville in November, 1607, and in the month of December Richard Johnson, William Brewster, Robert Rochester, and Francis Jessop of Worksop, a village about nine miles from Scrooby. Perhaps others were also cited but there is no mention in the ecclesiastical records of Clifton, Robinson, or Bradford, nor were any other persons than these named accused of Separatism or Baroism. The excellence and completeness of the ecclesiastical records at York for this period, the record of proceedings against the five named, make it probable that no other proceedings were actually instituted.

Neville was arraigned by the High Commissioners on November tenth, and charged with membership in a sect of Baroists and Brownists, with maintaining erro-

possibilities of fines, excommunication, and attachment, the failure to follow up the regular routine subsequent to citation are inconsistent with the initiative by the authorities in opening the case. When a decision to prosecute came from above, particularly when it came from London, action was prompt, thorough, and severe. Failure to follow up a case almost invariably means that the information was a presentment by individuals. The well attested animus of the people at Scrooby and the inferences from the records seem therefore fully to warrant the statement in the text.

neous opinions and doctrine repugnant to the Holy
Scriptures and the Word of God. He seems to have first
denied the charge and then to have proved it, by stoutly
informing the Archbishop and his officials that they were
an anti-Christian hierarchy, with other remarks which
they declared in the indictment to have been irreverent,
contemptuous, and scandalous. They committed him
to jail in the Castle of York for trial and further proceedings. The others were not tried because they were
not apprehended. Legal summons were served upon
them by an officer of the court sometime in November,
and they all promised to appear on December first.
They judged it expedient, however, to absent themselves, and on the twenty-second of April the court records prove that they were still at large. Bradford explains this. "For some were taken and clapt up in
prison, others had their houses besett and watcht night
and day, and hardly escaped their hands; and the most
were faine to flie and leave their howses and habitations
and the means of their livelehood."

It must be owned that from what we know of the
activity of the High Commission elsewhere, the treatment the Scrooby congregation received was far from
severe.[1] Indeed Neville was handled with considerable
charity. The procedure of the Commission had for
nearly a generation insisted that the culprit should take
the oath *ex officio*, and should not be allowed under any
circumstances to testify without taking it; if he steadfastly refused, he was to be committed tc prison until
such time as he did take it, and should thereupon be

---

[1] This again is a point of importance and the evidence about
the Commission's practice, on which it is based, is considerable in
amount, of unimpeachable quality, and varied in character.

tried, fined, and imprisoned for his offence. . Not long before Greenwood, Penry, and Udall, all of whom had been at Cambridge in Brewster's time, had been executed for this very crime of Separatism in London. Yet Neville was permitted to testify without taking the oath, and, though committed to prison for a time, was, after no long confinement, released without further examination or trial. He reached Amsterdam either with the Scrooby party or soon after. The proceedings against Brewster, Johnson, and Rochester were the merest routine. Even after several months' failure to appear, they were not adjudged contumacious and excommunicated, nor was the assistance of the temporal authorities sought to apprehend them. That much indeed was commonly done by the High Commission or the ecclesiastical courts in any case, however insignificant, where the culprit declined to appear. The Puritans in the South in fact completely disregarded such simple steps as these. Hundreds of the laity, both Churchmen and Puritans, cheerfully endured much severer treatment than this without qualms of any sort, as the records of the High Commission and of the Consistory Courts demonstrate at large.

Whatever others would have thought of it, the men and women at Scrooby objected to it vehemently; but we shall only partly understand their decision to leave England if we see in the exodus a mere flight from implacable authorities, or the simple expression of the fear of the consequences likely to be visited upon them for remaining in England. It is a great error to stress the hostility of the Church toward them and say that they were harried from the land. This action by the Church officers seems merely to have hastened the crystallization of their own religious dissatisfaction with conditions in England, for they went voluntarily. The Pilgrim movement was in truth a crusade for righteousness, a search for Utopia, a pilgrimage to the Promised Land. Their sufferings are those of Christian in *Pilgrim's Progress;* their trials and tribulations those which they believed all who follow the Lord Jesus truly must expect to endure. They were seeking no mere temporal peace, no mere freedom from courts and bishops in a temporal sense, no mere toleration of non-conformity, but a pure and congenial atmosphere uncontaminated by heresy and anti-Christ. "Their desires were sett on the ways of God and to enjoy his ordinances." The same impulse which now led them to leave England later caused them to leave Holland.

England was unclean. It was dangerous to remain there longer, for those who would worship God in all sincerity and purity must guard against the pollution and contamination of the Beast. They must not only themselves obey God's Ordinances, but they must steadfastly refrain from contact with those who derided and denied them. How could the new Church then remain at Scrooby, where the majority of the people opposed and resisted the Word of God, truly preached? How could they stay in England where the law of the land maintained in existence a vain hierarchy of anti-Christian prelates and forbade the worship of God according to His Ordinances? The vital objection to the Established Church was not so much its activity in persecution as its existence. To Robinson and Brewster the chief difficulty lay in the temporality of the Church—the hierarchy of Bishops and Deans, the laws and advowsons, the courts and judges, the ritual, ceremony, and apparel. It was all a relic of Paganism, there was no warrant in Scripture for any of it. It had been foisted upon an unsuspecting Church by the Papacy, but to accept it now when the Light had been separated from Darkness, when the revelation of Christ was seen, was to renounce salvation. To remain in contact with it was to risk defilement.

In one breath the leaders at Scrooby condemned the Established Church and the Puritan party in southern England. Indeed the latter were more guilty, if anything, than the prelates. They had seen the Light but had not followed it; the Truth had been revealed to them but they had chosen rather to walk in darkness, to soil themselves with pollution and to consort with the unclean, to hold rectories and cures in the Church of anti-Christ, to accept money for reading the Prayer Book, for wearing the vestments, for celebrating the communion. The very fact that the Puritan ministers strove so vigorously to remain in the Church, to secure the connivance of the Bishops at a few "irregularities," was sufficient in the eyes of these men to condemn them utterly.

The breakdown of the Puritan movement after 1604, the failure of the leaders to maintain a solid front against the Established Church, their acceptance of the Canons of 1604 and the Visitation Articles issued in 1605, the willingness of the majority to remain "unseparated," were indeed the significant causes of the separation of the Pilgrims from the Church and of their exodus from England. There was no longer hope of any regeneration in the Church itself. The influence of Bancroft with the King, the definiteness of the new Canons, made further reform from within improbable. Nor was there hope of regenerating the Puritan party. They had sold their heritage for a mess of pottage. There was no one left in England with whom the Pilgrims might hope to have communion. They were surrounded by scoffers and scorners, by the emissaries of anti-Christ, and by the Puritans who compromised truth in order to retain their stipends. All was wrong, all was uncongenial, unclean, and from it they fled.

The different view it is now possible to take of the general policy of Bancroft and of the beliefs and actions of the Puritan party in general is therefore a genuine contribution to an understanding of the Pilgrim movement and of the true impulse behind it.[1] When it was supposed that Bancroft's régime was one of great harshness and injustice, in which the most learned of the English clergy were ruthlessly deprived and driven from the Church, the emigration of the Pilgrims seemed to be logically enough the direct result of ecclesiastical persecution. They left England because they were not allowed to stay, because men of their opinions were persecuted by Church and State alike. As a matter of fact, the Puritan clergy were not persecuted nor did they leave the Church. Some sixty were temporarily deprived or suspended in 1604 and 1605, of whom the great majority soon conformed, accepted the tests prescribed by Bancroft, and continued to preach in their parishes without molestation. In the history of the Pilgrims there is no more vital and important fact than this— that the overwhelming majority of the Puritans ac-

---

[1] The evidence for this general view of the Established Church and of the Puritan party in England at this time has been developed in Usher's *Reconstruction of the English Church*, 2 vols., New York and London, 1910.

cepted the Established Church and remained members
of it, read its Prayer Book, and performed voluntarily
its ceremonies. They were the fathers of the men who
came to Boston, Salem, New Haven, and the River
Towns. Assuredly, we shall never grasp the story of the
early years in New England nor understand why Plymouth did not grow in numbers, as successive waves of
Puritans reached America, unless we bear constantly
in mind that the Pilgrims voluntarily left England to
avoid contact both with the Church and with the Puritans who accepted it. Indeed, the Puritans and Bishops
taunted the Pilgrims with running away from a persecution which did not exist, with silly fears of little things,
with an insistence upon indifferent matters. One and all
the Separatists denied stoutly that they left because they
were afraid, because they were driven out, or because the
temporal persecutions were severe. One and all they
asseverated solemnly their deep conviction that association with Church or Puritans was dangerous to spiritual
welfare, was a compromise with Truth, a failure to observe God's Ordinances.[1]

If go they must, the Scrooby congregation could not
long doubt whither to turn. The probable location of
the Promised Land was already clear. Two years before
Smyth's congregation had gone from their own little
district to Holland, and had found there, as they well
knew, spiritual comfort and a congenial environment.
The fact that these neighbors of theirs, farmers like

---

[1] The controversial literature is full of material on this point.
See in particular *Confessio Fidei Anglorum Quorundam in Belgia
Exulantium*, etc., 1598, preface; supposedly the work of Ainsworth
and Johnson; and Robinson's *Answer to a Censorious Epistle*,
1608; Ashton, *Works of John Robinson*, III, 405–420.

themselves, had made a livelihood in Holland proved to the leaders that the migration was not, as the rank and file thought, an adventure almost desperate, but one in all probability certain of success. The exodus seems to have been decided upon in the spring or early summer of 1607, and for it they soon completed their simple preparations. Land and houses most of them did not own, for they were tenants at will of the Archbishop. Such property as Brewster had he converted into money; and the rest followed his example. Household goods, clothing, books, they proposed to take with them. How many went is not known. Bradford's description of the journey to Holland is scarcely consistent with a movement of less than one hundred people, and the number of the congregation in Holland in later years makes this seem a probable estimate. The law forbade them to leave England, to carry money of any sort out of the kingdom, or to export goods without written authorization. It was extremely difficult to secure permission to emigrate without any intention of returning, carrying both money and goods. That was a permanent loss to the realm of which the authorities did not approve. Certain that permission to emigrate would be refused, primarily on economic grounds, they resolved to go without permission, and were forced therefore to flee like "criminals or conspirators."

"A large company of them" travelled overland to Boston in Lincolnshire, and there quietly arranged with a certain shipmaster to convey them and their goods to Holland. After considerable waiting at the out of the way place appointed, he finally appeared at night, took them on board, and then, to their astonishment and indignation, betrayed them to the customs' officers and searchers of the district. The latter rowed them ashore in small boats, searching both them and their goods with great thoroughness for the forbidden gold and silver, proceeding with the women so far that the men were highly indignant. Landed at the town, they were paraded into the market place, "a spectacle and wonder to the multitude which came flocking on all sides to behould them." This too the high-spirited Bradford could scarcely endure. Then their books and goods having been taken away, they were led before the magistrates, who committed them to honorable confinement, probably in the houses of some of the townspeople, while messengers hurried to London to ask the Privy Council for instructions as to further proceedings with them. They were used meantime with great courtesy, as even Bradford must confess, and were shown such leniency and favor as was possible. The Privy Council considered their offence unimportant, and sent orders for their release, so that after about a month's detention they were all sent back to their homes, except seven of the leaders who were kept at Boston to be turned over to the assizes. Of the latter Brewster was one. If they ever appeared before the judges, they were released, for we have no knowledge of subsequent trial, conviction, or confinement.

Indeed, a number of the party successfully reached Holland in the autumn of 1607 and some months later the rest of the contingent tried again to escape. They arranged with a Dutch captain, who owned his ship, to take them on board south of the Humber, where the coast was shelving and deserted. Thither the women and children with the baggage travelled in a boat or boats, apparently down the river Idle to the Trent, to the

Humber, and thence along the coast, while the men walked overland. The boats arrived a day before the ship, and, the sea being extremely rough and the women in consequence very sick, they put it into a little creek nearby to wait, until the gale should have blown itself out. The next morning according to arrangements the ship did come. The men also arrived, but the boats with the women and children were stuck fast on the shoals of the creek and their utmost endeavors could not move them. The shipmaster began to take the men on board, while waiting for the tide to come in, and the first boat load had already reached the ship, when suddenly a numerous and motley crowd from the country side, some on horseback, most on foot, some with muskets and some with older weapons, were seen approaching in the distance. The news had spread that somebody was escaping. The Dutch captain waited to learn no more, but weighed anchor, hoisted his sails, and departed, carrying the men who had gotten aboard, leaving the rest on shore, and the wives and children stranded in the creek. The latter were by no means the most distressed at the happening, because those on board had no money, no clothes but those on their backs, and were as much concerned at leaving their wives and children behind them as the latter were at being left. Bradford, Brewster, and the leaders were still on shore, however, like good generals, and, sending the majority of the men off to escape arrest, remained to take care of the women. The latter were weeping and crying, some for their husbands who had been carried away in the ship, others for fear of the consequences of the arrest, others again "melted in teares seeing their poore litle ones hanging aboute them crying for feare and quaking with could." Thus these dangerous conspirators were captured by the formidable force sent out after them.

Once taken, the local authorities were nonplussed to know what to do with them. The constables apparently hurried them around from one Justice of the Peace to another, from this court to that, only to make up their minds that the simplest escape from the dilemma was to connive at their departure for Holland. The Bishops and their commissaries, of whose hostility to the Pilgrims so much has been written, are not mentioned by Bradford, nor is there evidence to show their knowledge of the Scrooby congregation's flight. The only evidence concerns the officious meddling of minor local civil officials. Even they do not communicate with the ecclesiastical authorities nor the latter with them; they informed the Privy Council the first time, but not the second, and received from London orders to release the captives, not to punish them. Surely there is here no proof that State or Church was anxious to persecute the Pilgrims or drive them from England. A half-hearted attempt was made to keep them at home, but in the end they escaped with the connivance of the local authorities and without interference from Lambeth or London.

Thus in one way or another, after considerable anxiety and temporary suffering, all arrived safely in Amsterdam. Brewster and Bradford came among the last, having stayed to make sure that the weakest and poorest should successfully cross. Clifton arrived in August, 1608, and it seems probably that that month marked the end of the exodus. Real danger only the men who sailed away with the Dutch captain seemed to have encountered. Their ship met a great storm in the North Sea and for fourteen days was driven hither and thither at the mercy of wind and waves. For one entire week, they saw neither sun, moon, nor stars, and were unable indeed from the crude instruments they carried to make out where they were. Even the sailors were frightened, and once, with shrieks and cries, declared that the ship was sinking. The Pilgrims, according to Bradford, fell on their knees and prayed with such fervor and faith, that the ship weathered the storm and finally made port. United once more in Amsterdam, they held solemn services of humiliation and thanksgiving for their deliverance from the hand of the Spoiler.

CHAPTER III

Doubts of their ability to make a living in Holland had caused the emigrants many misgivings before the exodus, but the economic opportunities for such as they at Amsterdam were numerous, and the experience of other religious refugees from Germany and France, as well as from England, had demonstrated the feasibility of the experiment. Holland had made great strides in commercial development during the sixteenth century and no city had benefited from the general prosperity more than Amsterdam. The growth of the herring trade, the shift of the cloth industry from Flanders to Holland after the fall of Antwerp, the rapid increase of the Dutch merchant marine, plying between Europe and the East and West Indies, had created a great demand for unskilled labor of all sorts and kinds. Nowhere in Europe was there at that time a community in which a hundred pairs of hands could be more quickly or easily put to work.

All this the leaders of the Scrooby Church saw when they held council together in the summer and autumn of 1608 and debated earnestly arrangements for permanent residence. But these economic opportunities were to their thinking more than offset by the religious disadvantages. Amsterdam was "the Fair of all the Sects where all the Pedlars of Religion have leave to vend their Toyes." They knew themselves to be welcome, but they saw received with equal eagerness Anabaptists, Socinians,

Jews, Arians, and Unitarians, heretics quite beyond the possibility of salvation, with whom contact was even more dangerous and contaminating than with Papists and Episcopalians. To fill their cup of woe to the full, they concluded regretfully that the English Separatist Churches of Johnson, Ainsworth, and Smyth, were in grave danger of falling from Grace, and that the Dutch Reformed Churches were blind to the Light in the Word of God. These could not be congenial associates. They decided to seek some place where there were neither heretics nor English, some place where they should live as nearly as might be alone, and observe together the Ordinances of God whose perpetuation was the prime motive of their exodus from Scrooby.

After some hesitation they pitched upon Leyden as a permanent residence,[1] attracted by the fame of its University, by favorable economic opportunities in a flourishing city of fifty thousand people, given over to the manufacture of cloth, and in particular by the absence at Leyden of other religious malcontents. The Dutch Reformed Church they would have to contend with, but the cosmopolitan heretics at Amsterdam and the quarrelling English Separatists they would thus leave behind. An application to the magistrates at Leyden in

[1] Beyond the few inaccurate brevities in Mather's *Magnalia* and Prince's *Annals*, nothing was known about the Pilgrims at Leyden till the researches of George Sumner in 1842 and H. C. Murphy in 1859. The publication of Bradford's *History* in 1856 helped little for he gives no direct description of the life at Leyden. nor were Robinson's theological treatises of value for the narrative, the conditions of life, the membership, and the like. Our present knowledge, however, is the result of the elaboration of Sumner's and Murphy's researches by Dr. Dexter and his son in no less than eleven visits to Leyden.

December, 1608, or January, 1609, for permission to emigrate thither in the following May was granted apparently without objection on February 12, and in the spring
some hundred or more went thither under the leadership
of Robinson. Clifton, their first minister, remained
behind with some of the congregation, who were accredited to the Ancient Church of Johnson and Ainsworth.[1]

Unfortunately we know relatively little about the
Pilgrims at Leyden despite the almost incredible diligence
of Dr. Dexter and his son. The names of one hundred
and fifty-two men, women, and children have been
discovered who were certainly members of Robinson's
Church and the names of seventy-two who were in all
probability associated with the Church. The greatest
probable maximum number of persons, men, women, and
children, from 1609 to 1620 is four hundred and seventy-
three.[2] At Leyden were also one hundred and sixty-nine
English people during this period who may conceivably
have been associated with the Church but whose connection is not demonstrable. From a possible four hundred
and seventy-three and a less possible six hundred twenty-
six came the thirty-five who eventually sailed on the
Mayflower. In the Dutch records are also evidence of
some score of marriages and many births and deaths; the
places of residence of a considerable number of Robinson's congregation have been established with some
certainty. Thirty-three of the men became citizens of
Leyden before 1620. In 1610 the little group bought a
rather considerable house, in whose upper story Robinson

[1] The best and most recent account of these Separatist Churches
is C. Burrage, *Early English Dissenters*, Cambridge, 1912.
[2] See Appendix A on the number of Robinson's Church.

and his family lived, and in whose lower rooms the congregation met. This was their church. Some individuals purchased land from time to time; some bought houses; others built them; but beyond these bare details very little is known about the great majority of members and still less can be definitely established about their experiences together.

Certainly they found the life hard and the atmosphere uncongenial. After about seven years' residence—a time long enough to give the experiment a fair trial—they concluded that their conception of the Church could not be perpetuated in Holland, because of the unfavorable economic conditions and because of their inability to control civil and religious affairs. The unconscious pressure of an established community upon the fluid organization of the little congregation was too great to be withstood. It is upon this aspect of the life that Bradford lays greatest stress in his summary of the reasons for leaving Leyden. They seem to have had little difficulty in finding work, but extraordinary difficulty in winning more than a bare existence. The members of the Scrooby Church had been small farmers and husbandmen, perhaps nothing more than laborers on the farms of others, and they now found themselves in a maritime and industrial community without skill in the various enterprises conducted there and without the necessary capital to undertake others of their own. Indeed the only occupation they understood, agriculture, was not possible at Leyden. The skilled trades and highly remunerative occupations were controlled by craft guilds in the interests of their existing members, and the requirements for admission, rigidly maintained, invariably insisted upon Dutch citizenship, some little capital, and much experience. For those who were neither citizens nor had capital to invest such trades were out of the question.

Practically all found themselves condemned to labor extremely hard for small wages in the least skilled crafts. Some twenty became say weavers, making a sort of coarse thick cloth not unlike a very inferior quality of heavy blanket; eight became wool-combers; four or five became merchant tailors, wool carders, fustian weavers, hat makers, printers, while the remainder of the company in ones and twos were distributed among some forty other occupations. Nearly all of these involved hard manual labor for from twelve to fifteen hours a day. William Bradford became a fustian weaver. The only other thing we know about his life at Leyden is his marriage, December 10, 1613, at Amsterdam, to Dorothy May, a young girl of sixteen. She was the daughter of Henry May of Wisbeach, Cambridgeshire, England, who was probably a prominent member of Ainsworth's Church and who himself witnessed the banns at Amsterdam on November 9, 1613. She accompanied Bradford on the *Mayflower* but was drowned at Provincetown. Their only son, John, remained at Leyden, but reached Plymouth in 1627. Edward Winslow became a printer; Isaac Allerton a tailor; Robert Cushman a wool-comber; Jonothan Brewster, the eldest son of William, a ribbon-maker.

When William Brewster first came to Holland, he seems to have brought with him a larger sum of money and more household goods than the majority and was able with difficulty to eke out subsistence for some years from his slender capital. In 1616, forced to earn money in some way and unable to perform the heavy manual labor required by most of these occupations, he became a printer in partnership with another member of the congregation, Thomas Brewer, apparently not one of the Scrooby Church, but a later acquisition. The press did no job printing, as it is now called, nor did they keep an open shop where books were for sale, nor did they print books intended for circulation in Holland. The object was the publication in English of books intended for circulation in England, but prohibited by the Government. The edition, once prepared, was shipped to London to be sold by their Separatist and Puritan friends. Not more than sixteen volumes [1] represent their labor in the three years 1617, 1618, 1619, proving that the plant was by no means a large one and hardly a remunerative business. In 1619, Brewster printed David Calderwood's *Perth Assembly*, a description of ecclesiastical affairs in Scotland highly uncomplimentary to the English King and his ministers. The English Ambassador, Dudley Carlton, at once complained to the Dutch authorities and insisted that

[1] Mr. Dexter gives 16; Arber lists 15; Rev. O. G. Crippen lists 9 in the *Congregational Historical Society's Transactions*, December, 1901, 110–111. The results of Pilgrim research have yielded so meagre a return for so excessive an amount of labor, that students have tended to regard conjectures not obviously unwarranted as interesting and important. Indeed, it is to be feared that Dexter, Arber, and Ames have all more than once assumed bare possibilities to have been already demonstrated as truths. So in this case. Only two books bear Brewster's name; two more he admitted printing; two others Carleton, the English Ambassador, said that Dutch printers believed he printed. We have a definite total of four and a probable total of six. The rest listed by Arber and Dexter bear no imprint or mark of identification and cannot be demonstrated by evidence ever to have been printed in Holland, to say nothing of tracing them to the Pilgrim Press.

Brewster had broken the Dutch law by printing and exporting the book. Escaping the bailiffs with the aid of his friends, he migrated with his family to England, where he seems to have lived from July, 1619, until the *Mayflower* sailed. Brewer was apprehended, but eventually escaped serious penalty, primarily because the University of Leyden, on whose books he was enrolled as a scholar, was induced, perhaps by Robinson, to treat his case as one of university privilege. At all events, no more books were printed.

The net result of seven years of hard toil was discouraging—a bare subsistence. Upon the economic difficulties they shouldered their disappointment in the growth of the Church. The increase seems to us considerable. Not more than one hundred and twenty-five all told, men, women, and children, had come to Leyden and within ten years their number had perhaps doubled. At all events they were bitterly disappointed. They had expected the Ordinances of God, duly performed, to attract more adherents from England and from Holland. They felt sure that the solution of the economic problem would increase their number many fold and thus assure the permanence of the organization. For, argue as they might, they could not but admit that its permanence was threatened at Leyden. Though the adults were in the prime of life, they realized that they could not continue for many years such hard manual labor. The subsistence of the little community also made imperative work by the younger members, even by the children; all did some sort of manual labor, which had upon body and mind no less disastrous effects in the seventeenth century than it has now; and, while many of the children had borne cheerfully these heavy burdens, others had left home and become soldiers or sailors, and still others "some worse characters tending toward dissoluteness and the danger of their soules." Thus in one way or another, physically and morally, the strength of the little community was being sapped, its membership here and there drifting away, and its integrity as a community so sorely threatened that the leaders realized that its permanence could not be predicated at Leyden.

The road to economic success in Holland was all too clear. If they would but become Dutch citizens, join the Dutch Church, use the Dutch language, and renounce their English characteristics permanently, the craft guilds would open their doors, more remunerative employments would become possible, and some definite and permanent share of the great prosperity of the little country would be theirs. Incontestably, the price of permanence was the loss of their integrity as a group of Englishmen, speaking English, living in accordance with English customs, holding their services in the English language, and maintaining on alien soil as their most precious possession their identity as Englishmen. Already by 1620 thirty-three members of the Church had become Dutch citizens; many of the children used Dutch in preference to English; the adequate education of the children was possible only in the Dutch schools; and they saw that longer residence would make intermarriage inevitable. From all of this they shrank.

Yet as students we must see within these economic considerations the great spiritual truth which interpenetrates them, for the psychology of the Pilgrims is the most essential fact to grasp in their history. Without it we shall continually miss the key to the significant decisions. The rigid maintenance of separation from the English Established Church had been their main object in leaving England, but they now sought as well some environment in which their views of the intentions of Christ in regard to Church government could be developed and made permanent. They saw their children already less firm in the faith than themselves. They feared that the weakness of the flesh would cause many to forsake the Ordinances of God and either return to England to the bondage of the Established Church, or join the Dutch Churches in order to insure themselves something better than bare subsistence in exchange for a life of drudgery. Only in comparative isolation, they saw, away from the influence of other churches and governments, could they hope to create a permanent community where religious ideals and church government should be maintained in accordance with what they believed to be the Divine Revelation.

While at Leyden their ideas on government and doctrine had crystallized. There is no certainty that at Scrooby a Minister had been definitely "called" and church officers elected. We know nothing of decisions in regard to doctrine. Robinson joined them just before the emigration, and was himself so young a man and his convictions so recently achieved, that only in time did he reach definitive conclusions. Indeed it is at Leyden that the Pilgrim Church as we now speak of it was organized. Robinson then became formally Minister, Brewster was chosen Elder, while the deluge of controversies into which they were at once plunged compelled them to crystallize their notions of government and doctrine.[1] With the Dutch Reformed Church,

[1] These seem to have been vague and fluid. "In what place soever, by what means soever, whether by preaching the gospel

debating eagerly over the controversy between Arminius and Gomarius, they came at once into contact, and upon both of those theological distinctions they had to sit in judgment. The English Separatist Churches, too, at odds with each other and riven by internal dissentions, appealed to the new congregation for confirmation and support. Many and long were the discussions and arguments in the great house. Robinson was a really remarkable man of keen intellectual perceptions and wide learning, a leader in the truest and best sense of the word.[1] A man of great energy, a constant student, a diligent author, he played a decided part in all these controversies and speedily developed and organized his own ideas and with them those of his congregation. At the same time it is perhaps gratuitous to assume that Robinson's books represent literally the notions which Brewster and Bradford brought to Plymouth. They were hardly as advanced as he and were scarcely able to have deduced any such logical and complete array of theological opinions as are to be found in his books.

At the same time, from his books and from the Separatist literature in general, we can form some idea of Pilgrim worship, government, and theology at this time.[2]

by a true minister, or by a false minister, or by no minister, or by reading, conference, or any other means of publishing it, two or three faithful people do arise, separating themselves from the world into the fellowship of the gospel and covenant of Abraham, they are a Church truly gathered, though never so weak—a house and temple of God rightly founded upon the doctrine of the apostles and prophets, Christ himself being the cornerstone." Ashton, *Works of Robinson*, II, 232-3.

[1] Ozora S. Davis, *John Robinson, The Pilgrim Pastor.* Introduction by Professor Williston Walker. Boston, 1903.

[2] Walter H. Burgess, *John Smith, the Se-Baptist, Thomas Helwys*

The Service began with an entirely extemporaneous prayer by the Pastor or Teacher, no book or form of words being permitted. Then followed the reading of two or three chapters of the Bible in English, with a liberal paraphrase of the passage by the Teacher or Elder. A psalm was then sung in English without the accompaniment of any musical instrument. Next came the sermon, in which the Pastor expounded Doctrine or explained the application of Scripture to their individual conduct. A second psalm was sung or perhaps several, after which at stated times the Lord's Supper and Baptism were performed. Lastly a collection was made, the proceeds of which were devoted to the salaries of the officers and the needs of the poor. They used the Geneva Bible and Ainsworth's translation of the psalms in prose and meter, published in London in 1612. This they brought to Plymouth with them and used it there until 1696. It contained beside "singing notes, graver and easier French and Dutch tunes." Winslow wrote later with great enthusiasm of the volume of tone and the fervor of the singing at Plymouth.

Questions of discipline were commonly disposed of after the Sunday service by the Pastor and Elder, with the coöperation of the Church. They attempted to govern themselves and as far as possible to make the intervention of the Dutch authorities unnecessary. Disputes with each other, whatever the occasion, economic as well as theological, they decided in this Church meeting or by private conversation between Robinson and

and the First Baptist Church in England, with Fresh Light upon the Pilgrim Fathers' Church, London, 1911, pp. 364, gives special detail about Smith's Church at Gainsborough, and believes him the leader and originator of the Scrooby Church and its ideas.

those involved. Bradford boasts that they never bothered the magistrates of the city, meaning no doubt that this government was almost invariably successful. He also praises Robinson's wisdom in settling disputes. The Church was distinguished from the other Separatist Churches by the extent of the power possessed by the members of the Church in contra-distinction to the officers. The Pastor and Elder submitted to a majority vote all questions of importance and very many of no great significance.[1] The tendency at Amsterdam was toward an increase of the power of the officers, once elected, and the reduction to a minimum of the power of the congregation. To Johnson and Ainsworth, the people were ignorant of affairs and their decisions largely unintelligent or inexpedient. Discussions in meeting led to vehement quarrels and noisy disputes without commensurate result and some glib talker often succeeded in carrying a vote contrary to the intentions of the officers. Robinson and his followers, however, declared these objections of no moment and even permitted a discussion of the officers' conduct and their censure by majority vote of the members on any occasion.

Upon doctrine, their views were at once less original and less precise, a natural corollary of their complete absorption in the question of church government and the proper type of worship. They no doubt followed Robinson in his espousal of conservative Calvinism, ac-

[1] See Robinson's *On Religious Communion, Private and Public*, 1614. This is the most elaborate statement of his earlier ideas. His *Iust and Necessarie Apologie*, 1619, compares the practice of his congregation with that of the Dutch Reformed Churches and indicates their practice at the moment of emigration. Further light comes from the note drawn up for the Virginia Company quoted in Bradford's *History*, 44, 45 (Edition of 1898).

cepting fully the doctrine of the Elect, of Predestination,
and all that they involved. They also championed the
right of investigation in the Scriptures for all individuals
and soon found that this type of defense for their own
secession from the Papacy and the Established Church
involved permission to their own members to differ
from the Minister and the majority in their reading of
Scripture. Insensibly the influence of the Dutch and
English churches near them were modifying the ideas
of the rank and file, and stimulated a searching and
reading, a discussing and propounding, which not only
led "unstable wills and feeble intelligences" into dangerous waters but tended to keep constantly alive active
controversy as to the validity of their own fundamental
conclusions. Their own position contained the seeds of
dissension and dissolution. They saw the Separatist
congregations at Amsterdam, one after another, dissolved by the gradual defection of their members or
violently rent asunder by disagreement. They saw
the Dutch churches threatened with schism over the
Arminian controversy. Europe was too crowded with
churches and contentions. While they remained there,
dispute and recrimination, quarrelling and defections
of members would continue, if indeed they escaped
the fate of Ainsworth's and Smyth's churches. They
must find a place where they might isolate the fickle
and inconstant minds of the majority from other influences. "The place they had thoughts on was some of
those vast and unpeopled countries of America, which
are frutful and fitt for habitation: being devoyd of all
civill inhabitants; wher ther are only salvage and brutish
men, which range up and downl itle otherwise than the
wild beasts of the same."

CHAPTER IV

THE CRITICAL DECISION

Probably for some weeks, if not months, in the winter of 1616–17, exceedingly active discussions took place in the great house on the Kloksteeg which they used as an assembly hall. Many were terrified at the very idea of the New World and alleged the danger of shipwreck, the bad sanitation of ships at that time, famine, nakedness, and want.[1] Some supposed that "the change of air and diet" and, curiously enough to us, the drinking of water would infect their bodies with loathsome diseases.[2] Some, drawing no doubt upon the highly imaginative accounts of the early authors upon America, declared that the Indians flayed men with the shells of fishes, and cut off steaks and chops, which they then broiled upon the coals before the victim's eyes. From these terrifying images, the objectors passed to the great sums of money needed to outfit the expedition and the very pregnant argument that, if it had been difficult for them to make a living in a rich and populous country like Holland, what could they expect of a new world peopled only by Indians and Spaniards. Nor did they fail to dilate upon the lamentable failure of many at-

[1] Bradford is our chief authority. Winslow's account in his *Hypocrisy Unmasked*, London, 1646, is brief and adds little of value.

[2] Nevertheless, Bradford writing in 1643, records his surprise that the change of air and food, the "much drinking of water," all of them "enemies to health," should not have been fatal to most of them. *History*, 494.

45

tempts to settle the New World nor to expatiate upon the cruelty of the Spaniards and their treatment of the French Huguenots in Florida.

Bradford has eloquently phrased the argument of the majority to which he belonged. "It was answered, that all great and honourable actions are accompanied with great difficulties, and must be both enterprised and over-come with answerable courages. It was granted the dangers were great, but not desperate; the difficulties were many, but not invincible. For though their were many of them likly, yet they were not cartaine; it might be sundrie of the things feared might never befale; others by providente care & the use of good means, might in a great measure be prevented; and all of them, through the help of God, by fortitude and patience, might either be borne, or overcome. True it was, that such atempts were not to be made and undertaken without good ground & reason; not rashly or lightly as many have done for curiositie or hope of gaine, &c. But their condition was not ordinarie; their ends were good and honourable; their calling lawfull, & urgente; and therfore they might expecte the blessing of God in their proceding. Yea, though they should loose their lives in this action, yet might they have comforte in the same, and their endeavors would be honourable. They lived hear but as men in exile, & in a poore condi-tion; and as great miseries might possibly befale them in this place, for ye 12. years of truce were now out, & ther was nothing but beating of drumes, and preparing for warr, the events wherof are allway uncertaine. The Spaniard might prove as cruell as the salvages of America, and the famine and pestelence as sore hear as ther, & their libertie less to looke out for remedie."

Having thus threshed out the general issue of going to the New World, a solemn vote was taken and a majority voted in the affirmative. The debate now turned to the wide field of the superior advantages of one location over another. A minority, small in numbers but considerable in influence, was exceedingly anxious to settle in Guiana or in some part of the West Indies not yet occupied by Spaniards.[1] The fertility of the tropics would guarantee the subsistence of the colony; the climate would make unnecessary many of the provisions for comfort which a colder climate would make imperative; perhaps from the precious metals, unquestionably from trade, the wealth of the little community might be assured and its permanence guaranteed. The majority feared death from tropical diseases and the hostility of the Spaniards. Neither party thought Jamestown and the Chesapeake desirable. Why should they have fled from England, if now, after having suffered and sacrificed so much, they were to transplant themselves to a colony in which Episcopacy was already established?

The alternative plan to settlement in the West Indies at last reached expression in a definite determination, as Bradford says, "to live as a distincte body by themselves" in the general territory assigned to the Virginia Company by the royal charter, but in comparative isolation from the settlements already made. Protection from the Indians and from the Spanish they must have

[1] Raleigh's account of Guiana was not that used by the Pilgrims. Mr. Deane suggests in his notes to Bradford's *History* that Robert Harcourt's *A Relation of a Voyage to Guiana*, made in 1609, published in 1613-14, is the most probable source of their information. *Mass. Hist. Soc. Coll., 4th Series*, III, 27.

and it must come from some organized nation. Their marked desire to preserve their nationality, to perpetuate their English speech and habits, to prevent their children from becoming Dutchmen made residence in English territory a foregone conclusion. But they were anxious that this residence under the English flag should be nominal and not result in control by the state, which might in its own turn entail supervision from the English Church. Independence in ecclesiastical affairs they were determined to obtain and they saw clearly that it would involve a much more extended independence in temporal affairs than they could ever enjoy in England or in Holland, or indeed anywhere except in the isolation of a new country. For this reason the decision taken to go was at the same time a definite decision to take up permanent residence in the New World.

They saw at the outset therefore that everything would turn upon the question of subsistence. Their plan was simple but practical and was entirely in conformity with the definite knowledge already attained about the locality. For a great many years, relatively small ships had been accustomed to sail across the Atlantic from England, Holland, and France to fish on the Grand Banks for cod, to buy furs from the Indians in exchange for trinkets, and to return again in the autumn with a cargo of salt fish and pelts, which was without difficulty sold at a fair profit. Why should not a resident colony support itself upon precisely the same traffic? The men of the colony would spend the greater part of their time, not upon shore in the town and in the fields, but away from home engaged in trade. Houses there would be to build, fields to be tilled, conveniences must be made, no doubt clothing woven and prepared, but

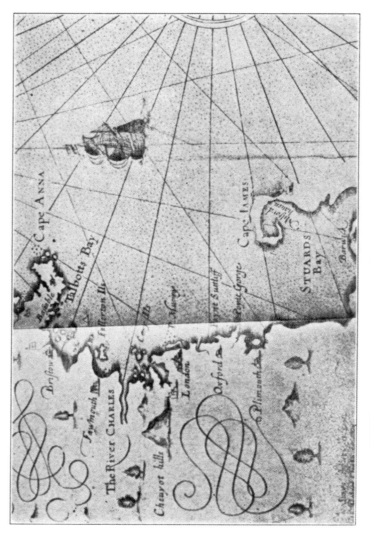

PORTION OF CAPTAIN JOHN SMITH'S MAP OF NEW ENGLAND, 1614

subsistence was not to depend upon the efforts of the colonists in America.[1] This was indeed a sound plan, entirely in accordance with the experience of Europeans in Northern America, and merely demanded of the Pilgrims the ability to do what others had done before them. Such examination as they made convinced them that the outlay of money, ordinarily involved in such a trading venture, was small and such as they themselves and their immediate friends could subscribe. The financing of the expedition was therefore not the aspect about which they needed most to concern themselves.

The vital issue seemed rather to be their ability to establish in the New World the kind of a political and ecclesiastical community they had in mind, free from interference from Europe or from resident authority in America. Argue as they would, they could not convince themselves that some kind of formal permission from the King would not be essential to ensure any degree of religious toleration. Their presence in the New World could hardly be kept secret and they feared that, if they landed without authorization, subsequent investigation would entail supervision and claims to the exercise of civil and ecclesiastical authority, which they had no intention of recognizing. Better to stay in Holland or return to England than incur the perils and expense of a voyage to America, only to find themselves under that same comparative constraint, from which

[1] This important point has not been sufficiently emphasized. See Bradford's own statements, *History*, 55, 72; the conditions with the Adventurers, quoted, *id.*, 57; Robinson's letter, quoted *id.*, 60; Cushman's letters, quoted, *id.*, 65, 67; Winslow, *Hypocrisy Unmasked*, 89, 90, London, 1646.

they had fled in England, and which they found still unsatisfactory in Holland.

They felt, too, that there was more than a fair chance, that consent might be obtained to such an arrangement as they had in mind, because of the importance in the London branch of the Virginia Company of Sir Edwin Sandys.[1] The Brewsters, father and son, had been postmasters at Scrooby during the period when the father of Sir Edwin had been Archbishop of York, and, while we may not perhaps assume that they had been friends of Sir Edwin as a boy, Brewster was at least known favorably to Sandys as a man of tried probity and ability. That Sandys had, like his father, strong leanings toward Puritanism was of course well known to them, and upon that fact they undoubtedly counted to enlist his sympathy in their project. Brewster should vouch for the seriousness of their purpose and their probable ability to found and maintain a colony. That the Virginia Company was more than anxious for Colonists they well knew; that it was more than ready to pay the expense of transporting to America those who were willing to go, they were also aware; they themselves therefore, who were not asking at this time financial support but merely the permission to "plant," ought consequently to receive a hearty welcome and liberal treatment. While they recognized that their comparative freedom under the Company's jurisdiction would

[1] Arber has elaborately reprinted in his *Story of the Pilgrim Fathers*, all the relevant material concerning the negotiations with the State, with the Virginia Company, with the Council for New England, and with the Adventurers. His attempts at meticulous criticism, however, should be carefully scrutinized, as should those of Ames, in his *Log of the Mayflower*, on this same phase of the narrative.

be entirely dependent upon their ability to finance the enterprise themselves, they entertained at this time no doubts upon this point.

In the summer and autumn of 1617, Deacon John Carver and Robert Cushman went to London to open negotiations with the Virginia Company, and carried with them Seven Articles, which were to explain the notions of the intending planters about religious conformity and toleration.[1] They would subscribe to the Thirty-nine Articles in the same sense in which the "Reformed Churches where we live and also elsewhere " accepted them. They would acknowledge the doctrine taught in the Church of England and its fruits and effects "to the begetting of saving faith in thousands in the land, Conformists and Reformists as they are called; with whom also, as with our brethren, we did desire to keep spiritual communion in peace; and will practise in our parts all lawful things." This vagueness as to the identity of those who were saved and of those with whom the Pilgrims proposed to keep spiritual communion was intentional. They would accept the royal supremacy without reservation, but added a not wholly fortunate clause, stating that "in all things obedience is due unto him either active, if the thing commanded be not against God's Word, or passive if it be, except pardon can be obtained." This certainly left them to judge whether the royal commands possessed or lacked Scriptural warrant. Similarly, they accepted the power of the Bishops and its lawfullness to govern the Church "civilly," and in so far as they derived that authority from the King, denying that ecclesiastical authority

[1] State Papers Colonial, I, No. 43. Copy. Most of the correspondence referred to in the text is quoted by Bradford.

could be exercised which the civil magistrate did not recognize.

The remarkable fact about these Articles is that Sir Edwin Sandys felt such statements would meet the approval of the King and the ecclesiastics. Carver and Cushman conducted themselves in a manner thoroughly agreeable to the authorities of the Virginia Company, who wrote in November an encouraging letter to Robinson and Brewster at Leyden. This drew from them in return rather more specific and open statements of their intentions and motives. They enlarged upon their industry and frugality, upon their readiness and ability to undergo hardship and misfortune with patience and equanimity. "It is not with us as with other men whom small things can discourage or small discontentments cause to wish them selves at home againe." The trials and privations of the New World did not terrify them, nor would the failure of the proposed colony be due to their remissness or want of diligence. They spoke in addition quite frankly of their Separatism. "We are knite togeather as a body in a most stricte & sacred bond and covenante of the Lord, of the violation wherof we make great conscience," and which they felt made them mutually responsible for each other's welfare and safety, and thus more than ordinarily satisfactory as prospective colonists. This letter too met with approval. The Seven Articles seem to have been shown to several members of the Privy Council in the month of December, 1617, or at the latest very early in January, 1618, for we find Robinson and Brewster writing late in that same month a further message of explanation to an eminent member of the Virginia Company, Sir John Wostleholme.

Three points, they say, had been raised by members of the Privy Council; their answer makes it evident that these concerned the institution of Bishops, the Sacraments, and their willingness to take the oath of Supremacy without qualification or reservation. They enclosed two replies, a brief statement which they thought more likely to meet approval, and a much more explicit statement which they feared the Bishops might not like; they requested their sponsors to choose between them. The most that they would concede in regard to the Church authorities was an acceptance of the provisions of the French Reformed Churches according to their public confession of faith. The Oath of Supremacy they agreed to take without reservation, if the authorities insisted upon it, but they indicated their preference for the Oath of Allegiance, a form expressly intended for Catholics who were attempting to make mental reservations in regard to the authority of the Pope, and to which therefore the Pilgrims would be able to subscribe with eminently clear consciences. These two points comprised the shorter form. The larger form particularized certain points in which they differed from the French Churches, and which proved beyond all possible question that the Congregation elected the Church officers, and that the government of the Church had nothing to do with Bishops nor provided any place for them.

The letter with its enclosure was forwarded to a well-known Separatist at London, Sabine Staresmore, who delivered it about the middle of February to Wostleholme. The latter read both the letter and its enclosures in Staresmore's presence, and then asked him, "who shall make them," meaning of course the ministers.

"'I answered His Worship that the power of making was in the Church to be ordained by the Imposition of Hands by the fittest instruments they had. It must either be in the Church or from the Pope and the Pope is Anti-Christ.' 'Ho!' said Sir John, 'What the Pope houlds good (as in the Trinitie) that we doe well to assente to but, said he, we will not enter into dispute now.'" He encouraged Staresmore to believe that what they wished could be obtained, but he told him quite frankly that it was utterly useless to present those documents.

Sometime during the next two months Sir Edwin Sandys, Sir Robert Naunton, then Secretary of State, and perhaps some other gentlemen, broached this question to the King. James asked how they expected to support themselves when they got to America. And their friends replied by fishing, " to which he replied with his ordinary asseveration, 'So God have my soul! 'tis an honest trade! it was the Apostles' own calling!'" He gave the gentlemen to understand that the idea met his approval. Sometime later, probably during the summer of the year 1618, he asked them to confer about it with the Archbishop of Canterbury and the Bishop of London.

Early in the autumn of this same year, the Church at Leyden learned of the unfortunate case of Francis Black-well. He had been an Elder in the Ancient Church of Johnston and Ainsworth at Amsterdam, with which they had already had so many dealings, and from which had come Bradford's bride and possibly other members of their own Church. When theological dissensions had riven the organization, Blackwell and part of the members had decided to try their fortunes in Virginia, and had journeyed to London preparatory to embarkation. There they had attended "a conventicle," had been apprehended, and found themselves in jail. This Blackwell's friends in London and Leyden could well have forgiven him had he not, as Bradford says, "glossed" with the Bishops, denied his Separation from the Church of England and its validity, and taken the oaths tendered him. The Bishops gave him their blessing, released him from jail, and sent him on his way to Virginia. Staresmore, whom Blackwell also implicated, wrote from the Counter Prison in intense indignation to Carver at Leyden. They also remembered that Johnston, Studley, and two other leaders of this same group of Separatists in 1597 had been shipped by the Privy Council to Newfoundland with a trading company, on the condition that they should never be allowed to return. When the venture failed, they had returned with the remnant of the colonists and had escaped to Amsterdam.[1]

The King's request that they should confer with the Archbishop and the Bishop of London therefore roused the suspicions of the leaders at Leyden. They decided now to give up any attempt to secure an explicit recognition of their religious non-conformity before leaving Holland. "If after wards ther should be a purpose or desire to wrong them, though they had a seale as broad as the house flore it would not serve the turn; for ther would be means enew found to recall or reverse it." Indeed they much regretted what they had already done and such incomplete revealings of their identity as had already been inevitable. The all important thing now was to confess nothing further, either of their intentions or their personnel.

[1] *Privy Council Register*, New Series, March 25, 1597. Hakluyt, *Voyages*, Ed. 1810, III, 242–9.

CHAPTER V

WAYS AND MEANS

None the less, throughout the autumn of 1618 and a considerable part of the winter of 1619 the discussions at Leyden continued.[1] In April, Cushman and Brewster again opened negotiations with the Virginia Company, but found considerable difficulty for a time in reaching any conclusion, because of the internal dissensions within the Company itself, until these were finally settled toward the end of April by the election to the Treasurership of Sir Edwin Sandys. His advent resulted in favorable action by the Company on May 26 on the Pilgrims' request for a charter, for which they applied in the name of Mr. John Wincob, "a religious gentleman belonging to the Countess of Lincoln." A patent to him was sealed on June 9, 1619. Technical anonymity was thus secured, but their connection with him was no doubt known to a considerable number of people. How far they proceeded

[1] The exact chronology and the sequence of events in this, as in the preceding chapter, can not be established by direct evidence. Arber in his *Story of the Pilgrim Fathers* and Ames in his *Log of the Mayflower* have made elaborate attempts to construct a detailed narrative, but the student should remember that neither has succeeded in most cases in suggesting solutions which are better than bare possibilities. The account in the text is based upon a fresh study of the material and differs somewhat in chronology and in sequence of events from the accounts hitherto published, but makes no pretensions to a finality which the character of existing material and the actual lack of evidence makes impossible.

during the summer of 1619 with their plans to utilize this patent is not known, but in the autumn news was sent them by Cushman in London of the extremely unfortunate results of the expedition to Virginia of Blackwell and their old Amsterdam friends which caused them to change their minds. The voyage had been long and tedious; so many had gone upon the ship that "they were packed together like herrings"; voyagers and crew had died for want of fresh water, from over-crowding, from lack of proper food. Blackwell was dead, wrote Cushman, the captain likewise; and the survivors had returned "with great mutterings and repinings amongst them."

Undoubtedly this news convinced the Pilgrims that their original plans could not be executed. A larger vessel would be essential and more considerable supplies of food and clothing, enough indeed to carry them well through the first year. Their own resources and the very limited financial competence of their immediate friends in Leyden and London were unable to cope with such a problem, and they concluded definitely that they must secure the coöperation of a body of men, resident in England or in Holland, sufficiently wealthy to provide the necessities, and sufficiently interested in the venture to insure the continuity of their assistance.[1] They must aim at more than subsistence. They must attempt a venture which would produce a profit.

They now received from Dutch capitalists or magistrates in January, 1620, an offer of conveyance to the New World, with a guarantee of continuous and adequate

[1] Such statements as this can not be supported by direct evidence but are implied by the sequence of events definitely established by the correspondence in Bradford.

support of so generous and definitive a nature that they scarcely dared refuse it. A suggestion was also made that they settle upon somewhat similar terms on the island of Zeeland at the mouth of the Rhine. Obviously, the fact that they were looking for capital to support a venture in America had leaked out in Holland. It was also known in London. In February or March there arrived at Leyden Thomas Weston, a London merchant, a Puritan if not a Separatist, a man already acquainted with some of them, and perhaps associated with their escape from England in 1608 or with the dissemination of books from the Brewster press. In his own name and that of other merchants, his friends, he promised them support for their voyage, drew up definite articles which they deemed favorable, and in particular gave them his personal guaranty that they should "neither feare wante of shipping nor money, for what they wanted should be provided." [1] He proposed no formal incorporation, for that would have disclosed necessarily the identity they were so anxious to conceal, but merely a voluntary association of the capitalists and the intending colonists. A patent this group of men already had, granted by the

[1] Of Weston's motives for this proposition we are utterly ignorant. The attempt of Ames, W. T. Davis, and others to explain his action is an excellent illustration of ingenuity overreaching itself. They couple this difficulty with the settlement at Plymouth instead of on the Hudson and "demonstrate" that Weston and Gorges planned to steal the colony, got it on board as best they could, and then bribed the captain to land it within the territory of the Council for New England, instead of in that of the Virginia Company. The only direct evidence associated with Plymouth, that of Secretary Morton, writing just before 1669, declares that the Dutch bribed Jones to land them outside the limits of their Patent! Both have been rejected by Arber, Dexter, and conservative students generally.

Virginia Company on February 2, 1620, to John Peirce and associates. While the use of this involved the abandoning of the Wincob patent already secured, it afforded complete anonymity, for the Pilgrims were in no way connected with the grantees at the time the patent was drawn.[1]

Weston proposed a partnership to last seven years for a venture in America of the type already decided upon by the Pilgrims. They should establish a permanent trading post at which they should live, from which as a base of operations they should trade with the Indians for furs, fish on the Grand Banks, cut lumber in the forests, and perhaps collect sassafras and other roots then salable in England. At this work the great majority should be employed. The rest were to build houses, till the ground, and insure the permanence of the trading post. The Adventurers, as capitalists were then called, were to contribute money, or provisions, or goods for trading, and thus finance the enterprise. Every colonist, or planter, as they were commonly called, was to be rated at ten pounds; every adult he took with him over sixteen years of age should also be rated at ten pounds or one

[1] Winslow in *Hypocrisy Unmasked*, pp. 89, 90, London, 1646, can be interpreted so as to imply the contrary. The records of the Virginia Company, the fact that the Pilgrims' negotiations with Weston were certainly subsequent to the request for the Peirce Patent, if not to its granting, the subsequent actions of Peirce himself, make the statement in the text seem more probable than other conjectures. We must not forget that Winslow and Bradford wrote long after these events, probably without the aid of memoranda taken at the time. The unreliability of human memory is well attested by the formal deposition of Miles Standish on oath in 1650, in a law suit to determine the priority of a land title, that he visited Boston Harbor in the summer of 1620! Goodwin, *Pilgrim Republic*, 237, note.

share of this joint stock. Money, or provisions, or goods
contributed by the planters or capitalists should also be
rated in multiples of ten. Thus the joint stock would be
created and on the basis of these shares the individual
Adventurers and colonists should eventually participate
in the proceeds.

Druing seven years the houses, goods, food, apparel,
and the like should belong to the company as a whole
and should be called the common stock, from which all
members of the colony in America should be provided
with necessities. Naturally they should do what they
could in America to add to this common stock and the
Adventurers pledged themselves to supply the remainder.
The proceeds of the trading and fishing were to be sold
in England for the benefit of the partnership, and it
was expected that the profits of the first seven years
would be sufficiently considerable to offset the original
investment, the subsequent necessary payments for the
maintenance of the colony in America, and afford besides a reasonable profit to the Adventurers. During
the seven years the colonists should work four days a
week for the Adventurers and two days for themselves,
the latter to be spent in improving the permanent plant
in America. When the question was raised as to what
notion of diligence and of effective coöperation the
merchants had, Weston gave them to understand that
he and his associates would gladly leave the question
of diligence to their own consciences. At the end of
seven years the colony itself, the houses and improved
lands, should become the property of the colonists. The
unimproved land should be divided between the Adventurers and the Planters, each to dispose of its share as
best it could, and the profits in money, in goods, or in

chattels should be distributed proportionately to the shares contributed by each Adventurer or colonist in money, goods, or his own value as a laborer. These terms were accepted. A paper stating the conditions was signed by the officers of the Church and by Weston for his associates, and a day was set for the payment of the money and goods which the Leyden members were to contribute. The Dutch offer was now rejected.

They now fell in April to a discussion of the very pertinent issue, how many could go and how many were willing to go. Even with the coöperation of the merchants, they saw that only a part of the Church could migrate and decided that, if the major part voted to go, Robinson, the Minister, should go with them, but that, if only a minority voted to leave, Brewster, the Elder, should accompany them. Explicitly they provided that each part was to form "an absolute Church of themselves" so long as they should be separated. The minority wished no questions raised as to the authority over them of the majority. After a long solemn meeting, a day of humiliation and perhaps another of fasting, after a sermon by Robinson many hours long, the vote was cast, and showed two parts nearly equal, the larger of which had elected to stay. They agreed together however that if the venture should succeed the majority should come at once to America, and on the other hand, if it should fail, the minority should return to Leyden with all speed. Now they fell to work upon the necessary arrangements. Property was sold, money collected, goods donated, both by those who were to go and those who were to stay. This during April and May, 1620. At the end of April or early in May a small ship of sixty tons, the *Speedwell*, was bought and refitted at Delfs-haven.

Meantime Weston had returned to London and had communicated to his associates the terms of the agreement. They pointed out at once that there was no collateral whatever to insure the repayment of the capital; inasmuch as the land and buildings were to become the property of the colonists at the end of seven years, a discharge of the indebtedness depended entirely upon the making of a profit in the meantime. While they seem to have had no doubts of the moral responsibility of the Pilgrims [1] and their willingness and readiness to labor hard in the common interest, they did very strongly question their ability to earn so great a profit. To put the venture upon a business basis, the objectors insisted that the tangible property at the end of the seven years, the improved lands and the houses, as well as the goods and chattels, must be subject to division or sale in the interests of Adventurers and Planters alike. Even then the merchants would risk much, for, if the venture was unsuccessful, they might still lose everything, although it was at the same time clear that, if the venture succeeded, they would on this basis make a much larger profit than they were entitled to under the existing agreement. They further insisted that the entire efforts of the colonists for the whole seven years must be devoted to the venture. The two days of work for themselves seemed to the merchants a loophole through

---

[1] It becomes now proper to speak of "the Pilgrims." It is certainly uncritical to term either the Scrooby emigrants or Robinson's Congregation as a whole "the Pilgrims" or "the Pilgrim Church"; until those who were finally to go had been separated from the rest, the true Pilgrim body had not come into existence.

which all profit would escape. Weston and Cushman, the Pilgrims' representative, did their best to convince the recalcitrant merchants, but in the end Cushman agreed to these terms. The Adventurers then elected a President and Treasurer and subscribed the necessary money and goods. Christopher Martin was chosen Treasurer and was to proceed with the colonists to America as representative of his associates.

When the news of Cushman's concessions reached Leyden, active discontent burst forth. The great majority of the Leyden Church had been agriculturalists in England and were familiar with the difference in status under the old manorial system of a tenant or villein, who had a right to a portion of his time for himself, and that of the serf who had no time to himself, had no property, and was without prospect of any. What Cushman had agreed to was something closely akin to serfdom; their legal status in America would be doubtful and complicated and certainly not that of freemen during the seven years. They were familiar with the practice in Holland and England of apprenticeship for seven years.[1] They also knew of the existing practice by which emigrants sold their labor for seven years to the capitalists who financed their voyage. The Leyden group were not in the least minded to land in America as indentured servants. They felt themselves no common laborers. As free men and not otherwise would they land. They must be further assured of possession at the end of the seven years of the improved lands and buildings which their labor had created. Some who had expected to go now withdrew; some who had paid in money wished it returned; a number of the more promi-

[1] Bradford, *History*, 58–62.

nent declared flatly that they would never leave Leyden under such conditions, and, taking refuge in the fact that Cushman had no explicit authority to sign such an agreement, declared it accordingly invalid. Of this decision they promptly informed Cushman and Weston in vigorous letters of protest and a long list of objections. Thus matters came to a stand in Leyden.

In London, too, matters were at a stand. The plan of operations, based upon the experiences of Blackwell's company, called for a simultaneous sailing of the Leyden colonists in the *Speedwell* from Holland and of the English group from London, for a meeting at Southampton, and a continuation at once of the voyage across the Atlantic, without delay or opportunity for investigation by the English authorities. Ostensibly certain merchants, one John Peirce and others, were shipping across the Atlantic in traditional style two cargoes of hired laborers. In Holland the *Speedwell* had been bought and fitted out, but in London nothing had been done towards procuring and fitting out the larger ship upon which the majority of the colonists expected to make the voyage. From Leyden came urgent letters pointing out the necessity of immediate action, so that the summer season, the favorable time for settlement, might be utilized, and so that they should not suffer want in Holland now that their property had been sold and their preparations made.

Weston and his associates remained undecided and on the tenth of June Cushman wrote a most discouraging letter to the group at Leyden, saying that nothing had been done, that they had underestimated the expense and difficulty of the venture, and could not land in America any such number of people with any such

CONTEMPORARY CUT OF SHIPS OF THE MAYFLOWER TYPE

amount of goods and food as they required. On that same day, however, apparently Saturday, the tenth of June, he succeeded in convincing Weston of the necessity of immediate action. That afternoon, they took a refusal of a very fine ship of about one hundred and twenty tons, and either that same afternoon or early on Monday were offered a much larger ship of one hundred and eighty tons, none other than the famous *Mayflower*, owned by one of the Adventurers, Thomas Goffe. A Captain Christopher Jones and an experienced mate were also hired. The provisioning of the ship went forward rapidly, the preparation of the company at London to sail upon her proceeded promptly, and by the middle of July all was ready.

Meanwhile, at Leyden, after a day of humiliation spent at Robinson's house, with prayer, fasting, the singing of psalms, a long sermon, much discussion, and probably some sort of farewell feast, they set forth on July 21–31, 1620, Friday, for Delfshaven, passing down the Vliet on canal boats, a journey of about twenty-four miles. Transshipping their belongings to the *Speedwell*, they spent the night in "friendly entertainment and Christian discourse," and on the next day took leave on the dock of such friends from Leyden and Amsterdam as had come to see them depart. They then went on board, and Robinson, "falling downe on his knees, (and they all with him), with watrie cheeks commended them with most fervente praiers to the Lord and his blessing. And then with mutuall imbrases and many tears, they tooke their leaves one of an other; which proved to be the last leave to many of them."

A fair wind carried them in four days to Southampton, where they found the *Mayflower*, which, sailing from London on July 15–25, had been there a week waiting for them. They also found Weston and Cushman, both most anxious that the articles as amended by the merchants should be signed by the principal members now arrived from Leyden. Long argument only developed excessive obstinacy on both sides and Weston finally, becoming very angry, told them "to look to stand on their own legs," and left for London without paying the port dues of nearly £100. Apprehensive of investigation by the authorities and the disclosure of their identity, they quickly sold some firkins of butter, raised the money, and thus cleared port. Their fears of ecclesiastical and temporal interference proved unfounded, for no investigations were made or questions asked at London, Southampton, Dartmouth, or Plymouth. At about this time Captain John Smith, who had done so much for the first colony at Jamestown, made some overtures to the Pilgrims. Good advice and information about conditions on the Atlantic coast he claims that he offered and that they rejected. Possibly he offered to go with them. At any rate they negatived that.

On the third of August (3–10) all was at last ready. They indited a final letter to the merchants at London, defended themselves as well as they might for not having signed the revised agreement, and offered to add to the conditions signed at Leyden a clause continuing the joint stock beyond the seven years, if "large profits" had not then been made. As Bradford notes in the margin of his *History*, it was well for them that the offer was not accepted. The company was then assembled and a long letter of counsel, advice, and encouragement, written by Robinson, was read to them; each individual was assigned his place in one of the ships; a Governor and two or three assistants were chosen for each ship, to have authority for the voyage, to distribute provisions, and generally to assist the officers of the ship. On the fifth (August 5–15) they set sail, but had not proceeded very far down the Channel, when Reynolds, the Captain of the *Speedwell*, complained that the ship was leaking. After search and discussion, they put in at Dartmouth, where the ship was overhauled from stem to stern and the leak mended. They again set sail and were scarcely out of sight of land when again Reynolds complained that the ship was leaking badly. Putting back to Plymouth, finding no important leak, they adjudged the ship faulty and, after some hesitation, took from her so much of the cargo and as many of the people as they could crowd into the *Mayflower*, and sent her back to London with some eighteen or twenty whose courage had already weakened. Later the truth came out. The refitting of the *Speedwell* in Holland had been badly done: the masts and sails were too large and overstrained the ship; when she was sold afterwards in London and refitted, she proved perfectly seaworthy. The Pilgrims later believed that the Captain and sailors of the *Speedwell* regretted their agreement to remain a year in the colony and crowded the ship with sail so that she might leak and be sent back. Certainly no one fact contributed so much as this to the difficulties of the colony in its first year. The successful execution of the original plans became now problematical in the extreme. On Wednesday, September 6–16, they finally left Plymouth and saw the coast of England sink out of sight, for the last time for most of them.

CHAPTER VI

There sailed from Plymouth on the *Mayflower* that sixth of September, 1620, one hundred and two passengers whose identity has been of greater interest to posterity than that of any other emigrants in history. The elaborate researches of the last half century have established many definite facts and a large number of highly probable conjectures about them. Only William Brewster and William Bradford can be traced from Scrooby and Austerfield in England to Leyden, and thence to Plymouth. Thirty-three others of the Leyden congregation, including children, sailed on the *Mayflower*, the other sixty-seven coming from England. Despite the numerical preponderance of the newer element, it was nevertheless always true that the Leyden contingent was the backbone of the colony. Among them were Brewster, Bradford, Carver, Winslow, Allerton, and their families. Among those sailing from London were Cushman, who returned with the *Speedwell;* Standish and his wife; Christopher Martin, one of the Adventurers, with his wife and two servants; Master William Mullins, another of the Adventurers, with his wife and two children, one of whom was Priscilla, and a servant; Master Stephen Hopkins and his wife, three children and two servants; and John Billington, with a wife and two children. The others were people of less interest. Among them were five children "bound" or apprenticed, two to Carver, two to Brewster, and one to Winslow.

It seems probable that the *Mayflower* passengers were thus distributed in their English homes. From the north of England came twenty-six; from eastern England forty-six; from southern England twenty-seven; from London seventeen; from central England seven; while the homes of fourteen are not yet ascertainable.[1] The vast majority, seventy-seven, came from four districts: from Norfolk thirty-two; from Kent seventeen; from London seventeen; and from Essex eleven. It is therefore clear that the majority of the *Mayflower* passengers not only did not come from Scrooby, but did not even come from northern England. The adult males numbered forty-four, the adult females nineteen, the young boys and girls under age thirty-nine, or about forty per cent of the whole number. There were twenty-six married men and eighteen married women, twenty-five bachelors and one spinster servant. There is every reason to suppose that only two of the adults were over fifty years old and only nine over forty. The mortality of the first year fell heavily upon them and left the colony in the hands of young men. Bradford was thirty-one, Winslow twenty-five, Allerton thirty-two, Standish thirty-six, and Alden only twenty-one. The Pilgrim Fathers scarcely deserved the appellation.

Of the ship on which they sailed we know little, for Bradford and Winslow merely refer to her as "the ship" or "the larger ship" and do not even give her name, but they do tell us enough to infer much about the general type of ship to which she belonged. She must have been about ninety feet long and twenty-four feet wide, carry-

---

[1] Dr. Dexter's geographical divisions are not those commonly denoted in England by the terms northern, southern, and the like. Dexter, *England and Holland of the Pilgrims*, 650.

ing a crew of between fifteen and twenty men. Of her
three masts, the fore and main masts were square rigged
without a jib, while the mizzen mast carried a lateen sail.
A high forecastle and a high poop deck left the middle of
the ship low. Broad of beam, short in the waist, low
between the decks and in her upper works none too tight,
she was what was known as a "wet" ship, and, being on
this voyage heavily laden and therefore low in the water,
shipped more seas than usual. At the same time, so
far as the Pilgrims were concerned, she was a decidedly
large, well constructed vessel entirely able to weather
the storms and sufficiently commodious to prevent any
danger from overcrowding. There was undoubtedly no
room to spare and from a modern point of view they
must have been decidedly cramped. They carried to be
sure no young cattle, and the poultry, swine, and goats,
which they possibly had, were penned up forward. Between decks much of the space was occupied by a shallop,
about thirty feet long when put together, but which they
were carrying in pieces. The passengers were distributed
aft in cabins and bunks, not in hammocks, while the
crew lived forward. No furniture is known to have been
brought. A whole fleet of ships, each several times
larger than the *Mayflower*, would have been necessary to
transport the supposedly genuine pieces which have
been claimed of *Mayflower* origin.

The staples of food were certainly bacon, hard tack,
salt beef, smoked herring, cheese, and small beer or ale,
for the Pilgrims were not total abstainers and followed
the practice, then universal in Europe, of a moderate use
of liquor. For luxuries they carried butter, vinegar,
mustard, and probably lemons and prunes. Gin they
also had and either brandy or Dutch schnapps. The

food was given out each day by the Governor and assistants of the ship and must have been eaten cold. The only opportunity for cooking consisted of a frying pan held over a charcoal fire, or a kettle suspended on an iron tripod over a box of sand. Much cooking for one hundred and two passengers and a crew of twenty or more seems highly improbable. There was also little opportunity for bathing or washing and when they reached America they must have been in sore straits for clean clothes. To cleanliness however they attached great importance and no doubt achieved a greater measure of it than was common at that time.

We know nothing about the voyage except the little Bradford tells us, which is enough to prove definitely that comparatively few incidents distinguished it. The wind was fair for a good many days and they suffered nothing more than seasickness. In mid-ocean they encountered cross winds and storms, during one of which the main beam of the ship sprang out of place and cracked a little. A consultation was promptly held as to the advisability of continuing the voyage and some were in favor of returning to England, but they produced a great iron jack from the hold, forced the beam back into place, and made it fast with ropes and timber braces. The officers and crew vouched for the soundness of the ship below the water line, pointed out that the voyage back to England was as long and perilous as the continuation to America, and promised to do what they could to make the upper works a little tighter. They stoutly affirmed that there was no real danger and so the outcome proved. Although delayed by high winds and seas, they came without further incident in sight of land on November 9.

The sailors at once identified the shore as Cape Cod and all knew at once that they were considerably north of the most northern limit of their patent, and that the Hudson River, which they had originally in mind, lay considerably to the south and west. They promptly turned south and, after some half day's sailing, found themselves among the shoals and breakers of the passage around Cape Cod. The Captain [1] extricated the ship promptly and a consultation was held upon the vital question whether or not to go forward. They decided to return to Cape Cod and to found their settlement somewhere on what we now call Massachusetts Bay, entirely conscious that they were thus abandoning their patent.

The reasons for this momentous decision have excited much curiosity and interest and have resulted in much speculation and conjecture, for the Pilgrims themselves tell us merely of the season of the year, the ship somewhat damaged by the voyage, the food running low, and the anxiety of Captain and crew to reach some haven for the winter without unnecessary delay. Beyond the fact that the mariners were insistent upon a speedy solution of the problem of settlement, we get no hint from Winslow or Bradford that any influence was at work other than the minds of the Pilgrims. Nathaniel Morton, writing in 1669 presumably from oral tradition at Plymouth, states explicitly that Dutch intrigue was responsible for this abandoning of the first patent, and

---

[1] R. S. Marsden in the *English Historical Review*, XIX, 669 ff. has exhaustively considered the question of the identity of "Captain Jones" and successfully raises the presumption that he was one Christopher Jones, and not Thomas Jones, a notoriously bad character.

later students have suggested a plot between Weston and Gorges to "steal" the colony from the Virginia Company. Both of these conjectures are of course based upon the assumption that nothing but treachery and terror could have induced the Pilgrims to land in New England without patent or authorization; both entirely disregard the failure of Bradford or Winslow to express the slightest concern for the change in plans. Bradford indeed explicitly says that the Compact, which they presently signed, was as legal and useful as the patent itself, and that they thought so at the time. If such was their attitude, certainly no treachery on the part of Jones or Weston is an essential premise of an explanation.

Is it not more likely that the patent was intended to legalize their departure from England, to secure the acquiescence of the authorities in their emigration? Must we not also remember that the patent gave them individually no rights in America whatever, but conferred all the privileges upon the merchants, with whom they had so decidedly quarreled at Southampton? If it was true that the Pilgrims landed at Plymouth without legal authority, they would have been equally devoid of legal authority in their own persons within the territory of the Virginia Company. It would have been possible for the merchants at any time to decline to recognize them longer as associates, to claim that they never had been their associates. What the Pilgrims wished was a grant of land in their own persons and they did not rest until they secured it. Moreover, the Virginia Company was either Episcopalian or unseparated and the Pilgrims could scarcely have regretted escaping its jurisdiction. Possibly, too, they knew that the Council of New England was about to be created, that the new company would be anxious for colonists, that Weston did know the grantees, and that a new charter on far better terms might be secured for a colony already planted in the New World. These are conjectures and for them there is nothing better than inherent probability. But are they not at least as probable as the elaborate structures of plots and treason hitherto suggested as explanations for this important step?

As the *Mayflower* returned along Cape Cod a number of the company, who had come on board at London, informed the leaders with no mincing of words, that the abandoning of the original patent left the leaders without authority over them, and that they should take the first opportunity to secure their freedom. To put an end to such murmurings—for the leaders did not for a moment suppose that they were providing themselves with legal authorization—a solemn Compact was drawn up and signed by forty-one adult males of the Company.

In ye name of God, Amen. We whose names are underwriten, the loyall subjects of our dread soveraigne Lord, King James, by ye grace of God, of Great Britaine, Franc, & Ireland king, defender of ye faith, &c. Haveing undertaken, for ye glorie of God, and advancemente of ye Christian faith, and honour of our king & countrie, a voyage to plant ye first colonie in ye Northerne parts of Virginia, doe by these presents solemnly and mutualy in ye presence of God, and one of another, covenant & combine ourselves togeather into a civill body politick, for our better ordering & preservation & furtherance of ye ends aforesaid; and by vertue hearof to enacte, constitute, and frame such just & equall lawes, ordinances, acts, constitutions, & offices, from time to time, as shall be thought most meete & convenient

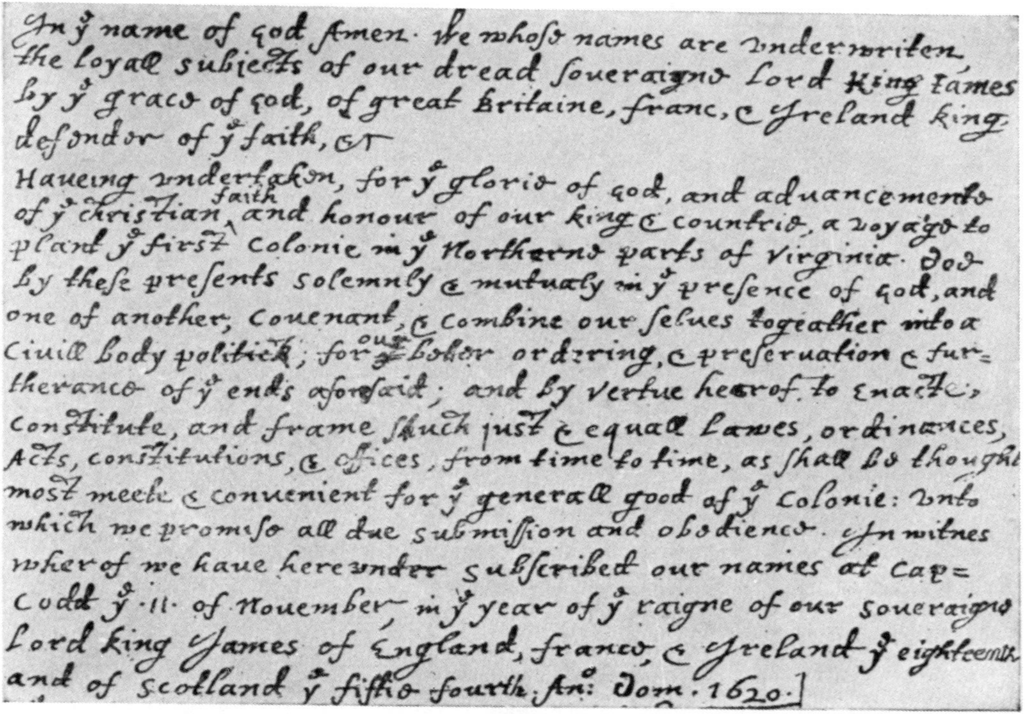
In ye name of God Amen· We whose names are vnderwriten,
the loyall subjects of our dread soveraigne Lord King James
by ye grace of God, of great Britaine, franc, & Ireland king,
defender of ye faith, &c.
Haueing vndertaken, for ye glorie of God, and aduancemente
of ye christian faith and honour of our king & countrie, a voyage to
plant ye first Colonie in ye Northerne parts of Virginia· doe
by these presents solemnly & mutualy in ye presence of God, and
one of another, Couenant, & combine our selues togeather into a
Civill body politick; for our better ordering, & preseruation & fur=
therance of ye ends aforesaid; and by vertue hearof to enacte,
constitute, and frame such just & equall lawes, ordinances,
Acts, constitutions, & offices, from time to time, as shall be thought
most meete & conuenient for ye generall good of ye Colonie: vnto
which we promise all due submission and obedience· In witnes
wherof we haue hereunder subscribed our names at Cap=
Codd ye ·11· of Nouember, in ye year of ye raigne of our soueraigne
Lord King James of England, france, & Ireland ye eighteenth
and of Scotland ye fiftie fourth. Ano: Dom. 1620.

THE MAYFLOWER COMPACT: FROM BRADFORD'S HISTORY

for ye generall good of ye Colonie, unto which we promise all
due submission and obedience. In witnes wherof we have
hereunder subscribed our names at Cap-Codd ye 11. of
November, in ye year of ye raigne of our soveraigne lord,
King James, of England, France, & Ireland ye eighteenth,
and of Scotland ye fiftie fourth. An°: Dom. 1620.

On November 11–21, the *Mayflower* anchored safely
in Provincetown Harbor and the leaders began definite
consideration of the sort of location required for the
future colony. They were to establish a permanent
trading post, which should maintain itself by fishing
and bartering beads, toys, and cloth with the Indians
of the district. Astonishing to relate, not one of the
passengers had ever fished nor, so far as we know, with
the exception of Standish, had any of them fired a gun
by anything better than accident. All had been farmers
in England, accustomed to the open fields and broad-
cast sowing, and in Holland all had followed some trade
or other. They were indeed so ignorant that they discovered spices in the thickets of Cape Cod and in the
first few weeks shot a bird which they took to be an
"eagle" and were frightened by "lions." They were
absolutely unprepared for the conditions they actually
found and brought really nothing except good constitutions, loyalty to each other, good sense, patience, forbearance, and devotion to a high religious ideal. They
lacked everything but virtue.

Nor had they brought with them the most necessary
supplies. Food they could not bring in large quantities
and they expected to depend upon the Indian corn or
maize, and were aware that they must obtain a supply
for planting from the Indians. They brought, however,
peas, beans, and seed for growing onions, turnips, pars-

nips, and cabbages. There was also a large stock of
salt, some clothing, some trinkets, and presents for the
Indians, and a few boots and shoes, brought by Mullins,
the father of Priscilla. Simple culinary utensils of pewter
or woodenware they brought with them, andirons,
candle molds, and the like. For wood cutting, cooper-
ing, and carpentry they brought an elaborate set of
tools, as well as equipment for a blacksmith's shop, and
an anvil. Guns, swords, and powder, with some side-
armor, breastplates, and cannon they also brought.
Everything considered, a remarkably adequate supply.
For agriculture they possessed only a few hand tools.
They brought no beast of burden, no plows, carts, or
harness of any description. For fishing they were provided only with nets and hooks so large that they could
not catch cod with them. Indubitably they were not
adequately equipped to found a colony, which would
depend entirely for subsistence upon what it might raise
in the New World. They were equipped to build houses,
cultivate gardens, catch fish in nets, and trade with the
Indians for furs. To find a location for such a colony
was now their task. This can not be too carefully borne
in mind. Had they been looking for a site for a settlement colony, which should depend primarily upon its
own labor in America for subsistence, they would probably not have pitched upon Plymouth.

They went ashore at once, and, wading and splashing
through the shallow water, first set foot on the soil of
the New World.[1] Fifteen or sixteen of the adult men,

---

[1] In the eighties appeared in London an historical work by the
author of *Julamerk*, a Mrs. J. B. Webb-Peploe, entitled, the
Pilgrims of New England. Some notion of the possibilities of
historical ignorance can be had from it. They land upon a pre-

well-armed, wandered about the shores of Provincetown Harbor for the greater part of the day, and we may well imagine with what mingled curiosity, elation, expectancy, and alarm these agricultural laborers and artisans from the domestic industry of Holland went out in the guise of explorers, adventurers, and soldiers. The location, however, was neither romantic nor adventurous. They soon saw that the land was a narrow neck of sand, interspersed with marshes and large ponds, certainly not the place for their settlement. On the thirteenth, they brought out the shallop and found many days' labor required before it could be seaworthy. Meanwhile the women washed clothes in the ponds, the men and children took exercise on shore, and several expeditions were made in the neighborhood.[1] The first, on November 15, led by Standish, Bradford, and Hopkins saw traces of game, of Indians, of previous Europeans, and marched up hill and down dale with great toil and fatigue. The unaccustomed armor chafed them, the weight of the guns tired them, and breaking through the heavy underbrush "tore our very armor to pieces." Some Indian fields, an Indian grave, the planks of a wrecked ship made into a rude house, an iron ship

cipitous granite strewn shore amid dashing surf, mountains high, in which the authoress instinctively bathes deep; they hunt wild horses (of which there were none, wild or tame in English America before 1624), and elect Carver *President*. The hero is an Englishman with sons named Heinrich and Ludovico!

[1] The winters of 1620–1622 were exceptionally mild; so were those of 1630–1631, while in 1645–1646 plowing was going on in February. The winters of 1637–38 and of 1641–42 were the coldest in forty years. Plymouth harbor was frozen solid and was crossed by oxen and carts for five weeks. It is fortunate they did not meet this sort of weather that first year.

kettle, such were the specific evidences of human habitation. Several caches of corn which they found, they took, for which they afterwards scrupulously paid.

Finally the shallop was ready and on November 27 the first trip was made under the leadership of the captain of the *Mayflower*. Weather conditions were highly unfavorable; snow fell, a cold wind chilled their bones, and the rowers in the boat were soon covered with ice from the driving spray and sleet. They coasted along to the Pamet River, which they at first thought a good site, found more caches of corn, more woods, sand bars, and ponds, and returned impressed more than ever with the unsuitability of the neighborhood and with the necessity of finding at once a permanent site. On December 6–16, the second expedition departed, in weather so cold that the spray from the oars froze on their clothes and one of their number nearly died of exposure. Far down Cape Cod they sailed and, after seeing more Indians in the distance, investigating empty wigwams, graves, and further caches of corn, they landed for the night and barricaded themselves, a little company of eighteen men, six of whom were from the crew of the *Mayflower*. At midnight they were disturbed by dreadful noises which they took to be those of wolves, but at daybreak further outcries aroused them and soon Indians were upon them. They were unprepared. Most of them had carried their armor and guns down to the water's edge in preparation for sailing and only Standish, Bradford, and a couple more had retained their fire arms. Two of them fired, checking the Indians for a moment, the other two holding themselves in readiness. The rest in considerable disorder and fear hurried for their own weapons, which they recovered without real difficulty, the Indians manifesting no real desire to meet the White Man in the open. From the trees the Indians continued to shoot arrows. From their own cover the Pilgrims returned musket fire. The chief of the Indians stood well forward under a tree and deliberately shot at the leaders with his arrows. They took equally deliberate aim at him, and after three misses, finally hit the tree above his head, whereupon he gave a great "shrike" and took to his heels. This ended the first encounter, as they called it, a fact which thrilled these simple countrymen inexpressibly.

December 8–18 was a hard day. They stood along the coast, steered toward the mountain of Manomet, which the sailors had pointed out from the ship at Provincetown as the landmark of the good harbor indicated on Smith's map. After some two hours' snowfall, the sea grew rough and the waves sufficiently violent by the middle of the afternoon to break the hinges of the rudder, so that two men with oars steered the shallop. At length, the lookout cried that he saw the harbor, and, crowding on more sail in an attempt to make the harbor before dark, they overtaxed the rigging; the mast split in three pieces, the sail dragged overboard, and they barely escaped capsizing. They were however near the entrance of Plymouth harbor and their diligence at the oars and the flood tide carried them through the harbor's entrance. Again they found themselves imperilled by the breakers, but the presence of mind of one of the sailors, who told them to pull sharply, the promptness of their own action, once more saved the little craft, and they soon ran into calm water under the lee of Clark's Island. After some hesitation, a few of the bolder spirits ventured ashore and, despite the sleet and wind, kindled a fire, of which they were presently extremely glad, for the wind shifted about midnight, the temperature fell sharply, and they had all been wet to the skin for the greater part of the day. This was Friday, December 8–18.

All night it rained. In the morning the rain continuing, apparently they marched around Clark's Island and there stayed all day. On Sunday, December 10–20, they rested. It was not until Monday December 11, Old Style, December 21, New Style, that they landed from the shallop somewhere on Plymouth harbor. Astronomical calculation shows that the tide was flood and that they could, despite the flats, have landed anywhere along the sandy shore. This date has been accepted for the greater part of the nineteenth century as the technical landing of the Pilgrims.[1] The weather was mild and sunny, there was no snow, and the ground was not even frozen. All the women and children and the great bulk of the men being still at Provincetown on the *Mayflower*, only eighteen men went ashore from the shallop on this day, of whom ten were Pilgrims: Standish, Bradford, Carver, Winslow, John and Edward Tilley, Howland, Warren, Steven Hopkins, and Edward Dotte. There were with them also two hired seamen not of the *Mayflower* crew, two of the mates of the ship, the master gunner, and three sailors. After sounding the harbor and exploring the shore at some length, they concluded that they had found a satisfactory location and returned to Provincetown, arriving December 13–23. Two days

[1] The anniversary speeches delivered at various dates are by no means devoid of interest and value and many will well repay a reading. A very nearly complete list has been compiled by Albert Matthews, and was printed in the *Publications of the Colonial Society of Massachusetts*, XVII, 387–392.

later the *Mayflower* sailed for Plymouth, but, because of the contrary wind, was unable to make harbor until December 16–26. The next day was Sunday, the first day of worship at Plymouth, conducted certainly on shipboard by Elder Brewster, and consisted no doubt of the singing of psalms, of heartfelt prayers, of the reading of the Scriptures and the expository work which was all that Brewster attempted. Thus ended the long pilgrimage from the Old World to the New. "May not and ought not the children of these fathers rightly say" wrote Bradford, "our faithers were Englishmen which came over this great ocean and were ready to perish in this willdernes but they cried unto the Lord and he heard their voyce and looked on their adversitie."

BIBLIOGRAPHICAL NOTES

Appearance of the Pilgrims. There is nothing which the student so much regrets as the entire absence of information as to the personal appearance of the Pilgrims. It is not merely true that we have no accurate or extensive information, we have literally not a suggestion as to whether Bradford was tall or short, thin or stout, black haired or light complexioned. Nor do we know what clothes they wore when they landed. Certainly not the hats, cloaks, and shoes characteristic of England half a century later. The numerous pictures can not longer be considered correct in detail and some of them represent scenes which can not now be shown to have taken place at all. One authentic portrait only exists,— of Edward Winslow, painted in London in 1651, five years after leaving Plymouth. The women, of whom so much has been written and imagined, appear in the contemporary accounts of Bradford and Winslow as mere names. From their own contemporaries we have not the slightest hint as to their character, influence, intelligence, or appearance. The critical scholar must confess this entire absence of material for the little details so much desired by posterity. Yet, after all, remarkable characters for sanity, intelligence, high devotion to Christian ideals are limned for us by the authentic narrative. The knowledge of their stature, weight, costume, and the color of their hair could add nothing to our estimate of their true worth.

Genealogical Bibliography.—Those who are anxious positively to establish their descent from the Pilgrims will do well to attempt no researches themselves, unless already skilled at such work, but to communicate with G. E. Bowman, 53 Mt. Vernon St., Boston, who has made the study of Pilgrim families and genealogy his life work. For those, however, willing to be content with something less than certainty, the *Mayflower Descendant*, a quarterly journal; *Pilgrim Notes and Queries*, eight monthly issues a year, both edited by Mr. Bowman, will usually give some clue to family relationships. Goodwin's *Pilgrim Republic* gives commonly full data covering the immediate descendants of known Pilgrims. *The New England Historical and Genealogical Register*, Peirce's *Colonial Lists*, Boston, 1881, the (English) Congregational Historical Society's *Transactions*, London, 1901, the various publications of the Massachusetts Historical Society, of the American Antiquarian Society, of the Colonial Society of Massachusetts, of the Old Colony Historical Society, are all valuable. There are also the *Pilgrim Newsletter*, Providence, R. I., published since 1909; and the Society of Mayflower Descendants of Illinois, which has published material since 1900. Much use must be made of the histories of great English and American families, of state, town, and county records, all too numerous to be mentioned here, as well as of all the Pilgrim sources which have been and will be referred to in this volume. Such researches commonly lead the student far afield into unexpected places, which is their chief charm for most genealogists.

CHAPTER VII

THE FIRST YEAR

The first stage of the great enterprise thus successfully accomplished, the difficulties in their path one after another surmounted, a greater problem now loomed before them—how could the transition from ship to shore be safely made and the colony established on the soil of the New World.[1] Monday, December 18, found the Pilgrims early ashore. That day and the two succeeding were consumed in eager and thorough explorations of the harbor, the rivers, the forests, and the soil. On the twentieth a vote was taken and the majority elected to build the new settlement on what Bradford called the "first site," evidently that selected by the leaders who came in the shallop a week or more previous. The name, Plymouth, they found on Smith's map of New England and retained it.

The site was well adapted for a permanent fishing and trading factory. Though the *Mayflower* was compelled to lie in the outer harbor on account of the shallow water at low tide, the harbor was deep enough for a ship of no

---

[1] Our information for this section of the narrative is singularly full and reliable. They sent back to England in the *Fortune* a detailed Relation of all that had happened since landing. It was printed in 1622 and was almost certainly written by Winslow and Bradford. It is conveniently reprinted in Arber's *Story of the Pilgrims*, together with Winslow's *Good News from New England*. Bradford's *History* adds important information on points not covered by these narratives, and on others, like the "general sickness," which they deemed it better to omit in 1621.

more than eighty tons to anchor near the shore. The second fact which impressed them was the number of fish they saw and the larger amount they conjectured would be present in the proper season. Whales they had seen off Provincetown; they had been told by the crew of the vast profit from the sale of the oil, and they judged in the sublimity of their ignorance that it would be easy to kill one. Seals also they saw and deemed valuable. Thus two prime requisites were answered. The amount of cleared land, on either side of what came to be called the Town Brook, also attracted them to the site. A good many acres of corn fields of the Patuxets, dead from the plague of three years before, were unused, and, after testing the soil, they concluded it to be rich and sufficiently deep. The small rivers and brooks emptying into the harbor provided an abundance of water, while at a distance of one-eighth of a mile stood abundant timber for their houses and for the cut lumber, which they expected to export to England, where wood was scarce and expensive. Furthermore, the site was protected by Nature, for on the east the harbor, and on the south the town brook in a little ravine prevented attack by the Indians. On the west an abrupt hill, one hundred and sixty-five feet high, gave them a location for their cannon commanding the only easy approaches to the new town from the open fields to the north.

After two days of storm and rain they set to work, on December 23, and for three days cut timber with great diligence. The difficulties of their task were considerable, for their headquarters, the *Mayflower*, was one and one-half miles from shore, and they must row back and forth constantly. They were compelled to carry the timber itself an eighth of a mile from the woods without draught animals to assist. There were in all only forty-four adult men, many of whom were by this time ill. The first Christmas therefore was spent in hard work, for, like most Protestant bodies of the time, the Pilgrims declined to celebrate the day because they could find no warrant for it in the Scriptures. Two more days of rain interfered with the work, but on the twenty-eighth they laid out the town along the brook, and assigned locations for a "common house," to be used as an assembly hall, and for several dwelling houses. After more rain and cold during the first week in January, the work went on at a more rapid rate and without intermission. Jones and his men went out in the shallop and after some ado caught three seals and one codfish. Apparently an expedition, whose prime object was the catching of fish, had arrived with no practical knowledge of the sort of fishing which New England afforded. On January 7, to facilitate the work, the company was divided into nineteen "families," thus putting the boys and servants under the supervision of the older married men.

So rapidly had they worked that by January 9, the frame of a "common house," twenty feet square, had been built of rough logs and the cracks filled in with mud. The roof they built in the succeeding days of thatch, after a fashion still common at Scrooby and Austerfield. On the fourteenth at about six in the morning, the lookouts on the *Mayflower* saw the new house on shore afire, but, the tide being out, the shallows and the high wind prevented their sending aid for some little time. A spark from a match in the house had set fire to the thatch, the high wind produced a quick blaze, which soon burned itself out without damage to the roof timbers or the frame. The house was packed with the beds of the majority of adult men, including several, like Carver and Bradford, who were very sick. All escaped from the burning building and regarded it as a special act of Providence, that the loaded muskets beside most of the men had not been discharged by the fire. The day being Sunday, no work could be done to repair the roof, and the rain poured dismally from a cheerless sky upon them, shivering in their roofless house throughout that long Sabbath. A week later the roof had been replaced and service was held on land by Elder Brewster for the first time. Gradually now as the weather permitted, and as the sheds and log cabins on shore were finished and thatched, the stores were moved from the ship to the shore, carried up the steep bank, and placed as they believed in safety. On the twenty-first of February, two cannon were gotten ashore by the help of the crew and located on the hill. Traces of Indians had been seen and the colony was alarmed.

Meanwhile,—indeed ever since the landing at Provincetown—a considerable number had been ill, and by February what Bradford calls the "general sickness" had stricken practically all the members. As their surprisingly good health on the voyage had been the result of the extremely careful arrangements, so now the cause of the "general sickness" seems to have been careless exposure, though not to the severity of New England weather, for the winter of 1620–1621 and the two succeeding winters were singularly open and mild. Both Provincetown and Plymouth harbors were so shallow that the *Mayflower* was anchored a long distance from shore, and a considerable number of Pilgrims waded back and forth, to the small boats every day, became thoroughly wet in the process, and had no satisfactory method of drying their clothes. The women, again, misled by the mild weather, washed clothes several days in the ponds at Provincetown and caught severe colds. The explorations in the open boat, the expeditions on the wet shore, resulted in further exposure. The result seems to have been tuberculosis of a surprisingly contagious and rapid type, called sometimes galloping consumption.[1] Whatever it was, the Pilgrims certainly caught it from one another and in December, six died, in January, eight more, in February, seventeen, and in March, thirteen. So dire was their distress that, during these months, no more than six or seven were well at a time, and only Brewster and Standish entirely escaped illness. On some days two or three died, and tradition has it that the graves accumulated so fast, that the Pilgrims leveled them with care, lest the Indians should be able to count and discover how greatly the little colony was weakened. Their devotion to each other during these exceedingly trying months is beyond all praise. Those who were able labored unsparingly night and day, carrying wood, making fires, preparing food, making beds, washing clothes, performing, as Bradford says, "willingly and cheerfully services which dainty stomachs could hardly endure to hear named."

The crew of the ship showed little sympathy for the Pilgrims in their extremity and even denied them a share of the few comforts they themselves possessed. Bradford therefore notes with considerable satisfaction the godless conduct of the crew when the disease fell upon them. The Pilgrims now ministered to their needs as best they

[1] Edward E. Cornwall, M. D., in *New England Magazine*, New Series, XV, 662–667. They were also much troubled by sciatica, rheumatism, and inflammatory rheumatism.

could, and so affected the boatswain, who, as Bradford notes, had often "cursed and scoffed at the passengers," that he cried out to them, "O, saith he, you I now see show your love as Christians unto one another, but we let one another lie and die like dogs." In all, forty-six died and only fifty-six were left alive of the original company. At the end of the first year, the number of survivors was fifty-one, twenty-three adults:—Bradford, Edward and Gilbert Winslow, Brewster and his wife, Allerton, Standish, Hopkins and his wife, Fuller, the surgeon, John Alden, and twelve others. Only one of the nine servants survived; only four out of fourteen wives; but ten out of eleven girls and fifteen out of twenty-one boys.

About the middle of March, when many had barely recovered from the worst ravages of disease, the men met at the common house to decide what action, if any, should be taken in regard to the Indians. Suddenly they saw walking down their little street, a solitary Indian, who advanced boldly and called out to them in English, welcome. He was entirely naked except for a leathern girdle and carried only a bow and two arrows. They stopped him as he was about to enter the common house, but he explained in broken English that he was a chief of Monhegan in Maine, where he had learned English from the crews of the fishing vessels. His name was, he said, Samoset. He talked with them pleasantly and at great length, and as the wind began to be sharp, they put a cloak about him. Presently he asked for beer. They took him to dinner and gave him some "strong water," with biscuit, butter, cheese, something they called pudding, and some duck, all of which surprised him not at all. He proceeded to tell them after dinner a great deal about the Indians of the district. In particular that the Indian name of Plymouth was Patuxet, that the whole tribe had died in a plague four years before, and that their nearest neighbors were a tribe of about sixty warriors. At night they would gladly have gotten rid of him, but, as he showed no inclination to leave, they determined to send him aboard the *Mayflower*. They were unable to get the shallop across the flats, and so lodged him with Steven Hopkins and watched him with care. In the morning he departed with many friendly expressions.

Two weeks later he returned with five tall savages, whom the Pilgrims entertained as best they could, much embarrassed because the day was Sunday and the Indians insisted upon dancing and singing. After a short but very friendly visit, they departed, Samoset remaining again overnight. On March twenty-second, a fine spring day, he came back once more, bringing with him the sole survivor of the Indian tribe which had formerly lived at Plymouth, a man called Squanto by Bradford, and Tisquantum by Winslow.[1] He had been captured some years before by an English captain, carried to London, brought back by the English to Newfoundland, whence Captain Dermer in a voyage the year before the Pilgrims landed had brought him back to Cape Cod. The two Indians brought news that Massasoit, the sachem of the tribes of Pokanoket, was on his way with his warriors to pay a ceremonial visit.

After about an hour of great excitement, some sixty

[1] Goodwin, Arber, and others have chosen to follow Winslow instead of employing the more familiar Squanto. I see no valid reason for supposing Winslow more accurate than Bradford in transliterating the Indian's name or in representing Pilgrim practice.

Indians appeared on the hill beyond the town brook, and, after some preliminary negotiations by Squanto, Edward Winslow, wearing armor and side-arms, clambered down the ravine to the ford of the brook, marched up the hill, and stayed several hours alone with the Indians. He presented Massasoit with two knives and a copper chain, with some sort of jewel attached, gave his brother a knife, and provided both with "strong water," biscuits, and butter. The "Emperor" ate and drank with relish and distributed what was left to his followers. After further speeches on either side, Massasoit with some of his warriors started down to the town brook. Standish, Allerton, and six men, armed with muskets, saluted, received him, and marched with such ceremony as they might up the street to one of the houses, in which they had placed a green rug and some cushions. Having seated the "Emperor," Governor Carver came to visit him, escorted by a small body guard, to the blowing of a trumpet and the beating of a drum. He kissed the Indian's hand and was kissed in return; they drank "strong waters" together, which made Massasoit "sweat for a great time thereafter." They fed him a liberal supply of meat, and then concluded with him what they called a treaty of friendship and amity. The business thus ended, Massasoit was courteously conducted to the brook and departed, Winslow now returning to his friends. Samoset and Squanto remained as guests of the colony for some little time, Samoset eventually taking up his residence with them.

On March 23, Carver was reëlected Governor for the coming year, but in the following month was apparently sunstruck on one of the warm spring days, and, weakened by illness and over-exertion, died. William Bradford was elected Governor in his stead. More eloquent testimony of the great value of Bradford's services during the past three months could not have been given. In England he had been but a lad, and in Holland had played no considerable part in the life of the Church that we can now trace. The voyage and the first few months at Plymouth displayed convincingly his great executive ability, and that calm, impartial mind to which Plymouth was to owe so much. Shortly before Carver's death, the *Mayflower* left for England and the Pilgrims were now thrown upon their own resources.

Under the guidance of Squanto they planted about twenty acres of Indian corn. The amount of labor involved was prodigious for twenty-one men and six large boys, all of whom had been sick the greater part of the winter. Goodwin has calculated that one hundred thousand holes were dug with a hoe or mattock; as they buried in each two or three alewives, caught in the town brook, they must have carried up the steep banks into the fields some forty tons of fish. A part of the labor of planting, which Squanto taught them, was the necessity of watching the corn fields to keep the wolves from digging up the alewives. The summer was occupied with expeditions to the neighboring Indian tribes for trade in corn and furs, and in the cutting of a great supply of clapboards, which was considerable enough entirely to fill the *Fortune* when she arrived in the autumn. It must be remembered that these clapboards had to be cut by hand with axes and saws and were then carried on the Pilgrims' backs into Plymouth and stored. In addition, they completed during the summer seven dwelling houses and four buildings for common purposes, including the common house and store houses. So prodigious an amount of manual labor will show how very seriously the Pilgrims took the pledge in their contract to labor four days for the merchants and two for themselves. In September, Standish, Winslow, Squanto, and eight men made a trip to Boston Harbor, which they very much admired, and sailed home well content with a considerable number of beaver skins which they expected to export to England.

It is difficult to imagine exactly what Plymouth must have looked like in its first year, but with the aid of a little plan left us by Bradford and the rather explicit testimony of their writings, we can picture to ourselves a small plateau of land, lying about thirty feet above the harbor, and sloping back to Fort Hill, one hundred and sixty-five feet high. "The street," as they called it (now Leyden Street), ran directly toward Fort Hill, at some little distance from the town brook, to the path which led up the steep incline. On the left-hand side, approaching from the harbor, came first the Common House, then lots assigned to Brown, Goodman, and Brewster successively; on the right-hand side, lots assigned to Fuller, Howland, and Hopkins. A highway at right angles to "the street" here intervened. The remaining space to the foot of the hill was divided into four lots on the left of the street, worked by Billington, Allerton, Cook, and Winslow, while the land on the right side of the street was divided into two larger lots, one held by Bradford and the other by Standish and Alden.

On these twelve lots were standing seven houses of logs, stuffed with mud, with heavy thatch roofs. The windows were made of oiled paper and the doors were probably hung on crude hinges of iron. Out beyond the houses, to the right of the street, lay the corn fields of the old Patuxets, and, on the other side of the brook, were also corn fields, though it seems likely that at this time the Pilgrims did not utilize them. The landing place from the ships lay well to the right of the street along the harbor, the famous rock, the only rock of any size (with one exception) within a considerable radius of Plymouth. The Pilgrims landed in reality, not upon a rockbound coast, but upon sandbars and mud spits, and this rock was the only landing place at which they could disembark without wading through the shallows. [1]

And now in the autumn an abundant harvest was reaped, and, with the houses thus completed and the fifty-one survivors in excellent health, a celebration was held. The first Thanksgiving dinner consisted of a plentiful supply of wild fowl, deer, and hasty pudding. Probably none of the butter, cheese, and biscuits brought from England were left at this time, though no doubt brandy and schnapps were still on hand. Some modern admirers of the Pilgrims will be surprised and perhaps distressed to learn that this historic feast was graced by the presence of Massasoit and his entire tribe. It lasted at least three days, and included not only several hearty meals but drilling, simple sports, and dancing and singing by the Indians, who played by far the most considerable and insistent parts. Not improbably the first Thanksgiving dinner much more nearly resembled an outdoor barbecue, attended by the entire population, than a grimly decorous meal, eaten solemnly by each family in its own house.

[1] Bradford and Winslow mention repeatedly during this first year wading ashore from the small boats and their inability to get ashore when the tide was out; evidently it was some time before they began to use the rock as a landing place.

CHAPTER VIII

THE PROBLEM OF SUBSISTENCE

Scarcely was the first Thanksgiving feast over than the problem of subsistence was raised anew by the arrival of the *Fortune* from England on November 20-30, 1621, with thirty-five new colonists, sent out by the Pilgrims' associates, but without tools, clothes, or food. For the succeeding two years the colonists were never for a moment free from the danger of starvation. Indeed, in the summer of 1623, the second band of newcomers, who landed from the *Anne*, found their friends "in a very low condition." "Many were ragged in aparel and some litle beter than halfe naked. . . . For food they were all alike save some that had got a few pease of the ship that was last hear. The best dish they could presente their freinds with was a lobster or a peece of fish, without bread or anything els but a cupp of fair spring water." [1] Winslow declared that he had often seen men staggering at noon from weakness induced by hunger.[2] Grimly the Pilgrims comforted themselves in the absence of bread with the words of Deuteronomy, that "man liveth not by bread only but by every word that proceedeth out of the mouth of the Lord doth a man live." [3]

For six years, from 1621 to 1627, questions of sub-

[1] Bradford, *History*, 175.

[2] Winslow, *Good News from New England*, reprinted in Arber, *Pilgrim Fathers*, 581.

[3] So quoted by Bradford, 175.

sistence and of trade, explorations, negotiations with the merchants, visits to and from the Indians, threatened quarrels with Indians and other white men continued to engross the attention of the Pilgrims and constitute a narrative difficult to follow as it happened day by day without loss of perspective and of a sense of proportion. The essential unity of the story can, however, be preserved by dealing in a topical fashion with the serious problems in the chronological order of their solution. The first three years, despite explorations, relations with the Indians, and other distractions, were almost entirely devoted to the question of subsistence. This happily was solved in 1623, to bother them no more. In that year, the Indian problem, never before dangerous or pressing, came suddenly to a head, demanded prompt action, and was also successfully and adequately met. While the Pilgrims had been by no means alone on the coast since 1620, it was not until 1624 and 1625 that attempts were made to sow civil and ecclesiastical discord at Plymouth and to induce the English authorities to undertake the supervision and examination the Pilgrims had from the first sincerely dreaded. These dangers past, their relations with the merchants, never satisfactory, came to an open breach in 1625 and necessitated in 1626 and 1627 a thorough reorganization of the little colony. Clarity and unity have therefore dictated the treatment of the problem of subsistence first, and it has been followed by consecutive and logical analyses of Indian relations, of the episodes of Lyford and Morton, and of the tangled negotiations with the merchants, from the original agreement signed at Leyden to the dissolution of the Merchant Adventurers and the creation of the Undertakers. While not free from objection, this treatment seems to meet in some measure the various requirements of a history which shall be something better than a brief annalistic sketch.

The sufferings at Plymouth have been only too little emphasized by the students of American history. So much has been said about the starvation at Jamestown that it is time we realized that the privation at Plymouth was as great and the devotion and forbearance greater. The explanation of these three years of suffering is not far to seek. The original plans, so carefully thought out in Holland for the little colony, had regarded as perilous a settlement colony which should maintain itself from the first upon the proceeds of its own labor. They had therefore decided to found a permanent trading post, supported during the first years of its life by supplies sent out regularly from England by the Adventurers, and paid for by the proceeds of the fish, furs, and lumber which the colony would return. The Pilgrims had felt able to pledge themselves to work four days in the week for the merchants, because they fully expected the latter to bear the real burden of supporting the colony, while they were working out their indebtedness. In addition, Robinson and the leaders had laid great stress on the importance of ownership by the colonists of one or more ships of from sixty to one hundred tons burden, so that their range of trading might be wide, and so that thus the ships themselves might carry the proceeds to England and bring back the provisions upon which the new colony was to depend. It seemed indeed a definitely safe venture:—nothing more than conducting from the New World the sort of trading voyage annually prosecuted from England and Holland by literally hundreds of fishers and traders.

From the first a profit was expected in excess of the cost of maintenance, so that in the course of seven years the debt of the Pilgrims to the merchants would be entirely extinguished, and they would then be at liberty to utilize the entire proceeds of the trade for their own support; this they would still expect to draw from England as they had in the early years.

The *Speedwell* was accordingly bought in Holland "to transport them, so to stay in the cuntrie and atend upon fishing and such other affairs as might be for the good and benefite of the colonie when they come ther." A captain and crew were hired to remain with the Pilgrims for a year while they were learning to operate the vessel. It was not until the spring of 1621 that the full scope of the calamity became clear which the return of the *Speedwell* had involved. It was not until the fifty survivors found themselves practically marooned in Massachusetts Bay that they entirely realized how radical a change of plan had been forced upon them, that they were now to attempt in fact the experiment which they had deemed in Holland too perilous possibly to succeed. The original plan had miscarried. Nor did they ever receive that prompt support from the Adventurers in England which they had felt it so important to secure when the original contract was prepared. The *Fortune* arrived in 1621 indeed, but with no food. The *Anne* came in 1623 but brought food only for its own passengers, and the subsequent ships brought no assistance except cattle. Both features of the original plan thus entirely failed. Here unquestionably lay the true difficulty of the Pilgrims. Had they expected to subsist from the first on what they could raise, not only would their equipment have been different, but the first contract with the merchants would have been as unacceptable to them as the second, and probably would have been deemed entirely unnecessary.

The great practical difficulty, however, presented by the problem of subsistence in these first years was the constant necessity of feeding more mouths than they had calculated upon. During the spring and summer of 1621, the supply of food, though never ample, seems somehow to have sufficed. Although provisions were low when the *Mayflower* reached Cape Cod, the death of half the company and of a considerable number of the crew made it possible for the survivors to hold out on an amount of food entirely insufficient for the original emigrants. In the autumn of 1621, their diligent labor was rewarded with a harvest, more than sufficient for all of their own needs for the coming year, and they celebrated the autumn festival in the true spirit of thankfulness. But within a few weeks the *Fortune* landed thirty-five new colonists, sent over by the Adventurers with neither tools, nor clothes, nor food. The labor of fifty active men and women was scarcely to be expected to suffice for the sustenance of thirty-five extra mouths, who had contributed nothing to the work of raising the food. Want at once stared the colony in the face. Half rations became imperative, and indeed it was doubtful whether the food could be made to hold out until the following harvest. They seem to have expected a ship from England with large supplies of food in the spring of 1622. Instead there arrived seven more men, the forerunners of a colony sent out by Weston on another ship, and whom he asked the Pilgrims to shelter and feed for the time being. Soon Weston's new colony itself appeared at Plymouth, some sixty husky men, who brought their own food to be sure, but who insisted upon levying toll on the Pilgrims' growing corn to supplement their own diet. There was thus constant necessity during the first two years of stretching the food supplies to meet entirely unforeseen emergencies. Nor should we forget that the entertainment of the Indians was a great drain on the slender resources of a community numbering only about fifty. Constant presents to Massasoit of food and occasional entertainment of anywhere from five to ninety Indians was no small item with a larder so insufficiently stocked.

All this would perhaps have been less serious had there been available any other source of supply in America for such food as the Pilgrims had been accustomed to eat. That none such existed the year 1622 proved only too definitely. In May, after the colony had been long upon short allowance, the food was literally gone, and desperate attempts were made by Bradford, Winslow, and Standish to discover some new supply. Nothing has more puzzled their biographers than this fact, that, in a land fairly alive with game, the waters of which were crowded with fish, the shores of which were strewn with lobsters, clams, eels, and oysters, in whose woods and fields grew quantities of edible berries, the Pilgrims literally starved. Perhaps one might say that our amazement results from the fact that they felt themselves to be starving when forced to eat shell fish and game. Some have supposed that the truth lay in their inability to catch the fish or kill the game, and it seems indeed extraordinary that they possessed no nets strong enough to hold cod and the other large fish which abounded, and on the other hand no hooks small enough to catch the fish which teemed in

New England waters. They came from a land of hunters to a land of game; they sailed from a land of fishermen for a land of fish; and seem to have been neither prepared nor able to kill the one or catch the other.

Certainly it was not for lack of firearms or of powder, because in 1622, when the need for food was greatest, Standish spent a good deal of time drilling small companies of men and allowed them to fire volleys and salutes in the course of the manœuvers. If powder was too scarce to be used in getting food, surely it would not have been burned in practice drills. We must perhaps remember that the small arms of the seventeenth century were exceedingly inaccurate in bore, and consequently that it was most difficult to hit an object at any distance, and particularly difficult to hit a moving object. The Pilgrims moreover had, with one or two possible exceptions, never used firearms, and needed a year or two of practice to become accustomed to their muskets. In their first encounter with the Indians, they tell us of potting at the Indian chief only half a musket's shot distance and of missing him again and again. They improved, however, for Winslow reports hitting a crow at eighty yards and a duck at one hundred and twenty yards, and in the autumn of 1621 four men killed enough game in one day to feed the whole colony for a week. Whatever the difficulties may have been in the first months, they were certainly overcome.[1]

We must perhaps ascribe something to the Englishman's well-known insistence upon his European diet and to his extraordinary dislike to accept any radical

---

[1] Bradford told De Rassiéres in 1627 that three men in a shallop could catch as much cod in the harbor in three hours as the whole colony could eat in a day. Goodwin, *The Pilgrim Republic*, 307.

change in it. There seems to be no doubt whatever that the Pilgrims resolutely refused to eat anything but the food to which they had been accustomed, until actual hunger drove them to it. Like all Europeans of the sixteenth and seventeenth centuries, their common drink in England and Holland had been small beer and they could not at first believe that the drinking of water would not be followed by terrible diseases.[1] Some considerable persuasion even seems to have been necessary on the part of the leaders to induce some to try the experiment at all. Previous experience had accustomed them to bread as the chief staple of diet and they seem to have believed it impossible to maintain health, unless one-half or two-thirds of all they ate was bread. They therefore seem to have eaten their bread in the accustomed proportion as long as it lasted, and then to have considered that a diet of shell-fish, water, berries, and game was literally starvation.

Otherwise it is difficult to explain the extraordinary efforts made to eke out the slender stores of grain which they possessed and to replenish them even at exorbitant cost. Expeditions were sent out to buy corn from the Indians and with some success, but the shallop was so small that the radius within which they could cruise prevented them from collecting any considerable amount of grain. The *Speedwell* would have allowed them to cruise from the St. Lawrence to the Hudson and to have

[1] Among objections made by those who returned to England stood prominently: "6. ob: the water is not wholsome." To which Bradford replied: "Ans: if they mean, not so wholsome as the good beere and wine in London (which they so dearly love) we will not dispute with them; but els, for water, it is as good as any in the world (for ought we knowe), and it is wholsome enough to us that can be contente therwith." *History*, 194–195.

tapped the abundant supplies of the Connecticut Indians. Some attempt was made to encourage the resident Indians to plant more corn on the expectation of selling it to the Pilgrims, but the tribes in the neighborhood had been too much decimated by the plague to sow any considerable area of ground. From the English fishing ships in Massachusetts Bay some food was procured during the summer of 1622. From the ships that put in at Plymouth something more was had, but from all of these sources only a very small total.

Nothing is perhaps more admirable in the whole annals of the Pilgrims than their generosity, magnanimity, and forbearance in these two critical years. They were under no obligation to feed and house Weston's seven men or to show hospitality to his colony of sixty when they appeared in July, 1622. Weston himself had already sold his interest in the Adventurers, and had quarreled with the Pilgrims so decidedly before they left England, that they could scarcely have been blamed, if they had felt that under the circumstances they could hardly share their pittance with him. But they made no protest and indeed sought to assist him in every way. Those of his men who were sick were kept at Plymouth until Fuller, the Pilgrims' doctor, had cured them.

The harvest of 1622, while reasonably good, again proved insufficient, largely because the depredations made upon the young growing corn by Weston's men and by the Pilgrims themselves had reduced its quantity. In the spring of 1623 actual starvation again was in prospect. The leaders now came to the conclusion that the true difficulty lay in the "common course and condition," in the contract with the Adventurers, and in the peculiar social and economic conditions which had resulted from it. Having rejected the revised agreement with the merchants, they had considered themselves the more obligated to observe the original stipulations. The Pilgrims, the Adventurers who came with them, and the laborers and servants had worked together for the common interest; all food and all supplies had been held in common; all the proceeds of the trading became common property. While the common stock by no means precluded the devotion of the entire labor of the little community to the raising of food, they had worked faithfully and conscientiously in the dressing of lumber and in the collection of furs, for the leaders were anxious to prove that under the first contract profit was possible. Then, in November, 1621, Cushman had arrived on the *Fortune* and had at last induced them to accept and sign the revised articles with the Adventurers, by which accordingly the work of the two succeeding years had been regulated. They were now bound to devote the whole of their time to work for the common stock, with a definite implication that the collection of goods to return to England was on no account to be suspended. This the Pilgrims accepted seriously. Their diligence must have been great and certainly a good half of their labor, if not more, went into the "many other imployments" which Bradford mentions.

The leaders now concluded that they could make profit for the Adventurers if supported from England, or that they could easily maintain themselves from the fruits of their labor in New England, if only the colony gave its entire time to the problem of sustenance.[1]

[1] Bradford thus translated Seneca:
"A greate part of libertie is a well governed belly and to be patiente in all wants."

They could spend six days a week in the employ of the merchants only at the grave risk of starvation. It was clear by this time that no regular supplies of food were to be looked for from England and they therefore determined to abandon work in common for a new system. As much land was alloted to each man and his family as it was thought he could possibly till; each was to retain for his own use the entire proceeds, but was on the other hand to be responsible for his own sustenance.[1] A great gain was immediately visible in the spring of 1623 in the amount of labor expended as well as in its efficiency. Many energetic and capable men had been unwilling to work as hard as they could, since they had realized that their energy would merely relieve the indifferent and the lazy from the necessity of working at all. Others had therefore shirked and had done as little work as they could, with the confident knowledge that the common store of food would give them as much to eat as the others had, and that the leaders were far too conscientious and merciful to allow even the laggards to starve. Those who had not worked before now began under the new system to work. Those who already worked, worked more; those who had done well, worked better.[2]

Moreover, the wives and children had complained of labor in the fields; several of the men had demurred at allowing their wives and young children to work for Adventurers in London and servants in America, and for young unmarried men whom they felt well able to look after themselves. Now the women and children gladly worked in their own fields and gardens, and felt no indignity nor grudged the pains. Thus in all these ways

[1] Bradford, *History*, 162–164.
[2] Winslow, *Good News from New England*, in Arber, 575–581.

an immense gain in the quantity and quality of labor devoted to the problem of subsistence was made. The whole colony in the year 1623 devoted its prime efforts to the harvest, with the very satisfactory and clear result that all doubts as to its future ability to maintain itself vanished. To anticipate a little, after 1623 no more considerable bands of new settlers arrived who brought no food. The newcomers formed also a smaller proportion of the colony than had the *Fortune* emigrants and therefore were a less serious problem. The artificial drains on the food supply ceased at the very time when they might more easily have been met. The satisfaction of the people under the new system was immeasurably greater, despite the fact that they had not been given ownership of the land, but merely the right to use it for a limited time.

Perplexities and fears continued still throughout the summer of 1623. After so great an amount of corn had been planted, drought set in for six weeks; during June and July practically no rain fell; and some of the colony began to despair, for much of the corn began to shrivel and wilt. There came news that a ship with supplies had been sent them from England but had been forced to turn back. Even the most courageous seem to have faltered a little during these trying weeks. Finally a day of fasting and humiliation was set. The Pilgrims assembled in the little meeting room on Fort Hill and prayed there continuously and fervently for eight or nine hours as the Scripture directed, "without ceasing." On the next morning gentle showers began and continued practically a fortnight. The harvest was saved. It is difficult for us to understand the theological significance they attached to this incident. It seemed to them literally a miracle wrought by God in their favor to indicate His blessing upon their enterprise. Just as the drought itself, with the months of famine which had preceded it, had signified the curse of God upon them, His desire to inform them that their enterprise did not meet His approval, so now elation, confidence in their correct reading of God's intention, came to them and never left them. From this moment they were convinced that God intended the enterprise to succeed.

When therefore, toward the end of July, the *Anne* arrived, and some days after, the *Little James*, the newcomers found a colony alert, full of determination and hope, little regarding the ragged state of their European clothes and their lack of certain staples of diet, which two years before they had considered essential. The newcomers were partly people sent by the Adventurers, partly members of the Leyden congregation who had come over to join their friends, and partly "particulars," who had paid their passage to the Adventurers, and who wished to settle somewhere in the vicinity and govern themselves. Now arose a burning question. The old settlers were very unwilling that the newcomers should be received on any basis which recognized their right to share in the new crop, for fear of a repetition of their fate in 1621 and 1622. The newcomers saw the condition of the old settlers and their lack of European food, and were afraid that, if the supply, which they had brought to last them until the following spring, should be shared with the old settlers, they too would be reduced to clams and Indian corn in the near future. This seemed to them akin to starvation. There were those too, particularly the men sent out by the Adventurers, who had expected to find rude houses, woods, and Indians, but who had also looked forward to good food and plenty of it, with cattle, milk, meat, beer, and the other staples of English diet. They were not at all sure that they wished to remain in the colony on any terms, and some of them were so outspoken and disagreeable, that Bradford sent them back to England when the ship returned.

After heated discussion, a settlement was at last reached. The old settlers should retain their crop entire, each man his own planting, should have no share in the new supply brought on the *Anne* but should be in no sense responsible for the maintenance of the newcomers. The newcomers were allowed to keep the entire supply of food they had brought, and gladly sacrificed any expectations they might otherwise have entertained of sharing in the supplies of the old settlers. They were allotted land to till, the produce of which they should keep. The "particulars," who came on their own account and who had had visions of building great houses in pleasant situations and of becoming suddenly rich from the fish and fur trade, speedily saw the error of their assumptions and came to terms with the colony. They received allotments of land within the limits of the town, agreed to acknowledge the authority of the Governor and the Assistants, and to obey all laws which had been made. They were freed from any obligation to collect furs or lumber in accordance with the agreement the Pilgrims were still observing with the merchants, but were accordingly debarred entirely from the right to trade with the Indians, so long as the contract with the merchants should endure. They were to pay a tax of one bushel of maize for every male more than sixteen years old. Eventually most of them became members of the colony.

The abundant harvest of that year put an end for all time to the fears of the ability of the colony to maintain itself, so long as its real strength and energy was given to the problem of subsistence. The credit for the solution of the problems of the first years belongs undoubtedly to William Bradford. As Brewster had been the outstanding figure of the English period, as Robinson had dominated the group at Leyden, so Bradford at once became the leader after the landing at Plymouth. While we must not forget the effective work of Carver, the undoubted influence of Brewster, or the able cooperation of Allerton, Winslow, and Standish, Bradford towers above them all as the true hero of the first years. The work of the Governor at that time must have been difficult and laborious in the extreme. He was foreman of a band of laborers and must allot them their tasks. He was an overseer, who must see that they performed them duly and well. He was storekeeper, receiving the proceeds of the work, doling out day by day supplies from the common stock. He was magistrate and policeman, rendering decisions, arresting offenders, punishing them himself. But beyond all question, his labors as foreman and overseer in the first three years took time, strength, tact, and patience to an extraordinary degree.

One last fright they had late in the fall of 1623. The harvest had been reaped and piled in the storehouses. Gorges's ship was in the harbor on its way back to England from Virginia. The seamen were on shore roistering, as Bradford says, in one of the houses, and had built a great fire because of the cold weather. The chimney was not sufficiently well constructed to resist the heat; the thatch burst into flames; and three or four houses were burned. The house, in which the fire started, was next the storehouse in which were all the provisions and the goods for trading with the Indians. Some would have thrown them out into the street, but others feared theft. So a trusty company was placed within, and the rest of the Pilgrims extinguished the sparks as they fell. In the midst of the tumult, a voice was heard that bade them look about them, for all near them were not friends. Shortly after smoke was seen rising from a shed near the end of the storehouse. There they found a firebrand, a yard long, thrust well into the refuse. Once more, they felt the judgment of God was in their favor.

Pory's Description of Plymouth in 1622. When this volume was about to go to press, appeared Mr. Champlin Burrage's *John Pory's Lost Description of Plymouth Colony in the Earliest Days of the Pilgrim Fathers.* . . . Boston and New York, 1918, pp. xxiv + 65. Edition limited to 365 numbered copies. Pory's brief letter (pp. 35–44) is by no means our earliest information about Plymouth, as Mr. Burrage seems to imply in his preface, for Mourt's Relation was written in 1621 and was published in London in 1622, but it is the first account by an outsider and was written in Jan. and Feb. 1622–23 about a visit in the previous June or July. The only interesting fact about it is Pory's omission of any information about the inhabitants or the conditions of life. True, we learn that they are a virtuous people, have built a strong stockade and fort, and are at peace with the Indians. But not a suggestion of their Separatism, of their straits for food, of their active dislike for the diet of fish, shellfish, game, and berries about which Pory discourses so volubly. He repeats Bradford's boast that the climate was so healthful that none had died for a whole year. This was the literal truth but concealed the fearful mortality of the first six months. Either they were able to hide from him the real condition of the colony as Bradford has described it or they persuaded him he could render them very material assistance by silence. Pory's letter to Bradford (*History*, 153–154) makes us practically certain that this letter tells not what he saw at Plymouth but what he and they judged it expedient should be believed in England.

CHAPTER IX

STANDISH AND THE PROBLEM OF DEFENCE

In the same year in which the problem of subsistence was so happily solved, another was disposed of, to bother them no more, the problem of defence. No phase of the adventure had so appalled the congregation of Robinson at its meetings in the large house at Leyden as the wilderness and its savage inhabitants. All the imaginative vagaries of Vespucius and the Spanish tales of Aztec and Peruvian barbarism came to them magnified and distorted in books about America which the credulous in sixteenth century Europe eagerly devoured. They saw illimitable forests and splendid fields, filled with furious hordes of savages, whom they seem to have supposed a sort of combination of all the monstrosities in the travelogues of medieval Munchausens. To be sure from fishermen and explorers who had actually been in America far less terrifying tales came to them. The congregation at Leyden was divided as to which should be credited, and even those who had scouted wild stories and had in consequence departed for America had not been without misgivings. As they stood on the deck of the *Mayflower* and inspected the quiet shores of Cape Cod, they shuddered as they thought of the possibilities. Bradford voiced this fear in no uncertain tones. Such fears were not unnatural in honest yeomen and peasants who had spent their lives behind the plow, loom, or printing press, who had never smelt powder fired in earnest, or seen beasts wilder than the North country cattle, nor life more dangerous than ruminative agriculture in the fens of the Trent, or manufacturing in peaceful Leyden. Wars and the rumors of wars in the sixteenth and seventeenth centuries had stalked about, knocking their heads upon the clouds, but real danger and adventure had passed the Pilgrims by.

Their apprehensions had found expression in an armament disproportionate to their means. They seem to have brought sufficient equipment for eighteen or twenty men, that is, for fully one-third of all the male passengers: quilted cotton coats for armor (the thickets of Cape Cod could scarcely have torn steel breastplates), several cannon, muskets of the older pattern, fired with lighted tow, and some snaphances, exploded by a flint which struck a spark in a pan of powder, all far more modern pieces than those commonly used in Europe for half a century. They had also secured the services of a professional soldier, an item of expense by no means negligible in their case. To talk thus about arms and the problem of defense for a little community of one hundred people, who found to oppose them Indian tribes of no more than fifty or sixty men, seems an exaggeration of language. We shall find warlike expeditions of six men, conspiracies threatening the life of the colony extinguished by eight men, battles fought, one might say, by Standish alone, like the first encounter. But weak as the Indians were, they were still sufficiently numerous to be a matter of concern to the Pilgrims. We must not forget that, after the "general sickness" of the winter of 1620-21, the little colony only mustered twenty-one men and six boys, and, even after the coming of the *Fortune* numbered not more than fifty, while even in 1630 the male population able to bear arms scarcely exceeded one hundred and fifty. If we think less of figures than of facts, less of the men concerned and more of the issues at stake, less of the safety of a single colony and more of the persistence of a certain trend of thought and of a certain example, we shall perhaps attain that measure of interest, in these first details with the Indians, which the Pilgrims themselves experienced.[1] The joyful fact was soon clear to them that they were in no danger of being scalped the moment they set foot on shore. The Indians seen in the first explorations ran with such celerity that the Pilgrims scarce caught sight of them. The First Encounter passed off without real danger, so that they were much emboldened and resolved in the future to show a stiff front. As the weeks passed, they concluded that the Indians of the vicinity really were peaceably disposed. Again and again two or three men had been alone in the woods or fields, had seen Indians sometimes nearby, sometimes at a distance, but had not been molested. The coming of Samoset and Squanto showed that there were many Indians who had seen white men before, who had received kind treatment, and were well-disposed. They learned also of others, like the Nausets, from whom Captain Hunt had kidnapped several men and carried them to England, and who were in consequence hostile to all white men. The traders and fishermen, French and English, who had voyaged up and down the coast

[1] The contemporary accounts written in the first four years deal at inordinate length with the Indians, their manners and customs, and with the events related in this chapter. The reader will find them conveniently reprinted in Arber's *The Pilgrim Fathers*. An older edition is Young's *Chronicles of the Pilgrim Fathers*. There have been various special reprints for bibliophiles.

for some decades, had thus made themselves known, but in the main their legacy to the Pilgrims was one of friendship and reliance upon the white man's good faith.

Indeed, during the first two years the Pilgrims seem to have been in no danger whatever from Indian hostility. The real danger lay in the probability that the Indians would consume their entire supplies of food. Far from it proving true that the Indians preferred roasted collops of human flesh, as the Pilgrims had believed in Holland, their liking for beer, strong water, biscuits, butter, and such other things as the Pilgrims could ill afford to dispense in large quantities, made their friendship more burdensome and really more dangerous to the immediate future of the colony than their enmity would have been. One village, some fifteen miles from Plymouth, in particular annoyed them by the continual resort of its population to Plymouth for food, lodging, and diversion. From fifty to one hundred Indians, male and female, might appear at any moment without warning and expect to be fed for two or three days.

From Squanto, Hobomok, and others, the Pilgrims soon learned the main facts about the Indians in New England. The Confederacy to which the Plymouth Indians had belonged was the Pokanoket, of which Massasoit was sachem, with residence at Sowams (now Warren) on Narragansett Bay. It included the small tribes of southeastern Massachusetts and eastern Rhode Island, numbered perhaps three thousand warriors before the plague of 1617, and only about three hundred after the visitation. The Patuxets at Plymouth had entirely disappeared in the plague and Massasoit's own tribe now numbered only about sixty warriors. To the north of them, around Weymouth, Boston, and Newton, was the Massachusetts Confederacy, composed of a considerable number of small tribes, which had been so decimated by the plague that scarcely one hundred warriors were left and its allegiance had been transferred to Massasoit. Further north in northeastern Massachusetts, southern New Hampshire, and the southern corner of Maine were the Pawtuckets, who had also been so decimated by the plague as practically to disappear from history by 1620. Central Massachusetts contained a few scattered and disorganized tribes, vassals of the Mohawks, while western Massachusetts, the whole of Vermont, and northern New Hampshire were vacant, having been depopulated in all probability by the Mohawks to furnish a hunting preserve.

From Narragansett Bay along Long Island Sound to the Hudson and as far north as the present boundary of Massachusetts was the most densely populated Indian district north of Mexico. Here were at least two powerful Confederacies, numerous, capable, and untouched by the plague—the Pequod Confederacy around the Connecticut River and the Narragansetts to the east of them. The total Indian population of New England in 1620 did not exceed fifty thousand and was perhaps not greater than twenty-five thousand, the great majority being in these two Confederacies and therefore in a district considerably removed from Plymouth. The Pilgrims did not know at this time the general distribution of Indians in the United States or realize that the powerful tribes of New England, rumors of whose prowess alarmed them, were after all weak, undeveloped, negligible, compared to the Iroquois nations, the Cherokees, and the Creeks. In truth, the Indians of the Atlantic coast were weak in numbers, inferior in development, backward in civilization compared to the Indian tribes of the interior. The Pilgrims stumbled upon a location where the aborigines were singularly weak, disorganized, and inferior in quality even for the Indians of the coast. Thanks to this fact and to the great plague of 1617, the question of defense was simplified.

Mere protection however would scarcely suffice. The Pilgrims saw at once that friendly relations with the Indians alone could create that profitable and continuous trade upon which such expectations had been built. Reasons of conscience also operated powerfully. They felt, as few Europeans did, the necessity of treating the Indian in accordance with the same ethical standard which they applied to each other. They attempted a scrupulous honesty and fairness which certainly exceeded the boasted ethics of Roger Williams and William Penn, both of whom in conspicuous instances over-reached the Indians in ways which most of us today would scarcely consider good business ethics. The Pilgrims even went so far as to hunt out and reimburse, the owner of a kettle of corn, which they took on one of their first expeditions along Cape Cod.

The Indian occupancy of Plymouth it was not necessary for them to extinguish by purchase or payments. Squanto was the only survivor and he lived with them until his death, well satisfied with the situation. Nor so far as we know did the other Indians subsequently raise claims. Many years later the extension of Plymouth beyond the limits of the original Patuxet occupancy did produce friction with Philip. The theoretical question of the justification of depriving the Indians permanently of their land caused the Pilgrims some considerable thought, but they answered it as nearly all Europeans have. They saw how slight was the attachment of the Indian to any particular piece of land; they sensed his lack of the conception of ownership; they realized that in the strictest sense no Indian ever used the land or developed its possibilities. They concluded that God had not brought them there without purpose, and that the conversion of the Indians would be more than ample compensation for the cession to them of a part of a domain too vast for the Indians to occupy. As Cushman wrote, the Indians "do but run over the grass as do also the foxes and wild beasts. They are not industrious, neither have they art, science, skill or faculty to use either the land or the commodities of it." [1]

The treaty, if such it can be called, made with Massasoit in March, 1621, was a simple reciprocal agreement of mutual aid and friendship. His people were not to hurt the Pilgrims nor would they injure his tribe. If any made war upon him unjustly (the Pilgrims were careful to specify the injustice of the war) they would help him. "If any did war against us" (and in this case Winslow left out unjustly) "he should aid us." They would each leave their arms behind when they approached the other's settlements. Thefts of tools or of food should be promptly restored and compensated. Offenders on either side were to be delivered up and they promised him that King James would esteem him as a friend and ally, all of which seemed to impress Massasoit. In the following

---

[1] R. C[ushman]. *Reasons and Considerations touching the Lawfulness of Removing out of England into the Parts of America* (1622). See also, "General Considerations for Planting New England" in Young's *Chronicles of Massachusetts Bay*, 275–276.

June or July, Winslow, Hopkins, and Squanto were sent on an embassy to Massasoit, partly as a visit of friendship to confirm and strengthen the agreement of March, partly because the Pilgrims were exceedingly anxious to see for themselves the size, location, and condition of Massasoit's tribe and of the country beyond Plymouth. Presents for the "Imperial Goveror," as Cushman called him, they carried,—a trooper's red cotton coat which they trimmed with lace, a copper chain and some other small things. This expedition to visit an unknown and questionable friend required perhaps more courage on the part of these men, who were not so many years before simple farmers and artisans, than we are inclined to credit.

Friendly treatment they everywhere met. Indeed the courtesy of the Indians was embarrassing. Some insisted upon carrying them across brooks, were anxious to carry their guns, accouterments, clothing, and the like, which the Pilgrims were afraid to entrust to them for fear they should carry them too far. After Massasoit had been informed of their coming and had returned to his chief abode, he welcomed them after the Indian ceremony, received the message, put on the coat and chain, and was exceedingly pleased in his simple way at the treatment. He then made a speech, of which Winslow tells us something, much of which seemed to consist of the statement that he was chief of such and such a place. Was not the town and the people his? Whereupon the whole assembly answered in unison that that was true, they were his. Thus he continued through the list of places of which he owned authority, and he repeated this series of statements some thirty or forty times, so that Winslow remarks, "As it was delightful, it was tedious unto us."

They then smoked together and Massasoit wondered that King James should be able to live without a wife, the poor queen having died the year previous. It grew late, the hungry Pilgrims longed for a substantial evening meal after their day's tramping and the long ceremony and speeches, but Massasoit offered them nothing, the reason, as they subsequently learned, being that there was nothing in the village to eat. He offered them however a share of his bed, a sort of framework about a foot elevated from the ground, upon which boards had been laid, with a mat of rushes upon them. He and his wife disposed themselves at one end and offered the Pilgrims the other. Two more Indians presently came and squeezed upon the framework, "so that we were worse weary of our lodging than of our journey."

Apparently no breakfast was served. At length, about one o'clock, Massasoit appeared with two fish he had shot in the stream with arrows. These were boiled and served, but, inasmuch as forty Indians beside the Pilgrims partook of this bountiful feast, their hunger was scarce assuaged. Massasoit, who seems to have enjoyed his own entertainment, was importunate and urged the Pilgrims to remain several days. But they determined to return to Plymouth, for the hardness and straightness of Massasoit's bed, the yelling and howling of the savages, the lice, fleas, and mosquitoes, made them doubt their ability to sleep while they remained. They were already so weak from lack of food and sleep, that they were afraid if they tarried longer, they would not have strength to reach Plymouth. They thus took their leave, to Massasoit's grief and surprise, and some miles away were entertained by other Indians with fish, a handful of meal, and some tobacco. At length, that night, they reached a river, where, despairing of anything to eat, they sent Hobomok ahead to beg Bradford to send out food to meet them. The Indians with them, however, caught a goodly store of fish that night, so that they had now plenty to eat, and thus, a day or two later, came back to Plymouth safe, but wet, weary, and footsore. This experience has been told at greater length partly because Winslow's account of it is so full, and partly because it is entirely typical of the Pilgrims' many experiences with these Indians.

In August, 1621, a tale was brought to Plymouth that one Corbitant, one of Massasoit's sub-chiefs, was plotting against him with the Narragansetts. Hobomok and Squanto were sent to find out the truth and word was presently brought back, that they had been captured by Corbitant, who intended to kill them both, for, as he told the Indians, if Squanto were dead, "the English had lost their tongue." Hobomok, who brought the word, told of breaking away from the circle of Indians and of seeing Squanto in their hands with Corbitant holding a knife to his heart. Upon this news the Pilgrims without hesitation determined to save Squanto if they might, and to avenge him if he were dead. They well realized that it would never do to allow the Indians to suppose for a moment that they were intimidated. They thus marched, ten men in all, on a rainy day, and, reaching Corbitant's little town, surrounded his house. The savages were exceedingly frightened and rushed around much distraught. Corbitant however was not there, Squanto was safe; and, taking him with them, they fired a couple of volleys to terrify the inhabitants and returned to Plymouth. In September, another voyage of exploration and intimidation was undertaken along Massachusetts Bay to the Massachusetts Indians whom they found demoralized and frightened. With some little difficulty, they reassured them and succeeded in exchanging a number of trinkets for a good many score of beaver skins. Squanto, Indian-like, wished to steal the clothes from the Indians' backs, a proposal indignantly rejected by Standish. But the Indians did not hesitate to sell their clothes, and the Pilgrims owned that the women, who decorated their bare bodies with twigs and leaves, were really more modest in their carriage than a good many Englishwomen they had known. Thus passed without danger or other incident the year 1621.

Early in 1622 a rattlesnake skin stuffed with arrows was brought into Plymouth by a messenger from Canonicus, chief of the Narragansetts, which Squanto explained was a challenge to war. After some debate, Bradford stuffed the skin with powder and bullets and sent it back by the messenger. The Indians seem to have been afraid of it and to have passed it around from hand to hand, until it was finally returned to Plymouth unbroken. Nothing came of it, but the Pilgrims felt it wise to erect pallisades around the little village. They began at the harbor and built a good sized stockade of dressed timber along the north side of the town, and thence along the north side of Fort Hill to the town brook, a distance in all of half a mile. The town brook ran through a rather steep and deep ravine and itself afforded natural protection on one side. There were in the pallisade four flanking bastions from which musket fire could rake the whole front. In these were the gates. Standish also arranged the fifty men now at Plymouth into four companies, each with an officer, put them regularly through certain evolutions, taught them to volley fire, and gave such additional instruction as there was time for. One squad was detailed as a fire battalion to put out fires should the Indians attempt that method of attack. During the spring further alarms of the hostility of Massasoit and of the Massachusetts Confederacy made them rather thankful for their stockade, even though the disquieting rumors proved to be unfounded.

In June they began building a fort, which they did not however succeed in finishing, perhaps because the remainder of the year passed quietly and uneventfully, except for the death of Squanto from sickness on an expedition to collect grain. His death proved a real loss despite his faults, of which they had for some time been aware. He would go to an Indian and tell him that the Pilgrims intended to kill him but that he could control the Pilgrims, and, if sufficiently propitiated, would save the man's life. He also told them that the Pilgrims kept the plague buried in the storehouse, which at their pleasure they might loose upon the Indians and destroy them. No doubt a certain profit accrued to him from these transactions and perhaps a certain friction between the Pilgrims and the Indians resulted, but unquestionably his assistance more than outweighed these disadvantages.[1]

In 1623 the only danger which the Pilgrims ever experienced occurred. A conspiracy, if we may dignify it by so large a name, seems to have been hatched between a number of the petty chiefs of the district and was intended to unite the Indians between Boston and

[1] What is known about Squanto had been brought together by C. F. Adams in *Three Episodes of Massachusetts History*, 23–44.

Narragansett Bay. The object was nothing short of the extermination of all the English, and as to the reality of the conspiracy there is perhaps no doubt. Whether the Indians could have executed it may well be queried. The cause of the trouble lay in the unfair treatment of the Indians by Weston's men at Weymouth. They stole food and skins from them, put them in the stocks, whipped them,—whipping the Indians always deemed a most degrading and extreme punishment. This in the days of their plenty and arrogance. As the winter had progressed and the food had become scarce, they had been glad to work for the Indians, carrying water and wood, tasks considered by the Indians unworthy of a man and fit only for women. This led the fiercer to despise them, so that they would come boldly into the camp, take their food out of the pot, and eat it before their faces. They stole the Englishmen's clothes, sometimes coming at night and snatching the blankets off of them, leaving them shivering on the ground. Such ill treatment of the Indians on the one hand, and such craven cowardice on the other provided the fuel from which this plot sprang.

Knowledge of it came to the Pilgrims from Massasoit. Standish indeed had noticed the insolence of the Indians as early as March, 1623, when they expected no particular treachery and certainly no concerted action. A chief named Wituwamat, one of the few remaining Massachusetts Indians and a "notable insulting villain" according to Winslow, boasted before Standish of his own valor, of the number of English and French he had slain, and of their weakness, because "as he said, they died crying making sour faces more like children than men." He then presented a dagger to a chief in Standish's presence, and delivered a long speech most of which Standish did not understand. His behavior however made its substance quite clear. Another savage seems to have been affected by this display and undertook to kill Standish that night, a fact the latter seems to have learned. There was nothing to do but to keep awake and Standish accordingly walked all night to and fro in front of the fire, the Indian asking continually why he did not sleep and Standish as regularly replying that he knew not why. Such incidents however the Pilgrims judged it wise not to deem serious.

The middle of the month of March word was brought to Plymouth that Massasoit was dangerously ill and Bradford detailed Winslow with one John Hampden, "Gentleman of London," who was wintering at Plymouth, to make a visit of condolence and sympathy.[1] The news reached them on their journey that Massasoit was already dead, and when they reached his village they learned that he was so ill that he was not expected to live. The wigwam was crammed with people, in the midst of which were the medicine men making a tremendous noise, while six or eight women were rubbing Massasoit diligently "to keep the heat in him." With some ado Winslow succeeded in putting an end to this treatment and managed to administer some of the simple but powerful drugs which he had brought with

[1] Upon the identification of this "gentleman" with *the* John Hampden, one Joseph Crowell, a shopkeeper at Plymouth, based a historical drama in five acts, written during the Revolution. Pocahontas appears as the daughter of Massasoit and with her Hampden falls in love. The Epilogue is delivered by Elder Brewster who prophetically sees new States arise and George Washington at their head "a shining Chief." *Mass. Hist. Soc. Proc.*, 2nd Series, III, 431, note.

him. Massasoit seems to have been suffering largely
from acute indigestion and auto-intoxication, induced
by too liberal eating. He was none the less suffering
great pain and would perhaps have died if Winslow's
simple ministrations had not been effective. The promptitude of his recovery produced a marvelous impression
of the Pilgrims' power and skill upon Massasoit and
upon his tribe and led him to reveal to Hobomok, before the Pilgrims left, the expected conspiracy.

On the twenty-third of March, the annual "court
day," the Pilgrims considered the course to be taken
to thwart it and finally delegated authority to Bradford,
Allerton, and Standish to deal with it as they thought
best. Standish was deputed eventually to rescue the
Weymouth colony. He took with him eight men, de-
clining a larger company on the score that more would
arouse suspicion and precipitate the execution of the
conspiracy before he could capture the leaders or warn
Weston's men. The Pilgrims left behind set to work
to complete the unfinished fort. Toward the end of
March then Standish appeared at Weymouth, found the
settlement unguarded, and broke the news to them of
their danger. The Indians soon learned of his arrival and
came in to see him. One bold fellow told Hobomok that
he knew Standish had come to kill him and the other
Indians. "Tell him we know it, but fear him not, neither
will we shun him, but let him begin when he dare; he
shall not take us unawares." Several of them went so
far as to sharpen their knives before him and to use
insulting gestures and speeches. The chief, who had
already dared Standish on a previous occasion, was
present and bragged of the excellence of his knife. He
said he had a better at home with which he had killed

both French and English. By and by it should eat and not speak. The ring leader, who was a tall, stalwart Indian, told Standish that, though he was a great captain, he was none the less a little man, while he, on the contrary, though not a chief, was a man of great strength and courage. Standish seems with great difficulty to have retained his temper and bided his time.

The next day he managed to draw these two, with two of their allies into a house, and, with three of his own men, went in after them and locked the door. He himself then grappled with the tall Indian, who had jested at his small stature, and presently killed him with his own knife. The other Indians were eventually dispatched, though after a very bloody battle, in which they received so many wounds that the Pilgrims wondered they could last so long. Hobomok, who stood by as a spectator, observed when it was over: "yesterday Pecksuot bragging of his own strength and stature, said, 'Though you were a great captain, yet you were but a little man.' But today I see you are big enough to lay him on the ground." The ringleaders being dead, the Pilgrims now sought to capture or kill as many more as possible. One young Indian Standish hanged and at least two or three others were killed. The next day Standish and his men saw a file of Indians in the distance, and a skirmish took place, after which the Indians fled. This was the end of the conspiracy, the other chiefs being too frightened to move. The majority of Weston's men Standish now provisioned and sent off to England in the *Swan*. He himself returned to Plymouth in safety and brought with him the head of Wituwamat, which was long exposed on a spike on top of the fort.

There can be no doubt that if Bradford was the great

figure in civil affairs, Standish was the dominant influence in dealings with the Indians. Winslow to be sure
did much, but Standish obtained a better knowledge of
the Indian dialects and was in addition a good deal more
active and resourceful man. The romanticists and poets
have dealt hardly with him, almost to the undoing of his
place in history.[1] He was perhaps no very dramatic or
romantic figure, for he was short, rather plump and
sturdy, and a little too old for poetic purposes. He was
admirably well placed however in the colony, and the
more one studies Pilgrim annals the larger he bulks, the
greater his ability seems and the more important his
services. His high personal courage, his resourcefulness,
his great physical endurance, his fiery temper, all made
him the leader needed to complement the more peaceful
and contemplative Bradford.

[1] In justice to Standish and his descendants and without disparagement to Alden and his, it should be said that the stories
commonly connected with them are based upon tradition rather
than upon evidence and have been rejected as unfounded by all
serious students of Pilgrim history, including the historian of the
Alden family. Augustus E. Alden, in *Pilgrim Alden*, Boston, 1902,
has brought together the available material and has skilfully
separated the evidence from tradition. He cannot trace the incident of Priscilla, John Alden, and the proposal of marriage in
Standish's name, upon which Longfellow's poem is based, beyond
Timothy Alden's *Collection of American Epitaphs and Inscriptions*,
published in 1812–14. See the uncompromising remarks of
Goodwin in his *Pilgrim Republic*, 566.

CHAPTER X

The Pilgrims had been anxious to settle far enough away from existing or prospective colonies to avoid the constant scrutiny of prying eyes and pricking ears. Their liberty to practice a form of Church Government, not regarded with favor either in England or in Holland, or even by their own business associates, had been a significant motive or emigration and now made essential at least circumspection, forbearance, and hospitality in dealing with all strangers and visitors. If possible they preferred to avoid inspection, but they dared not treat visitors so as to suggest that there was anything to conceal. They felt that they must be all things to all men, though they hardly anticipated that the first to give them real concern would be the very man who had been instrumental in financing the enterprise, Weston himself. During the first year there seem to have been no visitors at Plymouth and no danger of reports unfavorable to them other than those told by the crews of the *Mayflower* and the *Fortune*. In the second year, as already related, there came a colony, financed by Weston himself, sixty "lusty" men but an "unruly company," lacking in discipline, in energy, in practical ability, and in good sense, who were saved from a very real tragedy in 1623 by the Pilgrims. Presently, after his men were well on their way back to England, appeared Weston, who came back from England in a fishing ship disguised as a blacksmith. He sought to borrow from the Pilgrims

enough to fit himself out once more in an endeavor to
recoup his losses, and the leaders finally allowed him one
hundred beaver skins, which they lent him secretly, for
fear that the majority would have prevented the loan had
they known of it. With this, he fitted out a small ship
and began once more to trade, but promptly repaid them
in ill coin by divulging to some unfriendly to them the
fact, that, in letting him have the beaver secretly, they
had given him a great handle against them, with which
at any time he might set the colony by the ears. He
seems also to have sent back to England, in one way or
another, unfavorable and slanderous reports, which did
not tend to increase the harmony among the Adventurers.

In June, 1623, came the first sign of official interference
which the Pilgrims had had. A Captain West appeared
at Plymouth with a commission as Admiral of New England from the Council of New England, with jurisdiction
over all fishing and trading in those waters. The impulse
which led to his appointment was thrifty. A very large
fleet of fishing vessels visited the Grand Banks and the
coast of Maine from England, France, and Holland every
year, and it was thought that West might exact a considerable sum of each for a license to fish and trade.
These expectations failed to materialize, for the fishermen
with great unanimity declined to pay a farthing, and were
too numerous and too resolute for one man with a small
ship to coerce. In September, 1623, arrived Robert
Gorges with a colony, intending to begin a plantation at
Weymouth, already deserted by Weston. He brought a
commission as Governor of New England, with a council
composed of West, the Admiral, the Governor of Plymouth, and one or two other men. The commission

contained broad powers and indefinite phrases, but the most done toward executing it seems to have been the presentation of a copy to Bradford. The Pilgrims received him with extreme courtesy and hospitality. One purpose of his coming, he told them, was to arrest Weston for the disorderly conduct of his colony and for his subsequent behavior. When presently Weston appeared, he demanded an answer to the charges, which Weston minimized as much as possible. Bradford and the leaders were somewhat in doubt whether to allow Gorges to arrest Weston or not. To assist him was to recognize his commission as superior to their patent, a fact they were not anxious to admit openly or tacitly. To oppose him was dangerous. To assist Weston was to rescue an ungrateful rascal. Eventually they did in one way or another diplomatically prevent the arrest of Weston, for all of which Weston gave them small thanks, claiming that, though they were but young justices, yet they were good beggars.

Georges sailed away and considerably later sent a warrant to Plymouth for the arrest of Weston, raising thus the same question of the validity of his authority. Bradford, after some consideration, took exception to the warrant as "not legal nor sufficient," and indicated what eventually turned out to be vastly more to the point, that the arrest of Weston at this time would throw his men on Gorges' hands and cost him considerable money and trouble. Gorges however seems to have realized the legal issue, which caused the Pilgrims to hesitate, and sent an exceedingly formal warrant, signed and sealed, with strict orders to execute it at their peril. They judged it best to offer no further opposition, and accordingly executed it, only to prove the truth of their

former contention, that Gorges had created more
difficulties than he had solved. They were soon relieved
however of real apprehensions for their independence,
because Gorges concluded after a little experience that
the country did not answer his expectations. He returned to England and the people he had brought with
him for the most part either went back to England or to
Virginia. One, a Mr. Morrell, a minister, came to
Plymouth and stayed there for about a year, quietly and
circumspectly. Just before he left, he confided to Bradford that a right of superintendence over the Churches
of New England had been conferred upon him by the
Council, which he had judged it wise not to use. Thus
did their hospitable conduct deliver them from their
first peril.

Meanwhile there had arrived in July, 1623, on the
Anne, several colonists, who had paid their own expenses,
among whom were two men who subsequently played
considerable part in New England annals. The leader of
these "particulars" was John Oldham, who became
later a man of some importance at Boston, who developed an extensive trade with the Indians of Rhode Island
and Connecticut, and whose murder in 1636 led by a
pretty definite chain of causation to the fierce Pequot
war. Another was Roger Conant who became subsequently the founder of Salem. They were no sooner on
shore than they began to stir up trouble among the less
capable in the colony and to sow disagreement among
those who were not members of the Pilgrim Church.
The next spring there landed from the *Charity*, one
Master John Lyford, with his wife and four children.
He was a Puritan minister, had held a benefice in the
Established Church, had been ordained by a bishop, and

was now sent out by the Adventurers with the hope that they might thus provide the Pilgrims with more suitable religious instruction than Brewster's. Some students of Pilgrim history have seen in his coming evidence of a deep laid conspiracy to destroy the colony. There is no direct evidence of any such intention, although it is clear enough that after he had been in Plymouth a little while, he began an intrigue with Oldham, Conant, Billington, and other discontented spirits, to change conditions somewhat more to their own liking.

He was at first however exceedingly suave and deferential, and so admired the dispositions the Pilgrims had made, so lauded their diligence and industry, that they concluded him to be a man of discretion and judgment. He went indeed so far that Bradford feels it necessary to assure us that many were willing to witness to his desire to have kissed their hands, a sign of deference in those days due only to royalty and feudal lords. They alloted him as residence one of the houses in the town, made him a considerable allowance of food from the common store, and invited him to sit in the Governor's Council with the Assistants. When after some little time he came forward voluntarily and made a profession of faith which seemed acceptable to them, they received him into the Church very joyfully, firm in the belief that his protestations of his desire to abandon "his former disorderly walking" were sincere. John Oldham also came forward and voluntarily repented of his evil ways, professing that the arrival of the *Charity* had proved to him the falsity of his belief, that the Adventurers in England were about to desert the colony, and confessing that he had written a good deal to England about them which was untrue.

This harmony, however, lasted but a short time, for presently Lyford and Oldham began to hold private meetings of the weaker members, where a good deal was said against the Government as administered by Bradford, and the form and affairs of the Church. They insinuated that they had between them sufficient influence with the Adventurers at home to secure a change in both Government and Church. They were observed to write voluminous letters and to whisper and laugh with each other about them, so that when the *Charity* finally sailed Bradford judged it expedient to leave with the ship, towing the shallop behind in which to return. The ship's captain put into his hands, after sailing, the letters given to him by Lyford and Oldham. They contained, as had been expected, a type of statement which would certainly not redound to the credit of the Pilgrims in England and which, if brought to the attention of the Privy Council, might have led to an investigation with disastrous results. Copies were taken of some of the letters, the originals of the more important were kept, and copies of these sent on. They found among other things that one of the pair, probably on the voyage over, had not been above purloining letters addressed to them, which stated confidential facts they were very sorry to have known.

When Bradford returned in the shallop, the plotters were somewhat dismayed, but, hearing nothing for some weeks, recovered their boldness. Bradford and the leaders judged it best to give them all the opportunity they wished, for one letter contained phrases which led them to suppose that Lyford and Oldham intended to attempt something resembling a revolution in the colony. To this color was lent by the conduct of Oldham. When

presently he was ordered by Standish to take his turn
at the watch on the pallisades, he refused to go, called
Standish a rascal, and drew a knife. Bradford undertook
to restore order, whereupon Oldham "ramped more like
a furious beast than a man and calld them all treatours
and rebells and other such foule language as I am ashamed
to remember." They promptly confined him for some
time, censured him, and let him go. But when Lyford
presently instituted on Sunday a religious meeting attended by the various malcontents, the Pilgrims judged
that the time had come to call him to account. Bradford
accordingly summoned a general court of the colony,
which was naturally attended out of curiosity by every
soul in Plymouth. Lyford and Oldham were charged
with their letters and intentions and stoutly denied
everything. Bradford then produced and read some of
the letters, which seemed somewhat to confuse them.

Oldham now played their trump card and "caled upon
the people, saying My maisters wher is your harts? Now
shew your courage; you have oft complained to me so
and so, now is the time, if you will doe any thing, I will
stand by you." He was of course counting upon the
democratic constitution of Plymouth, where the majority
vote of the people prevailed, and he evidently expected
that the majority would swing to his side. Once assured
of a majority vote, his own election as Governor would
have been a simple matter. So would have been the
appointment of Lyford as minister and any change in the
laws displeasing to them. Much to their discomforture
not a man stood by them. Bradford, seeing that the
victory was his, proceeded to make the most of it, but
with a restraint and moderation admirable in contrast
with the intemperate language of Oldham and Lyford.

He acknowledged calmly the opening of their letters, but justified such an exercise of authority on the ground of public necessity. To demonstrate the truth of his assertion, the extremity of the need, and the justification of strict dealing with Lyford, he read the various complaints which Lyford had made and answered them. The complaints were clear proof of Lyford's guilt, but his suggestions for the future conduct of the Adventurers were damning and conclusive. They must at all odds, he said, prevent the emigration of Robinson and the rest of the Leyden congregation, and in particular must watch that they were not taken on board ship without the Adventurers' knowledge. It would also be an excellent idea for the Adventurers to ship to Plymouth enough people to outvote the Pilgrims in the General Court. This would be compassed easily enough by giving each bond servant, whose passage they paid, an indenture for a receipt of the amount of the passage, thus making him a free man and a citizen, in exchange for an assignment of the covenant to the merchants. This would give the servants power to vote at Plymouth without depriving the merchants of their services. A military man should also be sent, "for this Captain Standish looks like a silly boy and is in utter contempt."

The evident effect of the reading of the letters was such that Lyford felt it best to say, that the information contained in them he had received from the members of the Pilgrim company themselves. They charged him accordingly to produce his witnesses. When he gave the names, they promptly asked the men to testify, but they denied that they had ever said such things. The victory of Bradford was complete. Not one of the abetters of Lyford and Oldham stood the test. Indeed they seem to have come forward to add further condemnatory facts. By vote of the court, both men were censured and expelled. Oldham was to leave at once, though his wife and family were to be allowed to remain throughout the winter, or until he could make provision for them. Lyford was to be allowed to remain six months longer, with intimation that, if he should entirely reform, the sentence of expulsion might be revoked. Thereupon, after some time he made public confession in Church, and, if Bradford is to be believed, wept copiously the while, reproaching himself for all manner of evil against them and confessing "pride, vainglory, and self-love." Indeed they were inclined to believe in the sincerity of his professions, until a couple of months later another letter fell into their hands, written subsequent to his conviction, and which was meant to confirm to his friends in England the main tenor of the previous letters. In particular, he stressed the number of people who were not members of the Pilgrim Church, whom the Pilgrims would not permit to become members, and whom he declared to be therefore without the means of salvation. There was, he averred, no minister at Plymouth at all. He had nothing much to say when accused with this epistle, and they washed their hands of him. They fully intended to expel him as soon as the winter was over, satisfied with their victory and with the anxiety of most of his assistants to humble themselves before the Governor and their willingness to join the Church. It seemed as if the incident had served to unify the little colony and to produce a greater degree of coöperation between them than had ever existed before.

In the spring of 1625, Oldham returned without permission, apparently in the hope of finding support once

more. As usual their calm, diplomatic behavior was too
much for his fiery passion to endure, and he presently
put himself thoroughly in the wrong by abusing them
with strong language and insulting gestures. They lost
no time with him, arrested him promptly, and put him
in seclusion for a while. They then arranged to send
him to the harbor side through a double file of musketeers,
each of whom in Indian fashion was to hit him a blow
with the muskct end as he went by. While this scene
was being enacted, a ship came in from England bearing
Winslow with the news that the worst was only too true
about both Oldham and Lyford. They hesitated therefore no longer about expelling him, the less because his
wife had already confessed to some of them, that he had
been guilty on more than one occasion of licentious conduct, which the Pilgrims deemed unbecoming in any one,
much less a minister.

To her confessions was added the information Winslow
brought of the great scene in the Merchant Adventurers'
Council in England. Winslow had been much berated
for having accused Lyford and a meeting had been called
to hear the case and to decide upon the accusation which
Lyford's friends proposed to bring against Winslow.
Meantime the latter somehow procured knowledge of
Lyford's past, and arranged with two witnesses to be
present at the meeting. When therefore the Adventurers
had assembled in great numbers to try this exciting scandal, when the moderators had been chosen and the case
was well under way, Winslow brought forward his witnesses and proved an astonishing and shocking case,
wherein Lyford had ruined a girl while minister of a
Puritan congregation in Ireland. The case was, indeed,
if the facts were as Bradford reports, shocking, and the

effect upon the meeting was all that the Pilgrims could have asked. Their charges against Lyford were so infinitely less grave than this and so entirely what might be expected of a man sufficiently depraved to commit this other crime, that Lyford's own friends were compelled to censure him. He now left Plymouth and went further north, lived for a while at Salem, emigrated eventually to Virginia, and there died. And so, piously and triumphantly Bradford concludes, "I leave him to the Lord." The connotation as to Bradford's belief about Lyford's future habitation is indisputable.

In this same year, 1625, there came over Captain Wollaston, with some three or four assistants and a considerable number of indented servants, well supplied with tools and provisions, for the founding of a trading and fishing post of the type the Pilgrims themselves had intended to erect. Things, however, went badly with them and Wollaston took a considerable part of the servants to Virginia, where he sold his interest in their future labor for the seven years of their service. Having gotten what he believed to be good prices, he wrote to the partner left in Massachusetts to bring the rest of the band to Virginia. One of his assistants was Thomas Morton, one of the most interesting and dramatic characters in early Massachusetts history. He seems to have had some slight education in the classics, to have practiced law, certainly in a desultory way and perhaps a not altogether responsible manner, and to have possessed an unnecessarily liberal assortment of vices. The idea occurred to him of securing a colony of his own by the very simple expedient of stealing his partners' servants.

These men had all signed indentures in England,

agreeing to work for seven years in return for their passage money, and they still owed some five or six years of service. Morton seems to have gotten them thoroughly drunk and then to have pointed out to them, that, if they submitted to the authority of Wollaston and went to Virginia, their time would there be sold to the planters, and they would be compelled to work five or six years more. The simpler course was for them to decline to go and remain with him as partners and equals. They would thus become free at once and enjoy the fruits of an enterprise of their own. The idea commended itself to the laborers and they accordingly mutinied and turned out the assistants of Wollaston. Morton thus acquired a colony without expense, but also a colony in which he had no more authority than anybody else, and in which his lusty fellows promptly betook themselves to the vices of civilization. Merrimount, as they presently christened the settlement, became a sort of a drunkard's resort and gambling hell, very much of the type which were found on the frontier in the early days of the West. Drink flowed freely; licentious conduct with Indian women became the rule; and rogues and desperate white men, rascally Indians, and runaway servants began to drift into Merrimount from all parts of the coast. It became indeed a rendezvous for adventurers and piratical rascals and was in itself dangerous to the existence and welfare of the little settlement of honest men nearby at Plymouth.

Morton had however a really clever idea, despite its danger and unscrupulous character. He had realized of course at first that the Indians would sell beaver a good deal quicker for "strong water" than they would for trinkets, and that they would work a good deal harder to collect beaver enough for a complete drunk than they would for any other reward that the white man could offer. For a time he collected in this way a considerable amount of fur. He then saw that the Indians were greatly hampered in hunting by the primitive nature of their weapons and that if they could only be armed with guns and be taught to use those weapons skilfully, they would become deadly hunters, with a consequently amazing profit to him. He therefore began systematically to provide the Indians of the district with arms, powder, and shot and to teach them carefully how to use them, assuring them that all the alluring evils of civilization would be their reward after a successful hunt. The profits were all that he thought they might be, but a very obvious danger to the small bodies of whites in the vicinity became no less clear.

The Pilgrims had been reasonably safe, because their few firearms were immensely superior to the Indian bows and arrows, and because their stockade and fort protected them from any assault the Indians could very well make. There were however on the coast a considerable number of small trading factories, many of which numbered no more than a dozen or a score of men, and these found themselves seriously threatened by the bands of well-armed Indians, thoroughly skilled in the use of guns, who began presently to roam the woods of Massachusetts. There were therefore many good counts against Morton and many excellent reasons for disposing of him, beside the crowning iniquity of which the Pilgrims complained, the erection of a Maypole at Merrimount, which was duly celebrated in song and drunken ribaldry by Morton and his crew. Concerted action was planned by the Pilgrims and the other settlements on the coast, and, after summoning him twice by letter to reform his ways and forbear arming the Indians, they finally decided to deal with him by force.

Standish accordingly set out for Merrimount with a body of Pilgrims, well armed, and, if Morton is to be believed, captured him some eight miles from Merrimount and took him to a nearby house. Here, as Morton tells it,[1] they ate and drank heavily and slept therefore unduly soundly. Up got Morton in the middle of the night, stepped carefully over the keepers supposed to be guarding him, and escaped. The banging of the door roused them. "O! he's gon, he's gon, what shall wee doe, he's gon. The rest (halfe a sleepe) start up in a maze and like rames ran theire heads one at another full butt in the darke. Theire grande leader, Captaine Shrimp, tooke on most furiously and tore his clothes for anger, to see the empty nest, and their bird gone. The rest were eager to have torne theire haire from theire heads; but it was so short that it would give them no hold." Morton hurried through the woods back to Merrimount, where he made ready to receive Standish, whom he knew would follow promptly.

Bradford as was to be expected, gives a somewhat different flavor to the final incident. The Pilgrims landed at Merrimount from their boat and found that Morton had barricaded himself in the house and had armed his men. After a sort of Homeric battle of words and epithets between the two parties through the door, Morton and some of his crew came out to fight, but

---

[1] *New English Canaan*, ed. by C. F. Adams, for the Prince Society, 284–285. This is the most entertaining and amusing account of early New England and is certainly responsible for much of the attention Morton has received from students.

proved to be so exceedingly drunk that they were unable to keep their heavy muskets upon the rests which they set up in front of them when they fired. Morton, with a musket crammed half full with powder and shot, attempted to kill Standish, but the fiery little captain pushed the gun aside with his hand and arrested him. Neither, says Bradford, "was ther any hurte done to any of either side, save that one was so drunke that he rane his owne nose upon the pointe of a sword that one held before him as he entred the house, but he lost but a litle of his hott blood." Morton they brought to Plymouth, and presently shipped him to England with letters telling of his deeds. The worst characters of his colony were disbanded and dispersed, and, though Morton returned somewhat later, he bothered the Pilgrims no more. For, after a brief stay at Plymouth, he went to Massachusetts, where the Puritans recently come dealt with him with extreme severity. Thus were the tares uprooted in the New English Canaan.

CHAPTER XI

The year 1627 seems to be the turning point in Pilgrim annals, the year in which the solution of the problem of subsistence became permanent, and in which the future of the colony was practically assured. The anomalous contract with the Adventurers was cancelled and replaced by an agreement which freed the Pilgrims from economic bondage. The leaders undertook the payment of the outstanding debt, and, though not without misgivings, did possess a real confidence in their ability to discharge it from the proceeds of the really profitable trade they had already established. The individual allotments of lands and houses, already temporarily made, were at this time confirmed, and the members of the colony were able for the first time to know that what they had worked so hard to create was theirs in fact. The beginnings of a herd of live stock and of draught animals had been made and the allotments of cattle this year to groups of individuals was an important step in the improvement of agriculture and of the hitherto severe conditions of domestic life. Though not obtained until three years later, a part of this notable settlement was certainly the new patent of 1630, which vested in the Pilgrims themselves the title to their land. Surely no year, not even the first, records more significant and more important changes than the year 1627.

The position of the Pilgrims on landing at Plymouth

was peculiar. The patent from the Virginia Company they had brought with them was void of value at Plymouth. The contract they had signed with the Merchant Adventurers at Leyden had been repudiated by the latter, while the contract signed by the latter and Cushman had been repudiated by the Pilgrims. The land they stood on was not theirs. The tools and materials they worked with did not belong to them and were to be paid for by seven years of labor, like those of Jacob for Rachel, the conditions of which were yet to be agreed upon. Their associates in England, when the return of the *Mayflower* made their whereabouts known, at once procured from the Council for New England a new patent bearing the date June first, 1621.[1] This was granted to John Peirce, his associates, heirs, and assigns, the same in whose name as trustee the previous patent issued by the Virginia Company had been drawn. It gave him and his associates rather limited rights, without definite boundaries and with certain qualifications and conditions. The settlers under it were empowered to take up one hundred acres of land for every person transported from England in the original colony, if the colony persisted three whole years at one or at several times, and one hundred acres of land for all additional colonists, transported or transporting themselves during seven years and remaining three years thereafter "with intent to inhabit." The hundred acre plots were to adjoin each other, and were not to bè, as the patent said, "stragglingly." An additional fifteen hundred acres might be appropriated to maintain churches, schools, hospitals, and the like.

[1] The original is now at Pilgrim Hall, Plymouth. An accurate reprint, with notes by Charles Deane, is in *Mass. Hist. Soc. Coll.*, *4th Series*, II, 156–163.

Definitely this was a grant of a settlement colony, not for a trading factory, and knew no limit of location in New England other than that the land chosen should not at the time be inhabited by other Englishmen. Under it they might remain at Plymouth and move elsewhere. They had by this time seen Boston Harbor but evidently did not choose to move thither. They were graciously permitted to "truck, trade, and traffique with the Salvages," and "to hunt, hawk, fish, or fowle." They were also licensed to expel from their territory by force of arms and "by all wayes and meanes whatsoeuer," all persons who settled on their lands without special permission. A grant of incorporation was promised with power to govern the people transplanted, and in the meantime they should get along "by consent of the greater part of them." Feoffment was to be made when due notification of the location of the land had been legally certified.

The *Fortune* brought this patent in the autumn of 1621. Robert Cushman came as the agent of the Adventurers to secure the consent of the Pilgrims to the amended articles which had been rejected in England before sailing. After considerable debate and argument, the articles were accepted. Cushman thus returned to England with their promise to work a whole week in the interests of the Adventurers throughout the period of the seven years for which the contract ran. He was also to remain the agent of the colonists in England, and was to see that the new emigrants sent out to them and the goods intended for them were of proper quality and quantity. From the first the association of the Pilgrims with the merchants had been highly unsatisfactory to both, and, as time went on, the dissatisfaction grew greater rather than less.[1] That the *Mayflower* had brought back no cargo disgruntled the merchants in England exceedingly, with the result that the *Fortune* brought colonists but no food. The Pilgrims loaded the ship with clapboards and some furs, but it was captured by a French privateer on the way back to England, the whole cargo was taken off and thus lost. In 1622, there having been no return from the colony, its real straits not at all appreciated, the fact that a cargo had been shipped on the *Fortune* not yet known, the merchants met, disagreed, quarreled, and sent no supplies. Weston and Beauchamp broke with their associates, hired two ships themselves which they loaded with cargo, with a number of emigrants, and a patent for a settlement. The fortunes of the men sent to settle we have already seen, and the venture, so far as profit was concerned, proved a total loss.

Later in the year 1622, news of the value of the cargo the *Fortune* had carried revived the interest of the Adventurers, who contributed enough during the following winter to equip the *Anne* and the *Little James*, to pay the passage of more colonists, and to send with them sufficient food to carry them over till the next harvest. They deemed it wise not to rely wholly upon the energy of the Pilgrims in collecting a cargo, and provided that the two ships should make a fishing voyage after they

[1] The relations with the Adventurers are told by Bradford at great length in the *History*. There is also a fragment of his original Letter Book, containing some additional material, printed in *Mass. Hist. Soc. Coll., 1st Series*, III. A long letter, written by Bradford and Allerton on Sept. 8, 1623, has been printed in the *American Historical Review*, VIII, 294, and affords confirmatory details. This is the only original letter of this period which seems to have survived.

had deposited their colonists, and should thus collect
their own cargo. When the *Anne* arrived at Plymouth
in 1623, the courageous decision to abandon the common
stock had already been taken. They loaded the *Anne*
with dressed lumber and sent Winslow back to England
on the ship, bearing a letter to the Adventurers, and
with instructions to borrow money on the Pilgrims' account for the purchase of goods and cattle. The greatness
of the need and the feeble hopes they entertained of real
assistance were clearly writ in the letter. "We wishte
you would either roundly suply us or els wholy forsake
us, that we might know what to doe." They had, they
said, no intention of making an agreement with another
group of merchants, but would, if the Adventurers did
desert them, do the best they could for themselves.

To anticipate a little, in 1625 Standish borrowed £150
at fifty per cent interest and bought trading goods for
exchange with the Indians. In the year following Allerton was sent to England to procure £100 for two years.
He secured £200 at thirty per cent and a considerable
stock of goods. In 1626 Bradford and the leaders were
bold enough to purchase the whole stock of a trading
post at Monhegan, which had failed and was for sale.
A French ship was also wrecked on the coast and they
bought such of its cargo as could be saved. These facts
will make clear the extent of the Pilgrims' confidence in
themselves and the definite belief after 1623 that nothing
was to be expected from the Adventurers. The letters
of the latter were so contradictory, confused, and luke-
warm, that Bradford and the leaders were unable to
make up their minds as to the real status of the venture.

Nothing illustrates more vividly the discouragements
and difficulties which the Pilgrims and the Adventurers

both had to experience than the ill-fated voyages of the *Little James*, a small two-masted craft of forty-four tons, sent over by the Adventurers in 1623 in the hope of executing the original plan of fishing and trading from Plymouth as a base, in a vessel large enough to keep the seas. Bradford had immediate doubts of the sailors, whom he thought rude, and of the master whose honesty he seems to have doubted. His fears were only too well founded, for the crew had understood that the ship was to be a privateer, to cruise against French and Spanish vessels, and that they were to receive a considerable share of the prize money. The *Little James* did have a commission to capture ships, but the real intent had been to catch fish on the Grand Banks. When therefore the crew received orders from Bradford to undertake a fishing voyage, they threatened to mutiny and were finally pacified only by being paid wages out of the Pilgrims' meagre purse. The latter stocked the ship with great difficulty with trading goods and sent her around to Connecticut and Rhode Island, but the Dutch had forestalled them, the Indians had sold most of their furs, and the ship returned practically empty. Just before entering Plymouth Harbor, a storm broke upon her, the anchors failed to hold, and the crew saved her from going ashore on one of the shoals by sacrificing the main mast.

During the winter, with great difficulty she was refitted and, after pinching and paring to the utmost, the colonists managed to procure enough to send her on a fishing voyage along the Maine coast. There she ran into a storm, stove a hole upon a rock "as a horse and cart might have gone in" and sank. Sometime later, the captains of the summer fishing fleet offered to

raise the vessel, if the Pilgrims would bear the expense.
This offer they accepted and after considerable trouble
the ship was floated, repaired, and sent back to England
in 1624. There one of the adventurers, Thomas Fletcher,
promptly seized her for a debt the others owed him. In
1625, in hopes of making good his expenses, he sent her
with a much larger ship, the *Jacob*, to procure a cargo
of fish at Cape Cod.[1] This time the fishing was successful.
Though the larger ship was ordered to carry her fish to
Spain, the rumors of war led the captain to return to
England, where the cargo arrived inopportunely and was
sold at a loss. The *Little James* was captured in the
English Channel by a Barbary pirate and was carried
to Sallee where the captain and seamen were sold into
slavery. Needless to say, Thomas Fletcher was by this
time hopelessly bankrupt.

In 1624 the Adventurers, who still hung together, sent
out the ship *Charity* with a shipwright and salt-maker,
as well as some cattle and a patent for land at Gloucester,
Massachusetts. The shipwright was to build more coast-
ing vessels for the Pilgrims, in particular a ship large
enough to keep the sea during a storm and decked over,
while the salt-maker brought salt pans to make salt by
evaporation for sale to the shipping fleet which came
annually to the Grand Banks. The expectation naturally was that the profit on the sale of the salt would
be very great. The shipwright however died of fever;
the salt-maker seemed to the Pilgrims a vain and conceited fellow, who tried to make them think that boiling
sea water in a pan required some mysterious skill. They
were therefore not surprised when he made so hot a fire

[1] Some of the goods on this voyage were not to be sold for less
than seventy per cent profit.

underneath his pans that he burned the house, ruined the pans, and thus ended that part of the venture. The *Charity* also made poor work of fishing. The explanation to the Pilgrims was simple; the captain was "a very drunken beast and did nothing (in a maner) but drink & gusle, and consume away the time & his victails and most of his company followed his example." The judgment of God was upon such and they were only too definitely punished for their lack of temperance.

When the news of these misfortunes finally reached London, the Adventurers came to the conclusion that they could do no more. It was better to lose what they already invested than to throw more good money after bad. The Pilgrims had failed; fishing trips had failed, to say nothing of pirates and privateers. Accordingly in December, 1624, they wrote the Pilgrims and formally declared the partnership dissolved.[1] The causes they assigned were their losses at sea and the various debts they had been compelled to contract to support the colony in addition to the original venture. They also stated that for a year or two several of them had objected strenuously to extending further support to the Pilgrims on the ground that they were Brownists. They therefore stood in the way of the emigration to Plymouth of the rest of the Leyden congregation and had in particular prevented Robinson from leaving for America. The reasons were not so interesting to the Pilgrims as the tacit expectation that the Pilgrims were to pay the indebtedness of such Adventurers as still remained, which they computed to be £1400. Nothing definite was said as to future relationship between them and Bradford is silent upon the reasons why the Pilgrims judged it inex-

[1] Bradford quotes the letter in full, *History*, 240.

pedient merely to allow the matter to drop, as this letter
seems to have supposed it would.

Good reasons therefor are not far to seek. The existence of the debt, originally incurred by the emigration
itself as well as by subsequent expenses, was a legal lien
upon the lands, goods, and profits of the colony, and,
even if the Merchant Adventurers showed no present
intention to collect the money or to enforce their claims,
they might later at some inopportune moment insist
upon them, or what was worse, might sell them to others.
The Adventurers indeed were not a company nor incor-
porated, and an elaborate search of English records has
shown no trace of anything more formal than a purely
voluntary agreement between some seventy men. The
Pilgrims, however, felt it essential to extinguish all claims
upon them or upon their future labor. So many shifts
and changes had taken place; so many of the Adventurers
had abandoned their claims to which others had succeeded; some had sold to others; some had sold to the
Adventurers as a whole, that there was considerable
doubt as to what the legal situation was.

Nor should it be forgotten for a moment that the
Adventurers at this time held title to the land of Plymouth. The patent which had been obtained in June,
1621, in the name of Peirce had been quietly changed by
the latter in the following year to an obsolete English
land form known as a Deed Pole, which was written to
him, his heirs, associates, and assigns. It had the effect
of making him proprietor of Plymouth, lord paramount,
lord of the manor, after a fashion. The settlers were
to be his tenants; their lands, goods, and houses would
be his; and they would be subject to him as feudal lord
and to his courts and laws. The Adventurers, when they

learned of this stroke, were exceedingly indignant and tried to buy him out, but his price of £500 seemed to them exorbitant. In December, 1622, he fitted out an expedition to take possession of his new principality, but the ship was badly damaged by a storm and was forced to return. In February, 1623, another start was made, with additional passengers and freight crowded in, in the hope of recouping the losses from the delay. For two weeks the ship was at the mercy of a great storm in the Atlantic, her main mast was lost, much of her bulwarks torn away, and with very great difficulty she made her way back to England. The Adventurers themselves had expended on this particular voyage some £640, Peirce having undertaken the transportation of colonists and goods. Now he surrendered his stock as Adventurer to his associates and assigned his patent to the company.

The Pilgrims thus became literal tenants of the Adventurers with neither title nor rights in their own land, and were utterly dependent upon the latter for securing any in the future. It was now essential to make definite and clear their relation to the Adventurers. Somehow or other the title to the land and the right to govern must be vested in the Pilgrims themselves and that they realized could not take place until some settlement satisfactory to the merchants had been reached. Another reason of real significance also urged them to come to an agreement with the latter. They saw that until they had somehow or other freed themselves from these financial shackles, and had legally severed their connection with these men, it would be difficult if not impossible to bring to Plymouth the remainder of the Leyden congregation. The Adventurers stood in the way of the execution of the original plan and it was feared that they would continue to do so.

Allerton accordingly was sent to England in 1626 to borrow money, to bring back goods, and to reach somehow an agreement with the Adventurers.[1] This he successfully did on October 26, at a meeting to which the great majority of those concerned in the venture had been invited. They sold to the Pilgrims "all and every the said shares, goods, lands, marchandice, and chattels to them belonging." The document in which this transaction was recorded was intended to transfer completely the whole bundle of legal rights of any sort or description, which the Adventurers had or might acquire, in consideration for a sum of eighteen hundred pounds sterling to be paid in London in instalments of two hundred pounds a year for nine years beginning with Michaelmas, 1628. Some forty-two names were signed to the document. Eventually, further documents were signed and the bargain was bound and sealed on parchment. The Pilgrims further stipulated that the bargain was not to become void if they should default payment on the particular day and hour; they might be prevented by the weather or by enemies from reaching London in time and should not be penalized unless the fault were their own. They were therefore to forfeit thirty shillings a week for every week of delay. Thus, exulted Bradford, "all now has become our own as we say in the proverb when our debts were paid. . . . This wholly dashed all the plans and devices of our enemies both there and here who daily expected our ruin, dispersion, and utter subversion by the same."

[1] It may be that the proposition to buy off the Adventurers originated with James Shirley. See his letter to Bradford of December 27, 1627. *Mass. Hist. Soc. Coll., 1st Series*, III, 49.

How should the money be paid? After considerable discussion among the leaders, Bradford, Standish, Allerton, Winslow, Brewster, Howland, Alden, and Prence engaged to make the entire payment of eighteen hundred pounds within six years, and to provide the colony in the meantime with necessities from England, to be exchanged for corn at the rate of six shillings a bushel, if the entire trading privileges of the colony and all the facilities and stock of goods should be turned over to them for the purpose. This agreement, signed in July, 1627, gave them the name Undertakers. To the eight were added in November of 1628, four Londoners, Shirley, Beauchamp, Andrews, and Hatherly, who were to be the London agents of the colony. Isaac Allerton was to travel back and forth supervising the sale of the cargo and the purchase of new goods at both ends, being in each case the accredited representative of the parties absent. The Undertakers at once received possession of the shallops and the new trading sloop, of the fishing stage at Cape Anne, of the station on the Kennebec, and the trading station at Cape Cod, with a considerable stock of beads, hatchets, knives, and the like. This change was less radical than it seems at first sight because Bradford, Allerton, Winslow, and Alden seem practically to have managed the entire business of the colony since 1623, when the common stock was abandoned. It then became evident that if the majority were to work in the fields raising corn, they would not be able to trade or fish, and that it was better the majority should support some few of the men who would do what they could by trading toward raising money to meet their debt to the Adventurers. In 1627 therefore an arrangement was made explicit and legal which had already persisted for some little time.

It now became possible to make permanent the temporary agreements of earlier years in the division of land and houses. In 1623, it will be remembered, small plots of land, apparently not uniform in size, had been allotted to various individuals and families. In 1624 one acre had been allotted each family "for continuance" during seven years; no more than one acre had been granted in order that the colony might remain compact "for safety and for religion." Now in 1627 the horned cattle, which had come to the colony in the last three years, were assigned to twelve groups of people, who were among them to care for the beast and enjoy such use of it and perquisites from it as there might be. Abuse and neglect were to be charged against the whole group. Early in the next year the division of land was continued. Three hundred and fifty-six fields were laid out, covering some five square miles, and ranging from the Jones River to the Eel, with the village of Plymouth in the middle. Each family retained in the town the one acre plot already assigned to it and in most cases the house upon it, if there was one; the Governor and a number of the leaders received their houses and plots in recognition of their services to the colony. The large farms of some twenty acres each were now distributed by lot with some attempt to compensate those who drew the most distant. The meadows and fields upon which grass was growing were retained in common, and the poorer land seems not to have been distributed at all. Thus was permanency attained to general satisfaction. The status was also formally recognized of those who were *in* the colony but not *of* it, being either non-church members or adherents of other forms of non-conformity. While it is doubtful whether the right of these "Purchasers," as they were called, to the ownership of land was at this time recognized, their right of occupancy was conceded of lands to be assigned them, a definite recognition of their property in goods or chattels was promised, and their partnership in the enterprize admitted. Each head of a family and each self-supporting bachelor might by certain formalities become a "Purchaser," and accepted in return for his privileges one equal share in such part of the debt as the Undertakers did not discharge.

One of the most considerable tasks which the leaders now assumed, great in view of their other financial obligations, was the financing of the emigration of the remainder of the Leyden Congregation, now much reduced since the death of Robinson in 1625. The plans were made at Plymouth in 1627 as soon as the settlement with the merchants was complete, were prosecuted by Allerton and Shirley in London during 1628, with the happy result that in August, 1629, the first contingent of thirty-five came on the *Mayflower* and in the following May sixty more came on the *Handmaid*. The total cost reached £550. Only forty-seven, however, of the newcomers were from Leyden, the other colonists on these ships emigrating from England direct. Thus were the survivors at last reunited after so many troubles and losses both in America and in Holland.

Scarcely less significant and important an element in the new settlement was the patent secured from the Council for New England in 1629 and sealed on January 13, 1629–1630. This put an end to doubts about the Pilgrim title. It granted to William Bradford, his heirs, associates, and assigns a certain definite territory, practically identical with the present counties of Plymouth, Bristol, and Barnstable, omitting Bingham and Howe

and including a part of eastern Rhode Island. The grant
was made of course with reference to the Indian names
and was intended really to include the entire territory of
the Pokanoket Confederacy, an exceedingly vague district, and one whose bounds the names quoted in the
charter did not satisfactorily define, as the Pilgrims later
discovered to their disquietude. A tract of land on the
Kennebec near the site of the present Augusta, some
thirteen miles long and fifteen miles wide, on either side
of the river, was confirmed to them. The land was
granted in fee simple, and the language was so broad and
inclusive as to confer upon them every right possessed by
the Council itself, including the power of government over
the inhabitants and the authority to deal with intruders.
The only reservations were the coining of money and
shares of gold and silver for the Crown and Council for
New England, which, needless to add, never accrued.
The Council appointed Standish its attorney to deliver
possession to Bradford or his representatives. The ceremony was probably performed by the transference of
the turf, twig, and water of the most formal feoffment of
medieval law. The question however was later raised by
those anxious to dispute the Pilgrim title as to whether
such feoffment was capable of transfering the power to
govern and the right to enact and enforce laws. The
attempt in the following year to secure a royal charter,
confirming the grant of land and with an equally liberal
grant of authority, failed. In 1640 Bradford assigned the
Patent and all rights under it to the entire body of freemen of the colony.

CHAPTER XII

The Pilgrims had convincingly demonstrated no less significant a proposition than the practicality of the colonization of the New World. Posterity has dwelt upon their high moral qualities, upon their courageous daring, upon their religious idealism; their contemporaries were impressed chiefly by their economic success. Contrary to an impression only too widespread, the Pilgrims were not the first religious enthusiasts to sail for America, nor the first body of men and women of high quality and consecration to land in the New World. In the sixteenth century had come the Huguenots; several congregations of Separatists seem to have cherished the idea of emigration; Blackwell and a number of the Pilgrims' friends had actually sailed for the Chesapeake in 1618–1619. But just as there had been many predecessors of Columbus who had believed that the world was round and that one might sail from West to East, so the Pilgrims had had progenitors. Like Columbus, they were the first to succeed, the first to demonstrate the practicality of colonization. They planted the first permanent, independent settlement in the New World, in which the initiative lay with the emigrants and not with capitalists or kings. They were the first organized body of people to leave the Old World in expectation of continuing the life of their organization in the new. They proved that a small body of men and women, without capital or resources, and without governmental support, could maintain themselves in New England from the product of their own labor on the soil of the country without systematic assistance from England. They proved that even a small body of poverty stricken men and women could cut loose from Europe and safely take up residence in the New World, with every probability of being able to live without enduring too much physical hardship, and with every prospect of practical freedom from European interference. This was the economic fact the Pilgrims demonstrated.

The essential element was their undoubted weakness and poverty. There had come to New England in 1620 one hundred and two people, without equipment, expecting to be maintained from England and not from the proceeds of their own labor. They had expected to fish and to collect furs, to cut lumber, to export to the mother country materials whose sale would make possible the purchase of necessities they would consume in the New World. The whole project failed. The original plan was from the outset abandoned. Maintenance from the proceeds of their own labor in America became essential, even though the necessary tools and supplies had not been provided. Sickness came; half of them died. The promised aid from England did not materialize as promptly and as regularly as was imperative. The commercial ventures from which so much had been expected went wrong from the first. The *Mayflower* could carry no cargo; the *Fortune* was captured by pirates; supplies sent to them were lost at sea; their cargoes returned were unfortunately sold at a loss. It scarcely seemed possible that any body of men and women could have struggled with more adverse fortune or have received less effective assistance than they.

And yet, somehow, the little colony survived. Houses built by their own hands rose in considerable number, built of hewn plank with well thatched roofs. Behind them busy hands created gardens. Beyond in the fields the same untiring energy sowed corn and grain; in the woods lumber was cut to be exported; furs were bought from the Indians to be sold in England. By 1627 the accumulated misfortunes of the Pilgrims, the unsatisfactory support of the merchants, the efforts of wind, sea, and pirates had somehow not been able to prevent the little colony from prospering. They had landed deeply in debt, without any adequate store of even the necessities of life, with only a few carpenters' tools and rude agricultural implements, and a few guns and powder. And they had built a town, owned fields and trading stations, and had begun to accumulate a herd of cattle. Food, shelter, and clothing were assured them beyond doubt; profit even they knew they would make in the future. After the first great sickness the mortality had been small. One hundred and two had come in 1620 on the *Mayflower;* thirty-five had been brought by the *Fortune* in 1621, sixty by the *Anne* and the *Little James* in 1623, and of the one hundred ninety-nine there were alive in 1627, one hundred fifty-six besides some twenty or thirty laborers and indented servants who did not have the status of free men.[1] To be sure, some of those who came in the ships named had moved from Plymouth to other parts of New England or Virginia; some few originally in other parties had made their way to Plym-

---

[1] One hundred ninety-nine came; sixty-eight were born at Plymouth; fifty-eight had died; fifty-three had removed elsewhere; leaving one hundred fifty-six. Fifty-two had died in the first year and only six during the following six years.

outh and had there found welcome. There were fifty-seven men, twenty-nine women, thirty-four boys, and thirty-six girls at Plymouth in 1627 when the common stock was brought to an end and "the Purchasers" were organized. Forty-two of these people had come in the *Mayflower*. They possessed in common four cows, seven young heifers, four young bulls, eighteen goats, and, if Captain John Smith can be believed, a good many swine and poultry. A Dutch agent from New Amsterdam who visited Plymouth in this year for the purpose of opening trade, was particularly impressed by its general aspect of solidity, comfort, and prosperity. He thought on the whole they were materially better off than the Dutch and English colonists whom he had seen on the coast. Their morale and discipline were undoubtedly better and all augured well for the future.

What impressed their contemporaries was the essential fact which has made a place for the Pilgrims in history. They came to America to make homes, came with a definite determination not to return,[1] with a motive for residence more vital than commercial profit. In a pamphlet printed by Brewster in 1619, their purpose in leaving for America was defined: "That they might make way for and unite with others what in them lieth, whose consciences are grieved with the state of the Church in England."[2] A little later Winslow declared that they were leaving to show other Separatists "where they might live and comfortably subsist, and enjoy the like liberties with ourselves, being freed from antichris-

---

[1] Robinson and Brewster to Sandys, Dec. 15, 1617. Arber, *Pilgrim Fathers*, 285–286.

[2] Euring, *An Answer to Ten Counter Demands*, quoted by Dexter, *England and Holland of the Pilgrims*, 578.

tian bondage; keep their names and nation; and not only be a means to enlarge the dominions of our State, but of the Church of Christ also." [1] Of their extraordinary qualifications as home makers, they were thoroughly conscious, and Robinson and Brewster, writing to Sir Edwin Sandys on December 15, 1617, enumerated them as an inducement to the Virginia Company to assist the enterprize. "We are well weaned," said they, "from the delicate milke of our mother country; and enured to the difficulties of a strange and hard land: which yet, in a great parte we have by patience overcome. The people are, for the body of them, industrious & frugall, we thinke we may safly say, as any company of people in the world. . . . It is not with us as with other men whom small things can discourage or small discontentments cause to wish them selves at home againe." They knew they were different in principle and in quality from the great bulk of men and women who had come to America. They augured well from the fact.

They felt that colonies had failed in America hitherto because men had come to live in factories and trading settlements, meant to be permanent, but not regarded either by the settlers or by the authorities in England as homes, as desirable residences. Those who came were lured by hope of profit, by love of adventure rather than by the expectation of a hard but useful life in a new country.[2] They had not severed themselves from the Old World nor yet thought of themselves as no longer part of it. They had failed because they had come as sojourners only and because their motives were sordid. Some indeed had been worthy, but they had failed for one

[1] Winslow, *Hypocrisy Unmasked*, 89.
[2] Bradford, *History*, 35.

reason or another to gain a foothold. The Pilgrims came to succeed in founding a home or to die in the attempt.[1] Even the Merchant Adventurers who financed them seem to have been impressed with this phase of the Pilgrim venture, and urged them, even in their own moments of greatest discouragement, to hold out and demonstrate that colonization was possible. "You have been instruments," they wrote in 1623, "to breake the ise for others who come after with less difficulty; the honour shall be yours to the world's end."[2] "We are still perswaded," they declared in December, 1624, in the discouraging letter that severed relations between them and the Pilgrims; "you are the people that must make a plantation in those remoate places when all others faile and returne."[3] They were right. The Pilgrims did succeed. They taught the English people to look upon America as a habitable and desirable home for those dissatisfied in England. In that fact lay the true germ of the United States of America.

One other fact almost equally significant they also established. They came not at all to continue the sort of life they had led in Europe, to reproduce the same institutions they had known there, but to create a new commonwealth, "to live as a distincte body by them selves," as Bradford said,[4] to become, in the words of Robinson, "a body politic."[5] They brought with them

---

[1] "Yea, though they should loose their lives in this action, yet might they have comforte in the same, and their endeavours would be honorable." Bradford, 35. See also, 96, 97.

[2] Letter from thirteen of the Adventurers, Bradford, 174.

[3] Bradford, 242.

[4] *History*, 37.

[5] Robinson's final letter of counsel spoke of "your intended course of Civil Community;" "whereas you are to become a Body

the ideal of a new state, of a new "civil community," in which conditions political, religious, and legal should be different from those they had known in Europe. From their experience the Puritan leaders of the great emigration to Boston drew in 1627 the conclusion that the English authorities were ready to grant practical local autonomy to intending colonists. The Pilgrims indeed had been seven years in New England and neither the English King or the English Church had evinced the slightest intention to interfere with their conduct of their own affairs. The Council of New England, their immediate superior, had put forth certain pretensions but had made no consistent attempt to make them good. Here lay the germ of the future independence of the United States.

At the same time, we shall do well as students to recognize that neither the Pilgrims nor their contemporaries in the least anticipated such an independent political community as the United States was in 1789. If we suppose that the Pilgrims came to forget that they were Englishmen, to disavow their English allegiance, and to establish a state which should not fly the English flag or recognize the English King, we shall fall into a most grievous error. Indeed, was not their main object in leaving Holland to return to the English allegiance, to establish a community where their English habits and ways could be perpetuated under the English flag? The real difficulty lies in our failure to appreciate the fact that the notion of political independence and of popular

Politic, using among yourselves Civil Government." Arber, *Pilgrim Fathers*, 404. The plan for the colony under Dutch auspices speaks of the Pilgrims' desire "to plant there a new Commonwealth." Arber, 98. See also *Hist. Mss. Com., 8th Report, Appendix*, Part II, 45.

sovereignty, which underlay the constitution of the United States in 1789, was utterly foreign to the political thinking of seventeenth century England. There were perhaps a few students of Buchanan and Bodin who had some vague notion of sovereignty,[1] but the rank and file still thought in feudal terms, and their concept of independence was based upon a distinction difficult for the modern world to appreciate.

The Pilgrims were familiar with the manorial custom of Scrooby and with the practical immunity which they had enjoyed under the feudal Liberty, or exemption, owned by the Archbishop, from royal officers and courts and from county officers and courts. Allegiance they owed the King undoubtedly, as did the Archbishop; English citizens they clearly were; English nationality, language, habits they proudly owned; and saw no inconstancy in a frank and ready admission of all this feudal fealty with an entire autonomy in practical government. This same practical immunity from active rule by royal officials they expected to achieve in America by reason of the distance, and saw in it no seeds of political independence nor of popular sovereignty, nor dreamed of a written constitution and legislation. That they would be a civil community of a new type they seem to have known; that their relation to the English crown would be perhaps anomalous they realized, but that it implied any disloyalty or any renunciation of fealty, they denied strenuously to those who complained that they were seeking to be "several lords and kings of themselves."[2]   But they did prove that practical autonomy in civil government was to be had in the new

---

[1] Brewster possessed a copy of Bodin.

[2] Captain John Smith, *True Travels*, ed. 1629, 46.

world, that it would carry with it a lack of control and supervision in ecclesiastical matters, a very real exemption from anything more than nominal taxation. Emboldened by their example, the Puritan leaders of the Massachusetts Bay Colony attempted a government literally independent of the Crown save for allegiance. The legal concept of the relation of those first colonies to the Crown, as they themselves conceived it, was that of free and common socage, of feudal relationship, of the old tenure, not of a new political expedient.

Their economic success and their establishment of a civil government of their own were the direct causes of the colonization of New England on a great scale by the Puritans in the decade following 1627. Both proved to the Puritan leaders that men of wealth, of ability, of foresight, could easily, with the lessons of the Pilgrims to guide them, establish themselves in the New World safely and without apprehension of interference. The problem was simple, success was positive for a group as powerful and as wealthy as theirs, if as weak and poverty stricken a group as the Pilgrims had been able to survive. If therefore the founding of Boston and the expansion of New England became definitive facts in the history of the United States, if the strength of the Massachusetts Bay Colony and its size became a guarantee of the permanence of the English grasp of North America, the Pilgrims were their cause. With the motives leading individual Puritans to leave England, the Pilgrims had no immediate connection. They were themselves products of the economic and ecclesiastical history of England in the previous century, and not its cause. But it is perhaps not too much to say that had they not come, and had they not succeeded, the energy of the great emigration to Massachusetts would have expended itself elsewhere and the history of the world might perhaps have been different.

The direct influence of the Pilgrims upon the leaders of the Massachusetts Bay Colony is definitely and clearly established.[1] Six, and in all probability nine, of the guarantors of the Bay Colony had been members of the Merchant Adventurers who financed the Pilgrims and who knew therefore intimately the whole story. Goffe was an intimate friend of Winthrop. Pocock came to the Colony and was Deputy Governor in Massachusetts under Winthrop. There can be no doubt that Cradock and other leaders of the Boston Colony corresponded with the Pilgrims,[2] saw Allerton in England, and secured details from him in regard to conditions in America. There was also Endicott at Salem, who was intimately acquainted with the Pilgrims for nearly two years before the Boston Colony sailed. Anyone who will read even casually the minutes of the meetings of the Governor and Company of Massachusetts Bay for 1628–1629, and who will study the elaborate lists of necessary materials to be brought for a settlement colony, will have no doubt that the experience of the Pilgrims was the essential fact guiding those preparations. It is through Massachusetts, through New England, and through all that New England stands for, that the influence of the Pilgrims has been greatest.

[1] Ames, *Log of the Mayflower*, 56–58; Arber, *Pilgrim Fathers*, 322.

[2] Cradock sent a letter to Endicott by Allerton, Feb. 16, 1628, 1629, Young. *Chronicles of Massachusetts Bay*, 132. See also the General Instructions to Governor & Company, *id.*, 156. See also, "A Catalogue of such needefull things as every Planter doth or ought to provide to go to New England," in Higginson's *New England's Plantation*. Salem, 1908, pp. 113–114.

Many great achievements have been the work of men who understood vaguely if at all the significance of what they had accomplished. Not so the Pilgrims. Even before they sailed the leaders seem to have had an inkling of the possible influence their success might have. In later years Bradford rejoiced "That with their miseries they opened a way to these new lands; and after these stormes, with what ease other men came to inhabite in them, in respecte of the calamities these men suffered." [1] Winslow, in 1623, writing back to England, declared "That when I seriously consider of things, I cannot but think that God hath a purpose to give that land, as an inheritance, to our nation." [2] Exultant, they quoted from Isaiah: "A little one becomes a thousand and a small one a great nation."

[1] *History*, 165. Under the year 1630, he wrote: "So the light here kindled both to many, yea in a sorte to our whole nation," *id.*, 332. Sherley wrote to Bradford on June 24, 1633, "For had not you and we joyned and continued togeather, New England might yet have been scarce knowne, I am persuaded, not so replenished and inhabited with honest English people, as now it is," *id.*, 369.

In 1654, Bradford indited a poem, which has been printed in *Mass. Hist. Soc. Proc., 1st Series*, XI, 479, in which the following stanza occurs:

> "But them a place God did provide
> In wilderness, and did them guide.
> Unto the American shore
> Where they made way for many more.
> They broke the ice themselves alone
> And so became a stepping stone
> For all others, who in like case
> Were glad to find a resting place."

[2] Written in 1623. Arber, *Pilgrim Fathers*, 581.

CHAPTER XIII

Unquestionably the period from 1627 to the death of Bradford in 1657 was that most characteristic of life in the Old Colony, as it now came to be called. The ideal of the leaders had been realized; they had established a commonwealth in accordance with God's Ordinances and saw around them positive assurance of its future prosperity. The Adventurers had been bought out; title to the land was theirs; interference from King and Bishops had been avoided. The foundations of the Church seemed at last absolutely secure. They now undertook to shape the little community consciously in all its affairs and observances, political, economic, and social, as well as ecclesiastical, in accordance with what they understood to be God's direct commands. This is the characteristic period of life at Plymouth, the years in which the idealism of the earlier decades was impressed upon those men and women whose descendants so faithfully transmitted that abundant heritage to a great nation. To the study of that heritage we must presently devote considerable space.

For three decades there is little to tell beyond the tale of a slow, steady growth during peaceful years given over to the developing of the land, to the raising of cattle, to the improvement of agriculture, and to the founding of new towns. Gradually, better houses replaced those first erected; better furniture appeared;

clothing improved in quality and in amount; many of the little luxuries of English life became more and more common. To the Pilgrims themselves nothing could well have been more important or satisfying than this disappearance of the evidences of long, grinding poverty, but those who come to study it later are inclined to pass it impatiently by, intent on wars and rumors of wars which afford more dramatic material. A few landmarks should be mentioned and beyond them there is little to tell of happenings at Plymouth. In 1629 the first minister was "called" by the Pilgrims, an event in their eyes of stupendous import. In 1635, something like a code of law was attempted and in 1636 the form of government was crystallized, and laws embodying it were enacted by the General Court. From these years the political "constitution" of the colony dates. In 1638, came the Pequod War, to which the Pilgrims sent troops, by far the most important single venture undertaken in New England during that decade. The years 1639 and 1640 saw boundary disputes with Massachusetts, not settled for some decades, and the year 1640 the assignment of the Patent by Bradford to the freemen as a whole. The Undertakers also signified their willingness to surrender the monopoly of the Indian trade. The formation of the New England Confederation in 1643 regularized and stimulated constitutional relations with the more recent colonies. Beyond doubt the events next in importance were the loss of the four leaders to whom the colony had owed so much. Brewster died in 1643; Winslow left for England, never to return, in 1646; Standish died in 1656; and Bradford in 1657. Bradford's passing marked the end of an era in Pilgrim history and signified the triumph of changes in the character of life in the colony, which had been developing for two decades, but which had hitherto never been really apparent, much less dominant. The causes for the disappearance of the old Plymouth and for the rise of the new were fundamental and will presently engage our attention.

There can be little question that the most important event in Pilgrim annals during this important period from 1627 to 1657—far more significant in its effect upon Pilgrim life and ideals than anything which happened within the limits of the Old Colony—was the founding and rapid growth of Massachusetts Bay and of the other New England colonies. Not infrequently we come to realize that the really momentous influences in the development of a people are events in the history of other nations, questions of relative rather than of positive growth, the reflex and indirect results of vital happenings elsewhere, the relation of one community to those around it. It is not too much to say that the founding of Massachusetts Bay promptly altered in every conceivable respect the position of the Pilgrims at Plymouth, and established beside them a new community of such vigor, size, and intellectuality as to dominate insensibly and in time to transform the ecclesiastical, political, and social ideals of the older but smaller and weaker entity. No direct influence or conscious dictation was attempted, and the Pilgrims jealously watched for the slightest evidence of a disposition to interfere with their political or ecclesiastical independence and sternly, though politely, declined unsolicited offers of aid and assistance. The mere existence of the other colonies is the fact of which we must ever be conscious; Plymouth was no longer the largest settlement north of Jamestown, and that alone altered the value of every element in the economic, governmental, and ecclesiastical equation.

New settlements sprang up on all sides of Plymouth after 1628. New England soon counted people by the hundred, cattle by the thousand, worldly goods and supplies by the shipload. In the twelve years subsequent to 1628 no less than two hundred vessels brought emigrants, cattle, property. As early as 1634, four thousand inhabitants were grouped in about twenty towns and villages near Boston, with not less than fifteen hundred head of cattle grazing in the fields and four thousand goats browsing on the hillsides. By 1640, there were in the Massachusetts Bay Colony alone sixteen thousand people. Thriving and populous towns had sprung up along the Connecticut River, around New Haven, in Central Massachusetts, while others only less populous were located on Rhode Island, at Providence, and in what is now New Hampshire and Maine. The significant fact is not alone the great number of people who came and the extent of their worldly possessions; the area of the land they preëmpted and the extent of it they were able to utilize is scarcely less remarkable. In twelve years the new colonies became so numerous and powerful that the combined influence of the French, the Dutch, the Indians was seen to be clearly unable to make headway against them. The English language, English law and institutions became paramount on the soil of North America.

As the Pilgrim colony was the first to seek a home in the New World, so this great exodus of the Puritans to America was the decisive and final step in its preëmption for an English speaking nation. They came as literally complete communities, already possessed of all classes, kinds, and sorts of people. Administrators, lawyers, doctors, clergy are well known to have come, but there were also farmers familiar with the soil, craftsmen to produce the necessary articles of husbandry and to do blacksmithing and iron work, artisans capable of undertaking most of the simple processes of manufacturing. Industry in any proper sense or manufacturing for export they could hardly attempt for generations, but the new communities had been gathered together with a foresight, which made them ready to perform any task then regarded by Englishmen of that period as essential to life and happiness. Where at Plymouth, Fuller, the doctor, was the only one with professional training and he none too well educated as a doctor, even for that day, the professional men in Massachusetts were soon numbered by the score. Alden was the only man at Plymouth who really answered the description of mechanic, and he was at best no more than a cooper, and was quite incapable of undertaking the finer types of iron work. In Boston there were many able to perform most of the essential processes of blacksmithing and forging.

We cannot be quite sure but Brewster seems to have been the only Pilgrim with a college career and he did not receive a degree, whereas in the first shiploads that came to Boston were many university men, and by 1639 about seventy university graduates, many of them men of real distinction, are known to have been in New England. In 1636 Harvard College was founded, at a time when it is probable that at Plymouth children were still being taught by Elder Brewster and some of the women, and taught nothing beyond the rudiments. Strong personalities, rare at Plymouth, soon became numerous in the Puritan colonies. John Cotton, Roger Williams,

John Davenport, Thomas Hooker, John Eliot, were all
ministers of more commanding ability, magnetism, and
influence than any of the clergymen the Pilgrims were
able to attract, while Winthrop, Dudley, Eaton, and
Endicott were only a few of many laymen able to com-
mand respect by their intelligence and grasp of legal and
administrative issues. Indeed, more definite constitutional progress was made at Massachusetts Bay in four
years than at Plymouth in twenty. The size of the
colony alone forced the development of political institutions at Boston and brought to the fore instantly problems which the small size of Plymouth allowed to remain
dormant for decades.

The effect of the expansion of New England upon New
Plymouth was striking. Until 1630, the Pilgrim settlement had been the one stable and prominent colony along
the coast, the one reliance of the many factories, where a
few adventurers with perhaps a score of indented servants were seeking to collect furs or to dry fish. To Plymouth all these had looked for protection, for guidance,
and, what was still more difficult for the Pilgrims to provide, for supplies of food, of goods to trade with the
Indians, and for guns and powder. So rapid was the
change that within a year or two after the founding of
Boston, New Plymouth found itself no longer a leader
and scarcely an equal, already pushed somewhat to one
side. Ten years later it was the smallest and least powerful of a "congregation of plantations," most of which
already deserved the name of states, and the wealth,
numbers, and ability of each of which were far greater
than the Pilgrims ever dreamed of possessing. One would
have expected this disparity to have awakened real
jealousy and discontent at Plymouth. While we find

Bradford, Winslow, and Prence insisting upon due respect and theoretical equality in the various colonial
councils, we find them all rejoicing at such growth and
displaying genuine satisfaction that they themselves
had been its cause.

The history of New England is not a part of the subject of this book. We are concerned only with the influence of the Pilgrims on the other new New England
colonies, and with the reciprocal influence of the newer
colonies on the Pilgrims themselves. In a sense the remainder of our study will be concerned with this inter-
action and reaction, but it may be well to indicate here
that the direct influence of the Pilgrims on the other
New England colonies and upon their institutions after
1630 was slight, though perhaps far from negligible. On
the other hand, the influence of Boston upon Plymouth
was very great, gaining in importance as the century continued. Indisputably, the tendency was for the larger,
abler, more wealthy, and better organized unit to impose
insensibly and unconsciously something of its methods of
thought and procedure upon the smaller, weaker, and
less wealthy community. The loss of political independence by New Plymouth in 1691 was after all only the
official recognition of a gradual absorption of the colony
into Massachusetts Bay which became clearer and
clearer after the death of Brewster and Bradford. It
was not exactly that the authorities at Boston set out to
influence New Plymouth or felt that conquest, economic, social, or ecclesiastical was desirable, but the
characteristic differences between the smaller and the
larger units, which were so clear in 1630, began in the
decades after 1650 gradually to disappear. Something
must presently be said as to the claim frequently made

that the church organization of the other New England colonies was adopted or adapted from the organization at Plymouth. Here in all probability the Pilgrim idea predominated. The resultant unit, the Massachusetts of the Revolution, was neither Puritan nor Pilgrim, but a fusing of the two.

The founding of Boston at once changed beyond all recognition the problems of defense, of subsistence, and of profit at Plymouth. The size and importance of the Bay Colony made the problem of defense forevermore subsidiary and unimportant. As for subsistence, there was now always within easy reach food and European supplies more than sufficient to meet any possible demands of the Pilgrims. Starvation and want became impossible. Indeed, so much greater were the resources of the Bay Colony that the Pilgrims might easily have drawn from it luxuries in an overabundance had they been inclined or able. There was again created at once at their door a market for what the Pilgrims themselves had to sell and a source of supply for what they wished to buy. The dependence of Plymouth on England was practically ended and the failure of one voyage or the miscarriage of plans could no longer have serious results.

Very soon indeed an active interchange of visits and trade sprang up between Plymouth and the Bay Colony towns.[1] The relations between the two were dominated

---

[1] The evidence for the extent and character of the relations of the Pilgrims with the other New England colonies is more fragmentary, casual, and scattered than we could wish, but of itself, considering the extraordinary fulness of the records of the Bay Colony, must indicate a connection by no means extensive, regular, or systematic. This is precisely what we might expect from the rigid "separatism" attempted at Plymouth and the anxiety there to maintain absolute equality and independence with the newer

by the spirit of coöperation between brothers and equals. There was a certain amount of dispute and bickering over boundaries and over fishing rights at Cape Ann and in Maine, but on the whole the Pilgrims had little to complain of in the treatment accorded them by the newcomers. Winthrop and Dudley manifested the utmost respect for Bradford's counsel and advice, and Bradford was not slow himself to call upon Winthrop for legal suggestion in the case of Billington, who was accused of murder and was eventually executed. Fuller was sent to aid the sick at Salem in 1628–1629 and the Pilgrims on occasion received aid in dealing with undesirable characters, and, on occasion, gave it. Morton of Merrimount reappeared; Sir Christopher Gardner and Samuel Gorton were dealt with by coöperative action. A brisk trade in cattle very soon sprang up and the purchase in Boston by the Pilgrims of European goods, paid for in cattle and grain. Winslow seems to have developed something like a business in pasturing cattle and swine, sent down cross country from Boston. Before long the Pilgrims were paying merchants in England with bills of exchange drawn on Boston. As the years went on this method of exchange became more and more common. Indeed, from the first travel between the various little groups in New England had been active. Many of the first fur-trading groups visited Plymouth and the Pilgrims themselves looked in during the first year or two

but stronger colonies. Bradford tells us a good deal in a casual way and something more can be gleaned from the letters of Bradford and Winslow to Winthrop in the Winthrop Papers, printed in the *Mass. Hist. Soc. Coll.*, *4th Series*, VI, 156–184. The records and histories of the Bay Colony itself are singularly lacking in references to Plymouth.

ELIZABETH PADDY WENSLEY

upon all of the settlements on the New England coast. As soon as the Bay Colony was founded various members of both began changing residence. There was the whole wilderness to choose from, so that a man, dissatisfied with the land, water, woods, or companions in one place, found it a simple matter to transport himself and his goods to another. The population was really much more fluid in early New England than we commonly credit. A good many men were born in Plymouth, grew up in Boston or Lynn, lived a while in Rhode Island, Connecticut, or New York, paid a visit to Virginia, and died somewhere else.

The movement which founded New England was distinctly and decidedly one of immigration on a large scale, and was characterized by the movement of large groups of people rather than of individuals. Whole communities arose in England and transplanted themselves bodily with such of their possessions as could be moved. Towns, already settled and organized near Boston, grew dissatisfied and moved themselves and their belongings to the Connecticut River Valley. Nothing short of this movement of great masses of people and the resort to them in a continual stream of smaller groups could have created so rapidly such considerable colonies. Of this type of movement nearly all the New England colonies except Plymouth were the result. Even Rhode Island grew faster in numbers than Plymouth, which to the end was primarily the result of the slow, natural growth of a population, which came in the first years, and of the slow development of the natural resources of the district by the labor of its first comers. The original investment in money and goods was calculated in 1627 at about £7000, and after 1630 there was only a very gradual accession of people or of capital. Plymouth was the result of the unremitting toil of a small group of people upon a definite location. Unquestionably, it was an economic success, a fact regarding which more will be said presently, but the rate of growth in population and in wealth, in the increased acreage of farms and in the size of the fur trade could not be greater without the accession of large numers of people. Shipload after shipload came from England and settled elsewhere. Why did these immigrants not come to Plymouth? This is perhaps the most fundamental and essential inquiry in Pilgrim history. Why should only individuals have resorted to Plymouth? [1] Why should the little body of men and women who began the colony have been the only large group of settlers, and the men and women of 1691, with few exceptions, people of the second generation, themselves born in America? The inquiry is by no means simple, and contains the secret of the history of the colony after 1630.

The first fact to emphasize—though perhaps not necessarily the most important in answer to this question—is the alteration of the strategic position of Plymouth by

---

[1] This distinction should not be exaggerated into the statement, that there was no emigration to Plymouth. There were always a considerable number of newcomers in the colony, but the majority did not remain there, migrating more or less promptly to Boston or Connecticut, less commonly to Rhode Island. In the western parts of the patent, thriving towns grew up but were founded usually by settlers from the Bay Colony who introduced Puritan ideas and institutions. The Pilgrims looked at them askance, for they truly saw them to be aliens whose increase would endanger the predominance of the town of Plymouth, if not the perpetuation of the ideas for which they had already sacrificed so much.

the expansion of New England. Its economic opportunities were not comparable after 1630 with those to be
found elsewhere. It occupied no strategic position for
trading, for agriculture, or for communication. The
location had been selected without relation to the future
development of the country and to the part which the
colony might play in it. Indeed, the Pilgrims were at
first seeking seclusion and hoped to locate at a distance
from other colonies, on a spot which others would not
wish to utilize; and, though at first in a hurry to find some
place to winter, did not later, when they could easily
have done so, move the settlement to some better location. Once more we find the clue in the original plan of
founding a colony to be maintained from England with
the proceeds of the fish, furs, and lumber sent back from
America. No great accession of people was expected or
desired. Agriculture on a large scale was not contemplated until the colony was already deeply rooted.
Plymouth itself had been selected chiefly because the
first comers were too few and too weak to clear a large
acreage of new land. Its fields were for that very reason
"old land." The soil, never perhaps very fertile, had
been exhausted by constant cropping and only by regular
and perhaps excessive fertilization could be made to
yield at all. Around Plymouth itself there was abundant
good water, but the rest of the land granted by the
patent was too level to drain well, and there were in
consequence a good many marshes and bogs, as well as
a goodly area of sand. There was too much better land
elsewhere in New England for agriculturists to seek
Plymouth in great numbers.

For their first purposes the harbor had seemed excellent and strategically located. They had expected

to use nothing larger than small sailing ships of from thirty to eighty tons and for such craft Plymouth harbor was deep enough and large enough. But it was too shallow and too small to be used as a rendevous for fishing or trading fleets and never could become an emporium for trade with England or with the Atlantic Coast. Nor was it located strategically in relation to the supply of fish and fur after 1640. The Indian population of Massachusetts had been sadly decimated in 1617 and the gatherers of furs were few; the fur-bearing animals themselves had never been numerous and a decade of constant hunting between 1620 and 1630 had depopulated the woods; and the newer colonies occupied better positions than Plymouth for the control of such fur-trade as there was left. The Pilgrims were at once thrown back upon their fishing station at Cape Ann and upon the fur-trading station in Maine. They were now unable to export to England from their own immediate vicinity, and other colonies were better placed than they for the trade of the Grand Banks and of the Maine coast. Nor was Plymouth on the natural line of communications which emigration itself from one spot to another could follow. The Charles River valley was the true road to the interior of Massachusetts and Boston controlled it. The Merrimac valley was the true road to the interior of northern Massachusetts and New Hampshire, and Salem and Newburyport controlled it. The direct road between the Charles River valley and Narragansett Bay passed Plymouth by. The colony was therefore unable to benefit from the passage of settlers elsewhere, to serve as an outlet for their trade, or as a rendezvous for ships directed to them. Nor must the limited area assigned by the patent of 1630 be forgotten. There was not within its limits room for any considerable number of people, nor within the whole district enough arable land of good quality to have made possible the reception at Plymouth of such a colony as Hooker's, or even the addition of such a group as Williams soon gathered at Providence.

The extent of the disadvantages of the first site had become clear to Standish and Alden as early as 1631 and they had in consequence removed to more fertile land at Duxbury, in the teeth of strenuous opposition from their associates. They carried with them Brewster's two children, Collier, already a wealthy man, and others of importance. Brewster himself soon followed them. The General Court decreed in the following year that Plymouth should always be the seat of Government and that the Governor should reside there, but the removals and defections continued. Bradford stood stoutly for the maintenance of Church and Government at Plymouth and for the time prevailed. But year by year the agitation was renewed; and finally in 1644, after long and vehement debates, the majority voted to abandon the old site altogether and move to Nauset. Bradford, though outvoted, though deprived of the support of the other leaders already themselves deserters, determined to end his days at Plymouth, if he lived there alone. Thereupon, a goodly number decided to abide with him. The remainder, led by several men of prominence, including Prence, Bradford's real successor, did leave Plymouth and founded the town of Eastham, upon a location fully as disadvantageous as Plymouth except for the quality of the soil. Of the leaders, Bradford and Howland alone were left in the first settlement. Bradford's sorrow over this exodus found expression in a poem, "A Word to Plymouth," written in 1654.

> "O Poor Plymouth, how dost thou moan,
> Thy children are all from thee gone,
> And left thou art in widow's state,
> Poor, helpless, sad and desolate."

This lack of strategic position—the immediate result of the founding of the other New England colonies—was not the most important or most significant fact in explaining the failure of immigrants to settle at Plymouth itself or within the limits of the colony. The true reasons were ecclesiastical, governmental, economic, and social, and deserve treatment at considerable length.

CHAPTER XIV

THE DOMINANT NOTE AT PLYMOUTH

The ecclesiastical ideas of the Pilgrims are the key to the comprehension of their history and can be properly understood only in the light of the history of dissent in England both before and after the Pilgrim exodus. They alone explain the fundamental problems in Pilgrim annals—the emigration to Holland and to America; the aloofness of Plymouth from the other New England colonies; the failure of large bodies of new immigrants to locate under the Pilgrim patent; the peculiar features of political, social, and economic life; the inclusion of Plymouth within Massachusetts in 1691. The dominant note of Plymouth was struck by the Church and not by the State. There was to be a commonwealth founded upon "God's Ordinances" and not upon the devices of men. The Pilgrims were not merely Separatists but a peculiar variety of Separatists. The truth seems to be that at the time they left England they represented the radical wing of English Protestant dissent. Immediately after their exodus, both wings of the dissenting party ceased to develop along the lines they had chosen and espoused ideas either more conservative or more radical than theirs. The object of the Pilgrims was in fact to crystallize and perpetuate in the New World what we now see to have been a transitional phase of the Puritan movement in England.

It is only in recent years that the necessary evidence has come to light for the study of this first phase of the

Puritan movement.[1] Its first effective form was the
Classis Movement of 1582 to 1592. They felt that the
true interpretation of primitive Christianity had then
been found and vested the governmental authority in
the Classis of ministers, which was to define doctrine, to
perform various acts of discipline, to choose and con-
secrate new ministers, to appoint them to their places,
and the like. The Classis on the whole assumed the
duties which the Bishops had performed, but for the
laity there was as little place as in Episcopacy. If they
had been ruled, directed, and instructed by the Bishops,
they were to be none the less subordinate to the Classis.
While there was in these early years a very general feeling
that the Episcopacy was without warrant of Scripture
and was therefore to be denounced and supplanted, there
was also an almost universal belief that the Church could
and should be transformed rather than destroyed. The
method which seems to have met most favor was the
vesting of Episcopal authority in the Classis, of which the
Bishop should become a fellow member on terms of
substantial equality with the ministers. A variety of
suggestions and changes were considered which made
him something better than an equal, but in general the
Classis, and not the Bishop, was to exercise the authority.
The characteristic element in this phase of the Puritan
movement lay however in the retention, substantially
intact, of the existing Church organization and of the
great bulk of the existing observances and ritual. Stress
was laid upon the change or toleration of "things in-

---

[1] Usher, R. G., *Presbyterian Movement in the Reign of Queen
Elizabeth*, London, 1905; and *Reconstruction of the English Church*,
2 vols. New York and London, 1910; Burrage, C., *Early English
Dissenters*, 2 vols., Cambridge, 1912.

different," such as the sign of the cross in Baptism, the use of the ring in marriage, the wearing of the surplice, as changes highly desirable but perhaps not vital. For this transformation of Church government and for this change of practice and doctrine, the Puritan movement agitated with more or less energy and directness from about 1582 to 1604, when this phase of the movement culminated in the presentation of the Puritan cause at the Hampton Court Conference.

This definition of aims by the bulk of the Puritan party promptly led to the espousal of more radical ideas by the minority, which itself split up into several groups led by Brown, Ainsworth, Johnson and others. Most of them urged the rejection of Bishops altogether and the separation from the Church as a thing unworthy and unclean. There should be no paltering or compromising with the heritage of Popes. It should all be swept away and something better put in its place. The new Church government espoused by the radicals made place for the opinions of the laity in the choice of the ministers and even in the formulation of the creed, a fact of the utmost consequence. To these radical groups the Scrooby Church belonged. It was, however, organized at a period when many of these radicals had already left England for Holland and had separated not only from the Church but from the main body of the Puritans as well. It was a time moreover when the majority of the Puritans were to be tested for the staunchness of their faith, and when they were about, as the Pilgrims themselves would have said, to sell their Master for thirty pieces of silver and be branded with the mark of the Beast.

In 1604-1605, Archbishop Bancroft forced the issue of separation from the Church or conformity to its ob-

servances upon the reluctant Puritans. Those who
would not conform were to be deprived of their benefices
and there should be little if any toleration of tender consciences. Thus went forth the fiat. There is no fact in
Pilgrim annals so important as the conformity of the
overwhelming majority of the Puritan party at this
time. They did accept the laws and observances of the
Established Church. They found that they preferred to
remain within it, even at some little cost, rather than to
leave it. The few who were deprived, the more considerable number who were threatened with deprivation,
nearly all conformed within three years, read the prayer-
book, wore the surplice, followed the observances of the
Church, and retained their benefices. The Puritan
movement in England therefore continued as a movement
within the Church and the gulf between them and the
Pilgrims was already in 1608 impassable, for the Pilgrims
regarded as the very foundation of ecclesiastical polity
the separation from the English Church. As time went
on the main body of the Puritans came to feel an attachment for the Established Church just as the Pilgrim de-
testation of it was intensified; came to possess a real approval of its position, doctrine, and observances as the
Pilgrim disapproval became more and more vehement.
Those who came to New England in 1630 and after from
the main body of the Puritans were not men who could
sympathize with the views of the Pilgrims on Church
government or whom the Pilgrims on their own part were
willing to see settle at Plymouth.

The minority of the Puritan party had already by
1608 split up into a number of groups, some of which were
already abroad, and all of which continued to develop
doctrinal ideas which had not been approved, and in the

majority of instances not even considered, by the English parties in the decade 1595 to 1605, in which the Scrooby Church seems to have had its origin. One and all these radicals maintained an entire separation from the English Church. With practical unanimity they accorded the laity a share in Church government and discipline, and in particular in the choice of the ministry gave them voice. But, while the Pilgrims clung with an almost passionate devotion to the essentially negative doctrinal platform of the years 1590 and 1605, all other English sects, who could bring themselves to separate from the Church, proceeded to divagate in doctrine from the Church itself, from the main body of the Puritan party still in England, and from their own earlier doctrinal ideas. Questions of Baptism by immersion, the nature of the Eucharist, and a number of other issues of the first importance and complexity kept these little groups constantly in turmoil and dissension. Already before the Pilgrims reached Leyden, the earlier doctrinal position was assailed in the English Churches at Amsterdam and the change continued apace in the years the Pilgrims were in Holland. Indeed, they left Amsterdam to escape contamination and eventually departed for New England that they might be alone to develop their own particular ideas, choosing the wilderness because it seemed impossible to find anywhere in England or Holland a body of people who thought exactly as they did.

The potent fact is that none of those reaching the New World after 1620 professed that precise variety of dissent which the Pilgrims themselves were seeking to crystallize and perpetuate. The Pilgrims represented a transitional phase of the great Protestant movement, one whose duration in England itself was short, and they found themselves isolated, stranded, pushed to one side by the subsequent development of Protestantism both in England and in America. They maintained unflinchingly at Plymouth an ideal which had long ceased to have a numerous following in England. Here is the secret of that lack of numerical growth at Plymouth: there was no normal constituency in England or America from which they could draw adherents. Other religious malcontents found there no congenial atmosphere. On the other hand, there were plenty of colonies willing to absorb the Pilgrims' own dissenters.

The Pilgrims seem to have caught up a passing phase of the religious transition in England at a time when events were moving rapidly. They had found themselves at Scrooby practically isolated from other Puritan bodies and had therefore continued the primary impulse without subsequent modification by the thought and controversy which changed so greatly the other Puritan bodies. They were not part of the Puritan movement and disliked it. When they found at Amsterdam that contact with the English Churches there was likely to modify their ideas, they fled. They developed at Leyden quite alone and again at Plymouth quite alone. They had thus nourished in isolation a position which was itself a negation, nothing more than an uncompromising hostility to the Established Church of England and to the ordination of Bishops. They had also reached the conclusion that certain practices observed in England must not be performed, but otherwise in discipline, doctrine, and observances, they waited for further illumination. Their position was at once too uncompromising and too fluid. They had rejected the one Church and declined to accept the substitutes.

Nor did they occupy in America a logical and defensible position. In England, face to face with an Established Church, the denial of its principles and of its divine authority was a practical creed, capable of creating a tie of association, but in the New World, far from Established Churches, far from Bishops who were not menacing them, who had indeed forgotten about them, it became artificial and forced. Always a disruptive tendency rather than a cohesive force, it had separated them from the English Church rather than established them in a position of their own. It looked backward and not forward; it was destructive rather than constructive of a vital entity, endowed with energy of its own. For the generation of Bradford the old contention had real meaning, but for the second and third generations the bond became too weak to retain their allegiance, and certainly could not provide attractions for others looking for a positive and not a negative Christianity.

Nowhere does this isolation of the Pilgrims reveal itself more clearly than in their difficulties in finding a minister. In accordance with the agreement, Robinson, the pastor, had remained at Leyden and those who sailed on the *Mayflower* had been accompanied by Elder Brewster as Teacher. He expounded the Scriptures and held services of prayer and praise, but was forbidden by their previous conclusions to expound doctrine, to baptize, or to celebrate the communion. As Robinson's departure from Leyden was year by year deferred, and as the desirability of celebrating the communion at Plymouth became more and more obvious, Brewster wrote to inquire from Robinson whether he might not in the interim safely perform this vital service for the Pilgrim community. Robinson had replied with an unequivocal negation: no teacher might arrogate to himself the function of a minister.[1] When the news of Robinson's death in 1625 dashed the hope so long deferred, it is surprising that the Pilgrims did not exercise their power as a Church to call Brewster to the ministry. We know directly nothing whatever, but it seems probable that Brewster himself opposed the step and there was no other Pilgrim who possessed even primary qualifications.

The Church organization of the Pilgrims was indeed flexible. They considered themselves possessed of the power to ordain a minister and to choose all Church officers, to draw up for themselves a creed and to enact all necessary ecclesiastical legislation. They distinguished sharply, however, between the Church and the congregation. The former consisted of those adults who had been accepted by the others as consecrated to the service of God and able to give testimony of their faith. The congregation on the other hand included all inhabitants who did not decidedly espouse some other worship. The Church was the governing and disciplinary body and governed the rest. Its organization was voluntary and it seems to have possessed at Scrooby, at Leyden and in the early years at Plymouth, no financial organization. Contributions were made for the minister's support at Plymouth in land, food, and clothes, but there is no evidence that Brewster or any other worker was paid in the ordinary sense of the word until 1655.[2]

None the less the Pilgrims were nonplussed to find a

---

[1] Bradford, *History*, 200.

[2] S. S. Green, *Use of the Voluntary System in the Maintenance of Ministers in the Colonies of Plymouth and Massachusetts Bay*, American Antiquarian Society Proceedings, April, 1886. Separately printed, Worcester, Mass., 1886.

minister. When Allerton went to England on business in
1626–1627, he was to find a clergyman, but experienced
such difficulties in securing anyone whose views seemed
to harmonize with theirs, that he finally brought back
with him a man who soon gave clear proof of insanity.
Early in 1629 a boat load of Pilgrims, returning from a
trading expedition, found a Mr. Ralph Smith at a strag-
gling settlement on the coast. He had migrated from
England with his family and was much discontented
where he was, and, understanding that he had once been
a minister, they brought him to Plymouth and allotted
him a house and land. After some months they chose him
minister. He was an eminently good and respectable
man, but infinitely inferior to Brewster and to Winslow,
who seems on occasion to have officiated.

A few years later there came a man of "many precious
parts" in the person of Roger Williams. He had landed
at Boston, where having some words with Winthrop and
others, packed up his goods and departed. At Plymouth
he was well received; he liked the people and was liked.
He speedily proved his ability as a clergyman and was
called to the ministry. For a while all went well, but soon
he seems to have taken it upon himself to administer
some "sharp admonitions and reproofs" to the leaders,
and to have propounded some of those opinions for which
he was later expelled from Massachusetts Bay and for
which he became famous at Providence. He was "Godly
and zealous" the Pilgrims agreed, but "very unsettled in
judgment," and after a time migrated to Salem.[1] Bradford charitably concludes his account in his *History* with

[1] He left behind him an unpaid debt to Fuller, the Pilgrim doctor, for professional services, which Fuller "freely presented to
him" in his will. *Mayflower Descendant, I,* 28, 1633.

the words, "He is to be pitied and prayed for and so I shall leave the matter and desire the learned to shew him his errors and reduse him into the way of truth and give him a setled judgment and constancie in the same; for I hope he belongs to the Lord and that he will shew him mercie."

For some time after Williams' departure, they were without other ministrations than those of Smith and finally, perhaps growing tired of him, perhaps coming to some difference of opinion with him, they induced John Reynor to emigrate from England and become their clergyman. After a short trial, finding him like his predecessor mediocre in ability and temperament, they induced a really capable and magnetic personality, Charles Chauncey, to come to them from England. Unquestionably a learned and able man, the very sort of a man they needed most at Plymouth, he at once proved, like other energetic characters, to have proceeded in his thinking in a somewhat "irregular" direction. Soon he began to preach the necessity of baptism by immersion. They argued with him at great length, loath to let him go; called upon the Boston and Connecticut clergy for assistance. They were quite willing that he should hold such views about baptism as he wished, but he would not agree to stay with them, unless they were willing to admit that the tenet was as essential as he thought it to be. He went to Scituate where after a time of prosperity his Church again fell into controversy and dissolved. Reynor stayed with the Plymouth Church until 1654, when for thirteen years there was at Plymouth itself no pastor, Elder Cushman holding services as Brewster had in the first years.

It is hardly possible to overemphasize the importance

of the fact that the Plymouth Church was an attempt to crystallize a transitional step in the development of English dissent. Consequently they found themselves isolated, unable to increase their strength because there was no larger body of believers from whom they might draw adherents. So far as they could discover after 1630, there was not in all England one man of real ability who believed as they did, nor were there any laymen of real ability who came to Plymouth in any number to strengthen the Pilgrim state. True, the ability and commanding personality of Brewster and of Bradford was sufficient to maintain the original position during their lives, and to make Plymouth a decidedly uncomfortable spot for able men of different ecclesiastical persuasion, but the result could only be to preserve the position during their lives to lose it beyond a peradventure at their deaths. They bequeathed both Church and State to men who were intellectually too weak and too lacking in magnetism to maintain their peculiar ecclesiastical position against the strong current of opinion in the other New England Churches, there exemplified, as in England itself, by men of the first caliber.

Of Pilgrim practice and belief aside from Church government we have comparatively few reliable indications. About Robinson's ideas both before and after the exodus, we have the fullest possible details, but Robinson's opinions changed from year to year and exactly what version of them Brewster taught at Plymouth we do not know. Of the precise theological angle of Smith and Reynor we know still less. The first Church covenant of the Pilgrims we have, but it does not greatly assist us. "In the Name of our Lord Jesus Christ and in obedience to his holy will and divine ordinances. Wee being by the most wise and good providence of God brought together in this place and desirous to unite our selves into one congregation or church under the Lord Jesus Christ our Head, that it may be in such sort as becometh all those whom he hath redeemed and sanctifyed to himselfe, wee doe hereby solemnly and religiously (as in his most holy presence) avouch the Lord Jehovah the only true God to be our God and the God of ours and doe promise and binde ourselves to walke in all our wayes according to the Rule of the Gospel and in all sincere conformity to His holy ordinances and in mutuall love to and watchfullnesse over one another, depending wholly and only upon the Lord our God to enable us by his grace hereunto."[1]   No doubt the majority of these statements refer to Church government and there is certainly as far as doctrine is concerned nothing in it explicit.   We do know that the Pilgrims were stout Calvinists of a conservative angle, believed in predestination, and in the doctrine of the elect, and in all implied by both.[2]   Brewster possessed a considerable library, chiefly of expository works;[3] several men owned *Calvin's*

[1] This the First Church declared in 1676 was the original Church Covenant, so far as men alive remembered it or notes or letters could establish it.   Plymouth First Church Records, I, printed in full in *Mayflower Descendant*, V, 214–215.

[2] John Cotton, Jr., wrote to Mather on December 11, 1676, bewailing "the power of Satan in hurrying soules to hell through divine permission." It would seem that the conservatism of Robinson before 1620 had not been forgotten.   *Mass. Hist. Soc. Coll., 4th Series*, VIII, 241.

[3] A careful reprint of the original list is in *Mass. Hist. Soc. Proc., 2nd Series*, III, 261–274.   In *Ibid.*, V, 37–85, is a careful identification of these entries by H. M. Dexter.   There were three hundred and two English books and sixty-two Latin; ninety-eight expository, sixty-three doctrinal, sixty-nine practical religious books,

Institutes, the writings of St. Augustine, and the majority of theological tracts published in England of Puritan and Separatist persuasion before 1620, with some books of later date. Unfortunately, the libraries were too varied in character to enable us to conclude anything in regard to the theological views of the men who owned them. Of their ideas regarding the Godhead, the Trinity, the substances in the communion (the word eucharist they deemed Popish and offensive) we know nothing.[1] While they objected to the surplice, their ministers and elders wore a black gown with a white band, after the fashion of the French and Genevese. Winslow was imprisoned in England in 1635 for marrying people by virtue of his authority as magistrate.[2]

We are quite sure that they "called" their ministers and made Fuller, the doctor, deacon,[3] but by what pre-

twenty-four historical, thirty-six "ecclesiastical," six philosophical, fourteen poetical, fifty-four miscellaneous. The dates of publication seemed to Dr. Dexter most significant: fully seventy-five per cent were earlier than 1620, but the remainder were published in the years between 1621 and 1643, every year being represented except 1639 and 1642, and prove that Brewster continued to buy books. There was a treatise on timber, another on silk-worms (at Plymouth!), a volume of George Wither's poetry, Bodin, Bacon, Aristotle, Machiavelli, but no Shakespeare.

[1] In 1666, complaint was made to the Court of the "horrible blasphemy" "that Christ as God is equall with the Father but as Mediator the Father is greater than hee." This is not very solid ground for deductions covering Pilgrim belief on the Trinity. *Plymouth Colony Records*, IV, 112. The *Records* to 1650 contain nothing on such points.

[2] Bradford, *History*, 390–393.

[3] Over this, Morton made very merry in his *New English Canaan* (Prince Soc.), 297. They chose a man "that long time had bin nurst up in the tender bosome of the Church; one that had speciall

cise ceremony we do not know. There is every reason to believe that the real calling consisted in the trying test of long weeks and months of association, and not in any particular event. No doubt the candidate also made public confession of his faith, answered questions put to him by the older men at some stated and formal meeting, at which his calling was to be ratified. Surely their minds had been made up about the candidate before the formal election. Undoubtedly they judged his efficiency from such information as they had and tolerated no opinions other than their own. Previous ordination was for them worthless. The laity were admitted to fellowship in the Church only after stringent tests in private and in public. If we can judge at all from what was said in a later generation when the practice was abandoned, one qualification upon which they rigidly insisted was the ability of the candidate to give an account of his faith publicly and orally, assuredly a trying test for many a good soul.

The religious meetings were held first in the cabin of the *Mayflower*, probably throughout the first winter, though the first service was held on shore in the Common House in March, 1621. Then they used the lowest story of the new fort, which they finished in 1623, until about 1648, when the first meeting house was built at the back of Bradford's garden at the foot of the hill below the fort. The room or meeting house must have been simple in the extreme. We have no knowledge of the use of a pulpit at first; the Teacher or Minister probably stood and his congregation sat around him on stools or benches.

gifts: hee could wright and reede; nay more: he had tane the oath of abjuration which is a speciall stepp, yea and a maine degree unto preferment."

He prayed with his head uncovered, they stood with bowed heads, and they all closed their eyes during the prayer, a practice which visitors remarked as unusual.[1] For the Communion they probably used a table, brought from some one's house perhaps, though whether they knelt to receive or sat we have no authentic hint. Some dissenting bodies did, others did not. Baptism was performed in any part of the Church convenient; from some ordinary basin or dish. The use of a particular vessel would have seemed to them to smack of the ceremonies of the Established Church. The head of the child or adult was sprinkled with a little water from the fingers of the minister, who probably did not touch the child and certainly did not make the sign of the cross. They used in service the Geneva version of the Bible and Ainsworth's *Psalms*, which they sang in unison without the accompaniment of any musical instrument.

The Dutchman, De Rasiéres, told of their method of marching to service on Sundays and holidays. "They assemble by beat of drum, each with his musket or firelock in front of the captain's door; they have their cloaks on and place themselves in order three abreast and are led by a sergeant without beat of drum; behind comes the Governor in a long robe; beside him on the right hand comes the Preacher with his cloak on, and on the left hand, the Captain with his side-arms and cloak on, and with a small cane in his hand; and so they march in good order and each sets his arms down near him." [2] This was in 1627. A few years later Governor Winthrop,

---

[1] Arber, *Pilgrim Fathers*, 294; Bradford, *History*, 493; Morton, *New English Canaan*, Prince Soc., 334. This is a very obscure point, however.

[2] Reprinted in full in Goodwin, *Pilgrim Republic*, 308.

Pastor Winslow of the Boston Church, and some others, paid a visit to Plymouth and attended Church on Sunday forenoon. During the afternoon a further service was held, at which the guests from Boston listened with such composure as they might to Roger Williams, who had left them under somewhat strained circumstances the year before. Williams "propounded" a question in Puritan phrase. Pastor Smith then "expounded" it, after which Williams "prophesied," that is to say, preached. Bradford spoke and was followed by Elder Brewster and other Pilgrims. Winthrop was then invited to speak and was followed by Pastor Winslow. Deacon Fuller then reminded the people of the blessedness of giving; whereupon Bradford solemnly rose, proceeded to the Deacon's seat, deposited his offering, and the others in order of prominence followed him.

In the modern sense of the word, the Pilgrims were perhaps not tolerant, but surely a great deal of misconception has prevailed about their intolerance, and an amount of praise has been accorded others which they do not deserve. Certainly they did not allow people of all shades of opinion, of all walks of life, and of all varieties and conditions to reside permanently within their jurisdiction. In fact no man or woman was allowed to remain overnight without explicit permission, and those who proved themselves obnoxious in any way were promptly expelled without hesitation or delay. The Quakers received no charitable handling at Plymouth. At the same time the Pilgrims were hospitable to a fault and did give temporary refuge readily to all sorts, kinds, and conditions of men. If their rule seems unyielding, it must be remembered that it was enforced by Bradford in a very elastic and flexible way, with a serious attempt to mete out justice to all. So far as we know, while the Pilgrims were the only considerable settlement on the coast, no one was turned away, however unworthy, and many were kept for months of whom the Pilgrims would have been glad to rid themselves. In later years, when the other settlements outnumbered the Pilgrims ten to one, and there was little if any chance of people not finding refuge, the Pilgrims were less ready to permit those of whom they did not approve to make more than temporary visits to the jurisdiction. They were certainly as tolerant as any men of their time and under the circumstances perhaps more so than others.

At the same time, we shall much misrepresent them, if we suppose for an instant that they came to America in order to promulgate the idea that anyone might come to Plymouth and think what he liked, or to found a refuge for people who wished to disagree with them. On the contrary, they came to escape the necessity of tolerating those who disagreed with them, in the hope that they might be able to erect in America a temporal organization sufficiently strong to keep divergent minds at something better than arm's length. With that intention the age was entirely in sympathy. Toleration was not then believed to be a virtue and the conduct of Bradford at Plymouth is the exact counterpart of that of Winthrop at Boston, of Eaton and Davenport at New Haven, and of Oliver Cromwell in England. Toleration was then in the making and these men were making it. To it none contributed more than the Pilgrims, but they themselves did not know it, and would have denied it with asperity and vehemence, if they had been charged with it.

BIBLIOGRAPHICAL NOTES

Pilgrim Church History.   The excessive fear of interference from England and the determination to provide no *prima facie* evidence of failure to conform to the requirements of the Established Church perhaps explains the decision of the Pilgrims to keep no church records.   The first section of the records of Plymouth First Church consists of the manuscript of Morton's *New England's Memorial*, most of which was based upon Bradford's *History* and the rest of which is utterly unreliable.   The records proper begin in 1667 with Cotton's pastorate and have been printed in the *Mayflower Descendant*, IV, V, VIII, etc.   The histories and literature of the New England Churches in general either omit Plymouth altogether or barely mention it.   Neither Lechford's *Plaine Dealing* (Trumbull's Ed.) nor Morton's *New English Canaan* (Prince Soc.) distinguished between Pilgrim and Puritan practice, and devote only brief paragraphs to the former. There is some material in J. Cotton, *Way of the Churches of Christ in New England*, London, 1645, but the extent and accuracy of his information on Plymouth is open to question. John Cotton's *Account of the Church of Christ in Plymouth*, in *Mass. Hist. Soc. Coll.*, IV, 110, was not written until 1760, and refers principally to the period after 1667.   It quotes freely from Morton and the Church Records, though without acknowledgments.

H. M. Dexter's *The Church Polity of the Pilgrims the Polity of the New Testament*, pp. 82, Boston, 1870, is polemical rather than historical, assumes the identity of Pilgrim Church government and that of the Congregational churches of his own day, and attempts to prove from the New Testament that such was primitive Christianity.   Cotton's *Magnalia*, Book V, Part II, contains the Platform of Church Discipline of the Synod of Cambridge of 1649 which seems to have been approved at Plymouth in the last decades.   Explicit, direct, first-hand evidence on Pilgrim ecclesiastical history, we lack for nearly all points of first importance. From Bradford we see clearly the issue of Church government, the domination of the State by the Church, and get personal details about the ministers and their troubles. But upon doctrine, ceremony, discipline, we must infer, deduce, and piece together scattered fragments.

CHAPTER XV

The relation of Church and State at Plymouth was singularly close and significant. Already in Holland the Pilgrim leaders had seen that their failure to control the economic and political situation would ultimately result in a failure to maintain their ecclesiastical position and they left Leyden fully determined to create a state which should maintain and protect the Church. From the first therefore ecclesiastical necessity influenced the form of civil government and the temporal policy of the leaders. The perpetuation of God's Ordinances became literally the cornerstone of civil polity. At all costs the unity of the Church must be preserved, and no considerable accession of people to the little colony should be permitted, likely to outnumber and outvote those whose loyalty to the ecclesiastical ideal was already assured. Practically interpreted, this meant that the constitution of the State was to vest in the leaders authority over all existing colonists, a power to limit newcomers in number to a minority of the total population, and to exclude all those who did not seem likely to amalgamate in time with the Pilgrim Church. The experience with Oldham and Lyford confirmed the necessity and expediency of this decision and erected it into a cornerstone of constitutional law.

Such a civil policy was necessarily antagonistic to the physical growth of the colony. The leaders insensibly feared the accession of members, an increase in the number of towns, a division of the Plymouth Church into several Churches as tantamount to the disruption of the colony and the downfall of religion itself. ˙Able and energetic personalities they came to suspect and were chary of granting them a share of political power. The coming of the Puritans to Boston, they realized, afforded them much needed support and temporal assistance and they could not, despite themselves, but feel that these were their brethren. At the same time they wished no large accession of Puritans within the boundaries of Plymouth and they therefore framed a government and created a definition of political privilege, which should so far as possible discourage and hamper immigration.

Naturally, the type of civil government established at Plymouth, conditioned by this assumed necessity of defending State and Church from outside influence, vested practically unlimited discretionary authority in the hands of the Governor.[1] This they had at once concluded was essential, though they also appreciated the advisability of entire discretion in its use. This broad and flexible authority was conferred upon William

[1] The authorities for this topic are Bradford's *History*, the only source of much value for the period to 1636; the *Plymouth Colony Records*, 12 vols.; Brigham, *Laws of New Plymouth*, and the Records of the various towns. On the whole, the material for the constitutional history of Plymouth is singularly fragmentary and elusive in character and administrative practice as well as legal theory is peculiarly difficult to determine. The critical apparatus upon which this chapter is based became too elaborate and technical to permit its inclusion in footnotes. Some of the statements in the text are perhaps more positive than the direct evidence warrants, but attempts to qualify and explain made a chapter, even now somewhat long, entirely out of proportion to the rest of the book and resulted in an account which lacked clarity for the general reader.

Bradford in April, 1621. He promptly proceeded to perform such executive work as seemed necessary, usually after consultation with "a few"; and to arraign and punish such offenders as he and the few he consulted deemed essential. For the first three years the government at Plymouth scarcely deserved the name, for all functions seem to have been united in the person of the Governor, and those exercised were not primarily administrative at all. The fact of the Common Stock and the Agreement with the merchants imposed upon him the duty of regulating the labor of the community as well as the apportionment of the proceeds. He was in fact more an overseer of work, a foreman in the fields, a storekeeper who portioned out the common supplies and put away what had been collected or raised, than a civil officer of any recognized type. We are told that the whole body of settlers [1] met several times in those first years to consider public affairs and that a variety of decisions were reached, but no formal record was kept of what those decisions were, nor was any record kept for some fifteen years beyond such notes as Bradford saw fit to make. This fusion of executive, administrative, and judicial power in the hands of the Governor, this lack of formality, this unlimited discretion provided exactly that type of government best adapted to the needs of the Church. Whatever was required in its interests could be done promptly and without hesitation, and without permitting argument over its legality. Until the leaders knew better what regulations and forms the situation demanded, they proposed to hamper their discretion as little as possible.

Such a government was unquestionably an extraordi-

[1] Possibly with some exceptions; we cannot be sure.

nary tribute to the personal rectitude, the impartiality, the diligence, and the ability of William Bradford. By general consent all possible governmental power was vested for one year in one man, whose discretion was left practically untrammeled, except for such matters as he himself of his own free will saw fit to submit to the whole assembly, or dealt with in accordance with the advice of others. Such complete power over any community has rarely been vested in one individual for any length of time with that community's consent. Bradford held it with brief intervals from 1621 to 1657. The fact that his own *History* is our only authority for many aspects of life in the first years at Plymouth and the fact that his modesty led him to subordinate his share in the direction of events long concealed the extent of his influence.[1] Surely his energy must have been vast, his discretion remarkable, his ability commanding, or those stern and uncompromising men and women would scarcely have permitted him to regulate their affairs at discretion so long.

To be sure, such a government was possible only in a small community of homogeneous people, who agreed thoroughly upon the general aims of private and public life, and whose conduct was so invariably orderly that the amount of government required was reduced to a minimum. It is no disparagement of Bradford's ability or discretion to say that in most affairs the little colony

[1] When the Old Colony Club at Plymouth held its first solemn celebration of the landing of the Pilgrims in 1770, toasts were drunk "to pious ancestors," Carver, Morton, Standish, Massasoit, Cushman, but neither Bradford, Brewster, Winslow, nor Alden. This shows the very real ignorance about Pilgrim history which the traditions of Elder Faunce had allowed to develop at Plymouth itself. *Mass. Hist. Soc. Proc., 2nd Series*, III, 400–401.

certainly governed itself and ordered its own ways, with such complete regard to the common interest and to the proper share in it of each individual, that there was not a great deal of governing to be done. There was perhaps only one William Bradford, but quite as certainly there was probably never gathered together in one community, before or since, a body of men and women who averaged higher in diligence, in spirituality, and in law-abiding qualities than the Pilgrim fathers and mothers. Some who were *with* them, but not *of* them, gave Bradford uneasy moments, but the great majority certainly did not require to be governed.

At the same time, there can be no doubt that the ascendency of Bradford was so complete at Plymouth as to render the colony unattractive, for that reason alone, to those energetic leaders who emigrated from England after 1630 at the head of numerous colonists. There was room at Plymouth for but one Bradford and while he occupied the stage there could be no space on it for men who also felt themselves capable of directing large affairs and who were conscious of great ambitions. The leaders as well as the rank and file found Plymouth politically unattractive. Truth to tell, neither he nor the Pilgrim leaders dared share the direction of affairs with aggressive personalities nor even with the majority of the Plymouth Church. The ascendency of the Governor came to stand in their eyes for the supremacy of the Church over the State, for the protection and perpetuation of the Church itself; it became the visible sign of success in their great design in coming to the New World. To diminish that ascendency or attack it was to shake the foundations of religion and to disobey the Ordinances of God.

The unlimited authority exercised by the Governor was granted to him for a year by the whole body of those possessed of political privilege at the General Court of Elections, which met annually at the close of the year—according to the Old Style of dating used by the Pilgrims—about March 25. In practice, this General Court of Elections possessed what we should call today the sovereign power, for it exercised without appeal the supreme executive, legislative, and judicial authority. At the same time, it is abundantly clear that the Pilgrims did not look upon this as executive and that as legislative; there was so much to be done and they did it without bothering about constitutional subtleties. Not one of them had had a legal education and Brewster's experience with Davison had been diplomatic rather than administrative. It is scarcely less anachronistic to represent Bradford and Winslow invoking the sovereignty of the people or thinking in terms of the separation of powers than to imagine them diverting the Indians with moving pictures or exploring Plymouth Harbor in a submarine. The parties of the Civil Wars in England were about to work a revolution in political thinking, but the great majority in England were as yet unconscious of it when the Pilgrims were shaping their flexible and elastic constitution in the decades between 1620–1640.

The leaders consulted the majority less because of preconceived theories than because of the logic of facts. The acquiescence of the majority was absolutely essential and they deemed it wiser to assure themselves of it by putting questions of importance to a vote in an assembly, of which all men of any ability or position were members, and in which they were invited, nay exhorted, to express their opinions and preferences. It was easier to deal with the known than with the unknown and the "conspiracy" of Lyford and Oldham was crushed by the simple expedient of publicity.

Two strong precedents, familiar to them all, sanctioned this practice and strengthened their belief in its expediency. They had long discussed affairs of common interest in the Great House on the Kloksteeg at Leyden, where no less significant issues had been put to majority vote, after vigorous and free discussion, than the voyage to America, the location of the proposed settlement in North America, whether the Pastor should go, and the contract with the English merchants. The governmental issues at Plymouth were not essentially different in character and were intrinsically less important. The Pilgrim ecclesiastical organization, based upon Luther's priesthood of all believers and Calvin's right of the individual to judge for himself, contained the fertile seed of future American democracy; but those who first used it scarcely thought of it as governmental and recked little of sanctions and sovereignty.

While the administrative traditions of the rank and file were both vague and mixed, those predominant in Brewster's mind were the traditions of the Manor of Scrooby, where he had ruled autocratically as Steward, with the assistance of the majority of the inhabitants, who owed suit of court at the Court Leet. As Steward he had possessed a combination of powers very similar to those the Governor exercised at Plymouth; he had been responsible to an Archbishop who rarely interfered and had owed an allegiance to the King, which was satisfied in the sixteenth century by bare affirmations, for the "liberties" of the manor freed him and its in-

habitants from all immediate responsibility to the royal
courts and officers.   The laws of England he and the
suitors had construed in their own sense at the Court
Leet and they had been accustomed to adopt such regulations for their own affairs as they deemed convenient,
all without thought of disloyalty, independence, or sovereignty of the people. Their background was feudal
and not modern, but it did provide them with clear
enough precedent for their own right to manage their
own affairs without royal interference and at the same
time in entire consonance to the law.   They were to
obey the laws of England but they might interpret them
themselves.   We shall do well not to strain our analogies,
but is it not more probable that we hear the voices of the
suitors of the old Court Leet in the Pilgrim Compact and
in the legislation of 1636 than a conscious creation of a
new constitution, made by a people thoroughly awake to
modern ideas of popular sovereignty, and already im-
bued with a belief in their political independence of
England?

In practice, this decision to protect the Church at all
costs and thoroughly to test the loyalty and ecclesiastical
conformity of the newcomers before admitting them to a
share in the privileges of the State resulted in certain
differentiations in political status, which were not democratic as we understand the word.   Political equality
never existed in the strict sense of the word at Plymouth
during the lifetime of Bradford.   The General Court
possessed sovereignty but the leaders carefully provided
that too many should not be members.   No other definition of political privilege existed for many years than
membership in this Court and the qualifications for
admission were not definite nor made public.   Nominally,

new-comers were admitted with the consent of those already possessed of privilege, but the share of the forty-one signers of the Pilgrim Compact in government was from the first residual rather than direct or immediate. Bradford and Allerton, writing back to England in 1623 in answer to certain charges made against them by their enemies, declare "touching our governmente, you are mistaken if you think we admite weomen and children to have to doe in the same, for they are excluded, as both reason and nature teacheth they should be; neither doe we admite any but such as are above the age of 21 years and they also but in some weighty matters, when we thinke good." [1]

The few, in reality, were to govern at Plymouth and Bradford was their executive head and officer and the controlling influence among them. Just how many these were, we do not know. Undoubtedly the eight Under-takers were members, but how many more sat with them in the inner council we cannot say, probably not above fifteen in these earlier years. Membership in the General Court depended upon the ability of the man to convince them of his desirability or to prove to them, in their phrase, that he was godly, sober, and discreet. This meant that he must be eminently industrious, of quiet habits and ways, submissive and deferential to Bradford and other leaders, a Church member *in posse*, and one able to meet the rigid tests of moral conduct sure to be imposed upon him. After a time the members of the General Court came to be known as freemen, although the practice did not become general until after 1630 and was perhaps adopted as a result of the influence of Massachusetts. In 1633, when the first list of freemen

[1] *American Historical Review*, VIII, 299.

was recorded, it contained sixty-eight names; twenty-three more were apparently admitted freemen in the following two years, but in 1659, despite the growth of Plymouth in the meantime, the electorate of the whole colony was less than two hundred.

Below the Freemen were the Inhabitants, who possessed civil and legal equality with the freemen but had no political privilege. They included the heads of families and property owners, who had been accepted as permanent residents, and who were potential freemen. They paid taxes, were compelled to attend Church, were liable for military service, and possessed definite property rights, both to the use of land and to the personal property they accumulated. Although they could not serve as members of a jury, they had a right to be tried by one. Wives, all unmarried adult women, and all minor children took the legal status of the husband or father. Below the Inhabitants were the Sojourners, who possessed neither legal rights nor civil equality and could not hope to attain political privilege. They comprised those who had not yet been granted by the authorities the right of permanent residence, but who lived on from week to week at the Governor's discretion, and who might in time become Inhabitants, and after due period of probation Freemen. During the first decade, Bradford seems to have possessed personally the right to permit a stranger to sojourn, and to extend it or terminate it at discretion, without the formality of consulting the other leaders.

All of these three classes, Freemen, Inhabitants, and Sojourners, were to our thinking free men. They were masters of their own time, able to go where they would. Below them in the Pilgrim scale were the unfree, those who did not possess legally the control of their own destinies. These comprised indented servants, who had hired themselves out to others, either in England or in America, for a term of years, in order to pay their passage or to discharge debts accumulated in America. With them, though not exactly of their class, ranked domestic servants, of whom there were a few at Plymouth, and those who had hired themselves out as servants, though not for a specified term of years or by a written contract. There were also a number of apprentices, mostly minors, the number of whom increased considerably as time went on. There were besides many Indian servants and a few Indian slaves, mostly captives taken in war. Not improbably the unfree at Plymouth were as many as one-quarter or one-third of the total population and in the early years perhaps a more considerable proportion.

The crystallization of constitutional law and practice at New Plymouth was slow, primarily because the leaders found elaborate formalities unnecessary in so small a colony, but in large measure because they feared the effect upon the welfare of the Church of surrendering their discretionary power. From 1621 to 1624 the only constituted authority was the Governor and one Assistant (Allerton). In 1624, at the request of Bradford, four new Assistants were created and elected, making a Governor and a Council of five, in which the former had a double vote. In 1633, the growth of the colony and the additional administrative work led them to add two more Assistants to the Council, making seven in all. The Governor remained, however, as before, almost supreme depository of authority and was at once Executive, Treasurer, Secretary of State, and Judge, for the power of the Assistants to act upon their own initiative seems to have been either non-existent or exceedingly small. Explicit provision was made that these "offices were annual," that is to say, the grant of power was apparently renewed each year and the office itself would have lapsed but for the vote of the Court continuing it.

Not until 1636 was any definition of the powers of the Governor or Assistants attempted or any codification of what they understood the law to be written on paper. The definitions now provided by no means deprived the Governor of his old discretionary authority. He was to execute the laws and ordinances; he was empowered personally to arrest and imprison at discretion any citizen or stranger, and to examine all persons whom he felt to be suspicious. No limitations upon this authority were imposed, no more exact definition attempted. He was expected speedily to bring to trial before the Court of Assistants, or before the General Court at his discretion, such persons as he might apprehend or such cases as he did not feel he could settle himself. The Assistants were his deputies, might take his place temporarily, but possessed individually no executive authority, except as he might from time to time see fit to delegate it to them. Sitting collectively with the Governor, they possessed the right to advise him, and probably had the right to be consulted, though the law did not say so. The legislation of 1636, if it deserves the name, did not alter the discretionary aspect of government at Plymouth nor did it perceptibly reduce the power of the Governor. It was in fact little more than a statement of what the practice had become during the régime of Bradford. After 1633, the latter was not Governor every year, but he continued to be one of the Assistants when he was not Governor, and, until his death in 1657, exercised a controlling influence in the state.

The judicial power at Plymouth rested in the early years with the Governor. He decided himself such cases as he felt he could and received such assistance as he asked for, but apparently no such aid was compulsory. Whether or not in the first years a case could have been appealed from Bradford himself to the Governor and Assistants and from them to the General Court on the initiative of the defendant is exceedingly doubtful. The method of trial in these first years is sufficiently clear from the cases of Lyford, Morton, Billington, and others. There were apparently no lawyers at Plymouth and no defence in our sense of the word was attempted. The Governor or his deputy was at once judge and prosecuting attorney. There were no set examinations and no definite legal forms were observed. None of the Pilgrims had had legal training and they could not therefore very well observe English forms with which they were not familiar. The practice of the Manorial Court at Scrooby Brewster knew and no doubt they followed it as closely as they could. In criminal cases, an oral charge was made by the Governor or his deputy of the case against the prisoner. An oral reply was permitted him, and the question and answer continued quite without restriction and without formal oaths, taken for judicial effect, and without anything that would have been considered in England pleading to the jurisdiction. Written pleadings were not essential but witnesses were informally called by the Court or by the accused without restriction.

Civil cases, where two parties appeared, were apparently tried by the parties themselves, each of whom stated his case to the Governor or to such aids as the

Governor had asked to sit with him. No plaintiff or defendant can have had much difficulty in getting before the Court and the little community at large the true facts about his case. It must be remembered that judicial work in a tiny community, where everyone's goings and comings and practically his inmost thoughts were known to the community as a whole, was a comparatively simple matter. In 1634, the General Court provided that actions of debt or trespass involving less than forty shillings value should be tried by the Governor and Assistants. This was little more than a definition of what had always been true and had chiefly the effect of preventing appeals of such cases to the General Court itself. This raises the presumption that such appeals had become common. In 1636, the judicial competence of the Governor and two Assistants was affirmed for the trial of civil cases under forty shillings and of all criminal cases where the penalty was a small fine. Provision was made for the empanelling of a Grand Jury to present offences and the Governor was formally denominated Prosecuting Attorney. In 1666, this minor jurisdiction was handed over to the Selectmen of the towns. In 1651, the Governor was empowered to create one of the Assistants Deputy-Governor. This, however, was merely the confirmation of an existing practice and was due perhaps to the growing infirmity of Bradford. Not until 1679 was a Deputy-Governor formally elected.

Serious crimes at Plymouth seem to have been few. Murder, arson, burglary, as distinguished from pocket-picking and the stealing of tools, were very rare. A few cases of vagrancy are reported but seem rather to have been what we would call laziness or a technical charge by which to apprehend a man, otherwise undesirable, than real crimes. Inasmuch as one of the capital crimes at Plymouth was "diabolical conversation," some latitude of interpretation of the criminal law was essential. This throws considerable light upon the Pilgrim "criminal code" in the absence of what were elsewhere regarded as serious crimes. There is evidence on every page of the records of a serious attempt at fairness, justice, and mercy. A spirit of general forbearance is evident, which one would not expect to find, considering what has been so often said about the Pilgrims and about the intolerance of Bradford and his followers in particular. They did not follow the letter of the law too strictly and they were far from heartless. Many complaints were discharged; many penalties were mitigated; many fines never collected.

The relationship between the colony of Plymouth, the Pilgrim Church, the town of Plymouth, and the other various towns and Churches of the colony is one of the most abstruse of all the difficult problems in Pilgrim institutional history. Bradford unquestionably intended that colony, Church, and town should be one and the same, and always opposed a grant of authority to a new town or the recognition of a new Church as a tendency sure to diminish the authority of the leaders at Plymouth and certain in time to disintegrate the original Pilgrim Church. Until 1630 there seems to have been no attempt to leave either the Church or the town of Plymouth which was not easily and immediately suppressed by the leaders. The foundation of Duxbury in 1631 by Standish and Alden, and its recognition as a town in the succeeding year, seems promptly to have resulted in the creation of a government for the town of Plymouth separate from that of the colony. In 1633 a Constable was chosen for the town, and in the following year persons were appointed to lay out highways. In 1643 raters of taxes appeared, but not until 1649 were Select men chosen, and not until then therefore was there a real executive for the town of Plymouth and work performed there by other officers than the colonial government itself. There were by that time several towns in the colony, all of which recognized the authority of the General Court, the majority of which consisted still of the freemen of Plymouth itself. It exercised an instant and searching supervision over the new towns from the very first, and so far as possible seems to have restricted their competence to the allotment of land and of cattle, the repairing of fences, the hiring of men to herd cattle, and the like. How much further their powers might have extended at this early period the records of these towns do not tell us. In all probability the work required was simple in the extreme and did not comprise more than the primary common interests just mentioned.

As early as 1638, six towns beside Plymouth had already come into existence and a good deal of opposition was apparent to the "sovereign power" exercised by the General Court of Elections, on the ground that the majority of freemen were resident in Plymouth anyway, and that the freemen resident in other towns could attend only at so great a sacrifice to themselves as practically to leave the political authority with the leaders in Plymouth. Indeed, there can be little question that the leaders had hoped that this situation would retain men at Plymouth and prevent the foundation of other towns. Their attempts to supervise stringently the constitutional arrangements of the new towns had been probably undertaken to discourage the resort of people thither and to bring those who had already gone back to Plymouth, if it were possible. They deemed it best to agree however in 1638 to the formation of an assembly of towns, in which Plymouth should have four votes and the other towns two each, to be cast by delegates elected by the freemen. The new Assembly was to legislate but found its power considerably circumscribed by the necessity of propounding a law at one court and of considering it at the next. Probably this was due to the desire of the delegates to discuss the measure with their constituents at home and to return to the next meeting with instructions for action, but it inevitably resulted in delay and obstruction. The new Assembly was to sit four times a year, and the Governor and Assistants, now called the "Bench," were to form a sort of upper house. The members from the towns, called at first "committees" and afterwards "deputies," formed the lower house.

The two houses, however, commonly sat and voted together, the decision being by majority vote, the "bench" being counted with the "deputies," a practice which persisted until the end of the colony. The General Court of Elections retained its sovereignty, and its relation to the new Assembly is difficult to explain, for it certainly still retained the power of passing laws itself, and still annually chose the Governor, Assistants, and Treasurer, when that office was presently created, and, after 1643, the Plymouth Commissioners of the New England Confederation. The General Court sometimes repealed the laws passed by the Assembly, although it became presently more common for the latter to legislate, and for the work of the General Court to be restricted to the election of officers. Except for the towns, there were no other sub-divisions in the colony until 1685, when three counties were created, whose boundaries were substantially those of the present counties of Plymouth, Barnstable, and Bristol. The control therefore remained to the death of Bradford substantially in the hands of the freemen of Plymouth itself, who used the General Court as their principal constitutional weapon. Here again was a fruitful source of discontent among those resident in the colony and a frequent cause of dissatisfaction among newcomers.

CHAPTER XVI

ECONOMIC PRIVILEGE, 1627–1657

The Pilgrim leaders early saw that the possession of economic privilege must be the reward of orthodoxy. It should be the visible pearl of great price which alone could compensate the Elect of God for the toil and effort necessary to establish His Church in the New World. Nor were they slow to realize that it would be an influence by no means to be despised in leading the timid and ignorant to investigate with a whole heart the ecclesiastical propositions they held to be so true. The withholding of economic privileges must be the gleaming sword with which the faithful could and should defend and preserve the purity of the Church and the integrity of the State. It was the one weapon which definitely reached the worldly, the selfish, and the objectionable. To make living difficult for them at Plymouth, to make profit impossible, was the one means of rendering Plymouth so unattractive that they would depart voluntarily, and thus relieve the leaders of the necessity of a forcible expulsion, which was only too likely to attract attention from Bishops and royal officials whose inquiries it might be impossible to avoid and equally impossible to satisfy. Economic privilege, therefore, like civil rights, was to be dependent upon Church membership. The period, both in Europe and in America, was one of strict economic regulation on the part of the state and the maintenance was universal of a great variety of exclusive privileges and concessions. Economic regulation was not new to those at Plymouth. There was no place indeed in New England where economic privilege was not dependent upon conformity to the Church, but there were few colonies where the ecclesiastical and civil prerequisites of a share in the economic privileges were as stringent or as consistently and rigidly enforced. The small size of the colony throughout its history, the fact that it included for more than ten years only one town, made a degree of regulation possible which could not have been maintained in a larger community, differently placed and differently governed.

The one thing of value in early Plymouth was land. Ownership was impossible, because the title was vested in the Adventurers till 1629 and then till 1640 in Bradford, finally reaching the whole body of freemen as a corporation, not as individuals, in 1640. The first allotments of land for individual use were made by the Governor, with the confirmation of the General Court. Probably the dispensations were for the most part Bradford's personal judgment, perhaps because any division of land prior to 1627 was contrary to the agreement with the merchants and the majority were quite willing to let him shoulder the responsibility of a breach of that agreement. Until 1640, the vast majority of people therefore did not own land, but possessed instead temporary rights of occupancy. These had been assigned annually to the various individuals by the Governor and Assistants, and then, as towns were organized, by the town authorities. This allotment of land became the most important event of the year, the surest method of reward or punishment for past conduct, the effective measure of an individual's status and rights. Attempts to evade it or to supply omissions from it were not un-

common and were ordinarily occupancy without permission or purchase from Indians. The latter transactions were invariably denied validity, unless the previous
consent of the General Court had been obtained. It was
quite obvious that to recognize the possibility of such
purchase by individuals was to accept the superiority
of the Indian title to their own patents from the King.
They claimed later that they had originally bought the
land as a whole from the Indians and therefore could not
accept subsequent purchases from individual Indians as
valid. Cases however appeared every few years and
were always dealt with sternly.[1]

The monopoly of the trading rights also was vested
in the leaders, certainly until 1640. The Indian trade
was never open to the main body of settlers during the
first twenty years of its history and perhaps not for two
or three decades thereafter. The Common Stock had
provided for its monopoly in the joint interest of the
merchants and the settlers and for its control until 1627
by the leaders, who were to allow the majority absolutely
no individual share in it whatever. Between 1627 and
1634 the leaders continued to hold this monopoly as
Undertakers, or until the debt to the merchants should
be finally paid. This clearly involved more responsibility
than privilege on their part. They assumed a supposedly
crushing financial burden without obtaining a privilege
then estimated as a fair equivalent. After 1634, for
some years they continued to control the trade for a
variety of reasons. To their monopoly of the land, of
the fishing, and of the fur trade, the leaders promptly
added a stringent control of such other economic privileges of value as appeared.

[1] *Plymouth Colony Records*, IV, 44, 49, 58, 59, etc.

The first commodity exported to England was dressed lumber, and when, after the allotment of land and the practical abolition of the general stock in 1623, individuals were free to work as they pleased, the General Court decreed that no one should sell or transport lumber without the permission of the Governor and Assistants, that no handicraftsmen, tailors, shoemakers, carpenters, joiners, smiths, or sawyers should do any work, either in Plymouth or outside, for any strangers until the needs of the Colony itself had been met. The Governor and Assistants were to accord the necessary permission, when in their judgment the condition of the colony warranted it. The General Court again decreed in 1626 that no corn, beans, or peas should be transported or sold out of the colony without the Governor's and Assistants' permission. After live stock was imported, the regulation promptly appeared that no animals were to be sold out of the colony.[1] From the first in all probability the Governor had regulated prices of most goods produced in the colony as well as of all goods imported from England. Wages had also been fixed by the Governor and Assistants, and in January, 1635–36, the General Court confirmed this power, but required them to consult with and secure the consent of certain men named.[2] In practice these regulations covered the entire economic activity of the colony. Nothing was done or could be done which was not subject to the direct control of the leaders.

Nor did the leaders hesitate to increase, diminish, or withhold the shares of various individuals in accordance with their estimate of the man, and in particular of his orthodoxy. Four degrees of economic privilege are very

[1] *Plymouth Colony Records*, I, 13.
[2] *Ibid.*, 36.

sharply outlined. There were first the leaders themselves, a group of from eight to fifteen, sometimes larger or smaller. They allotted themselves the best land, the best cattle, the best meadows for hay, and kept in their hands for nearly twenty-five years the entire trade with the Indians and all fishing rights. A second group contained the remainder of the Church members, to whom were made allotments of land and cattle entirely desirable, and in the main such as they wished, located where they on the whole preferred, unless too many chose the same spot. These seem to have had, after the first fifteen years, the option of sharing in the Indian trade, if they were also willing to assume a corresponding part of the financial responsibilities of the colony. They seem ordinarily to have preferred to leave both the trade and the debts to the leaders. A third group, definitely inferior, were the Inhabitants. These were the potential Church members, people deemed sufficiently sober, godly, and discreet to be allotted land and to be permitted to pursue agriculture under such restrictions as the leaders deemed necessary, but with no chance to share in the trade of the colony.

Below them were a fourth group—the unprivileged—those who were not considered as possible Church members or citizens, who received no land, who had no right to cut hay on the town meadows, who were to work as directed and who were to be ruled. These included all temporary residents of the colony, all people on probation pending a decision by the leaders as to their desirability, and all the servants, bond servants, apprentices, minor children, and slaves. In a considerable number of instances, the leaders seem to have concluded that some individuals could never be anything better than servants and they did not hesitate to require them either to work for some freeman of the colony and thus to cease "living disorderly," or to leave the jurisdiction. The time of probation before an Inhabitant might become a Freeman, or one of the unprivileged might become an Inhabitant, was entirely discretionary with the leaders. There was apparently no rule about it, and there were certainly no formal, written, or publicly acknowledged qualifications of wealth or status, the attainment of which automatically conferred right to examination and election. The requirements were highly elastic and clearly varied with the individual. Sometimes they had no hesitation at all and acted promptly on a newcomer's arrival. In other cases, men stayed for months or perhaps years without even receiving an allotment of land. Some bond servants, having served their five or seven years, were then told that they were undesirable and could never become Inhabitants. No legislation was ever necessary; no executive or judicial enforcement needed; it was a perfectly simple matter to pass over the individual when the next allotment was made, and a failure to obtain land was equivalent to degradation to the status of servant or to banishment.[1]

The lengths to which the leaders were prepared to go is shown most clearly by the case of the town of Sandwich. This was one of the towns founded in the 30's and recognized with reluctance. It was based upon a grant of land to certain Freemen and Church members of Plymouth, who proposed themselves to form the nucleus of the town. They gathered around them a considerable number of people, allotted land, admitted men as free-

[1] The Colony and Town records give these annual allotments in great detail.

men, and completed their organization in such ways as
seemed to them expedient. In 1639 the General Court
proceeded to investigate their conduct. The record
states that "they have not faythfully discharged that
trust reposed in them, by receiveing into the said towne
divers persons unfitt for church societie, which should
have beene their chiefe care in the first place, and have
disposed the greatest part of the landes there already,
and to very few that are in Church societie or fitt for the
same, so that without speedy remedy our cheifest end
wilbe utterly frustrate."

One can scarcely have a clearer statement of the basis
of society at Plymouth nor more definite proof of the
object with which the leaders still believed the colony
had been founded. A month later the General Court
passed sentence. No more people were to be admitted
to the town of Sandwich without the consent of the Minister and the Church. Such of the Inhabitants as had
already been admitted, but had been adjudged undesirable, were to sell and leave. Nor was any more land
to be allotted by the town without the approval of one
of the Assistants of the colony, from whom the Freemen
of the town should receive advice and direction.[1] The
leaders of the colony practically cancelled the entire
arrangement, which the Freemen to whom the grant had
been made had already instituted.

On the whole there seems to be good reason to believe
that the people accepted this dictation of economic
privilege by the leaders without much objection and certainly without open revolt. There are throughout
Pilgrim history signs that individuals disliked and dis-
approved of this policy and of its results. From Weston,

[1] *Records,* I, 131, 134.

Oldham, and Lyford, we pass to Morton, Christopher Gardiner, Samuel Gorton, and a considerable number of less distinguished individuals. These were however all newcomers, the majority of whom left of their own accord. From the people of Plymouth themselves for more than fifteen years, we have practically no trace of resistance or even of a determination to share in the regulation. After 1634 a certain amount of discontent seems to have gradually made headway among the freemen and Church members, upon whose votes the leaders depended and whose acquiescence was essential in the conduct of the colony's affairs. When the original grant to the Undertakers expired in 1634, the privilege was continued from year to year and from court to court, apparently without opposition, the records indeed indicating that the leaders believed the trade not very valuable and that the great majority at Plymouth did not wish to follow it at all.[1] At the same time the leaders punished those who infringed upon their privilege with promptitude and stringency.

In March, 1639, however, the Grand Jury, impanelled for the usual purposes, brought in what was tantamount to an impeachment of the leaders. "1. Wee desire to be informed by what vertue and power the Governor and his Assistantes doe give and dispose of lands either to particular persons or towneshipps and plantacons.

2. Wee further desire to be informed what landes are to be had or is reserved for the purchasers as hath beene formerly agreed in Court too.

3. Wee further desire to be informed of the undertakers of the trade what wilbe allowed to the colony for the use of the said trade during the years past.

[1] *Records*, I, 31, 32, 54, 62, 126.

4. Wee further desire to be informed why there is not a Treasurer chosen for this yeare, as other officers." [1] At the next General Court, Bradford and his partners, so the record states, notified the colony that they would not pursue the trade longer than the following November. They seem to wish to convey the impression that they had in the meantime been doing the colony a distinct favor by holding the privilege at all. Of the discontent and dissatisfaction which the Grand Jury record undoubtedly revealed, we hear nothing further, perhaps because in December, 1640, it was agreed that any freeman who wished to trade with the Indians might make the colony an offer for the privilege.[2] If no suitable offer was made, the Governor and such persons as he should select were to hold the privilege. Apparently the leaders themselves retained the right, though it was not now one to which they attached great significance or from which they made much profit.

There seems to be no better place than this to record the fate of the Undertakers in their final dealings with the English merchants. They assumed in 1627 the whole debt of the colony—some £1800—which none but themselves at that time believed could be paid. They also shouldered the entire expense of transporting to Plymouth the rest of the Leyden Congregation, some £550,[3] for which the colony never reimbursed them. The privileges they received included the fishing post which had been in operation near Gloucester ever since 1623; the fur-trading post on the Kennebec which had proved profitable for several years; and a trading route across

---

[1] *Records*, I, 119, March 5, 1638–1639.
[2] *Ibid.*, II, 4.
[3] Bradford, *History*, 297, 299.

Cape Cod to Narragansett Bay by which they reached the Indian tribes on Long Island Sound. With the Dutch also arrangements for an exchange of commodities had been made in 1627.[1] The rebuilding of one of the shallops in 1626 had provided them for the first time with a vessel decked over and large enough to venture into Massachusetts Bay and around Cape Cod.[2] The following year they established a trade in wampum, which seems hitherto to have been unknown to the Massachusetts Indians, and which turned out to be exceedingly profitable.[3] This and the trade with the Dutch led them to give up the attempt to supply the English fishing fleet, which came annually to the Grand Banks, and also the trade they had pursued with the struggling planters up and down the Massachusetts coast. Conditions, they complained bitterly, were changing. Where they had at first been able, with a yard of cloth or a few cheap English trinkets, to buy a fine skin or several bushels of corn, they now found that the Dutch and French had "demoralized" the Indians by paying a real equivalent, a wicked practice which the Pilgrims much deplored as showing a lack of imagination and a proper degree of business acumen. The Indians were demanding hatchets, knives, iron kettles, powder, guns, with the result that the degree of profit in the trade had fallen off considerably.[4]

They now launched forth in 1628 and 1629 upon a series of costly ventures, all of which failed. One was

---

[1] Bradford, *History*, 281; *Mass. Hist. Soc. Coll., 1st Series*, III, 52, 55, 56.
[2] Bradford, *History*, 253.
[3] *Ibid.*, 281.
[4] *Ibid.*, 283, 287.

their own fault, a fishing voyage undertaken without
sufficient calculation or judgment and pursued without
the necessary knowledge of fishing essential to success.[1]
As Bradford said, fishing had always been fatal, and
indeed out of it from first to last they seem never to
have made a farthing. Allerton, whom they had made
their agent in England, now brought back to Plymouth
a considerable bill of goods which they had not ordered.
For the most part these were clothes and household
utensils, which ranked as luxuries. They had strictly
ordered him to purchase only a moderate amount of
trading goods to exchange with the Indians for more
beaver, and felt that to buy more for themselves was
highly inexpedient.[2] They were anxious to devote every
pound of money to the extinction of the debt. He not
only failed to do this, partly through the importunity of
Shirley, one of the English partners, but he also implicated them in a venture on the Penobscot by one Ashley.[3] He then borrowed in England considerable sums
of money at fifty per cent interest [4] which he invested in
trade; he chartered one ship and purchased another for
trading voyages to New England.[5] The whole involved
a total expenditure of something over £7000, an aggre-
gate sum, borrowed and invested by one man in two
years, as large as the entire sum which they calculated
had been spent in creating the colony up to that time.

In 1628 their debts, outside the main debt to the
Adventurers of £1800, were not over £400. In 1630

[1] Bradford, *History*, 312–313, 319–320, 324–325.
[2] *Ibid.*, 292–294, 303–304.
[3] *Ibid.*, 309–310.
[4] *Ibid.*, 311.
[5] *Ibid.*, 320, 325, 327.

they were not less than £4000, and in all probàbility
more.[1] In the meantime, Allerton had also obtained for
them as partners, four English merchants to whom goods
could be consigned and who would purchase and ship
to them in return whatever they wished. The association
was from the first unfortunate and disappointing and
grew more so as the years elapsed. In 1630, the Pilgrims
were driven to renounce Allerton as their agent, though
with misgiving and regret because of his marriage to
Brewster's daughter, and their very great concern for
Brewster's feelings.[2] They applied themselves at once
diligently to the collection of beaver and its shipment to
the English partners, Winslow undertaking Allerton's
task and performing it with extraordinary tact, ability,
and care. In 1633, they set up a trading post on the
Connecticut River,[3] much to the disgust of the Dutch,
who believed themselves to have secured already a right
to that trade. They threatened to fire upon the Pilgrim
ship, if she should attempt to go up the river and establish a post above them, thereby intercepting the Indian
trade. This however the Pilgrims courageously did and
derived some considerable satisfaction from the discom-
fiture of the Dutch. It must be added that they viewed
that type of proceeding very differently when an Englishman attempted to create a trading post on the Kennebec
above their own. Him they suppressed and unfortunately
one of his company was killed.

Now came a series of misfortunes. In 1635 the French

---

[1] Bradford, *History*, 347.

[2] *Ibid.*, 305, 329. On final episodes of his history see pp. 348–349,
358–359.

[3] *Ibid.*, 372–373. The trade was very lucrative during 1633–1634;
ibid., 375, 385, 409, 410.

captured the post on the Penobscot, which the Pilgrims had continued after the bankruptcy of Ashley, and an expedition which they equipped to retake it was a ludicrous failure.[1] In 1636, there appeared around the post on the Connecticut the first of the Massachusetts colonists. They denied the validity of the Pilgrim purchase from the Indians and were with much ado gotten at last to permit them to retain a small fraction of the land, though, apparently without any scruple, they appropriated the whole Indian trade.[2] Now came the crowning misfortune of all. The Pilgrims learned that Shirley, chief of their English partners, had not been honest with them. They calculated that they had shipped him beaver to the value of £12,150,[3] that their indebtedness on the score of Allerton's failures was not in excess of £4000, the original indebtedness to the Adventurers was £1800, and they were therefore astounded to discover that the other three English partners had not received any of the proceeds of the sale of the beaver during the last few years, and that Shirley himself regarded them as still in his debt. Protest they did, but they deemed it better to extinguish his claims and paid him in 1642 £1200.[4] Even then they were not entirely freed from charges and claims. In 1646, however, they at last owed no man.

The difficulty seems to have lain in the fact that they

[1] Bradford, *History*, 350, 396–398.

[2] *Ibid.*, 407.

[3] *Ibid.*, 412–413. Bradford, like so many of his contemporaries, was a poor mathematician. The true total was £12,530, assuming the annual totals were correct.

[4] Bradford, *History*, 446–448, 477–486. Bradford gives a multitude of details on this dreary business failure, but it has not seemed wise to devote space to them.

believed others as far above taking advantage of them in business as they were themselves incapable of dishonesty. Allerton, Shirley, and Beauchamp professed what the Pilgrims believed to be "true religion," were all Church members, and the Pilgrim leaders simply could not conceive that these men would try to overreach them. They made Allerton legally their agent in a document so sweeping that they were bound by everything he did, without the possibility of an explanation or renunciation. When they broke with him, they demanded the return of the document. He was unable to produce it; but, instead of demanding from him a written release, they accepted his verbal promise to obtain it from Shirley in England. Shirley retained the paper, the Pilgrims never did receive it, and on the strength of it Shirley eventually forced them to pay a very considerable sum of money for an undertaking into which Allerton entered after they had disowned him. The most unfortunate of Allerton's ventures had been explained to them at Plymouth by Allerton and Hatherly in terms which completely convinced them of the former's innocence. They accepted his verbal statement that they were not bound to accept the venture as their own if they did not wish to, and that he and the London partners would be entirely responsible for it, if they in turn would allow them to dispose of the cargo which the ship had brought. Accordingly the Pilgrims paid him a considerable sum for part of the goods, and allowed him to sell the remainder in Boston. Somewhat later they received a letter from Shirley and a statement from Winslow declaring that the responsibility had been theirs and not Allerton's in the first place and that the loss was now theirs in the second place. Nor would the English partners make allowance for the money paid Allerton in accordance with the verbal agreement.

Such was the result of a failure to insist upon written documents in every case, and to insist upon a strict and prompt accounting every year, instead of allowing the English partners to keep the books as they pleased and have an accounting at the end of a term of years. Indeed, the ignorance of the Pilgrims about business seems almost incredible, and their carelessness would seem almost criminal, if it were not so entirely obvious that it proceeded from inexperience and from guileless faith in the integrity of all Church members. They attempted literally to deal with Allerton and Shirley in accordance with the Golden Rule, and, even after it became clear that Shirley was robbing them, gave him the benefit of the doubt, and sent two or three more shiploads of beaver, all of which he promptly appropriated to his own use. Not only were the Pilgrims out at pocket, but they never entirely regained their confidence in their fellowmen.

Before 1640, the fur trade had fallen off considerably and was no longer particularly profitable. The settlement of New England had driven out the fur-bearing animals and the hunters upon whom the Pilgrims had depended. The Kennebec had been sold by the colony to individuals; the post on the Penobscot had been captured by the French; the Connecticut trade had been lost by the settlement of the Valley Towns; the trade route across Cape Cod was no longer profitable because the Rhode Island and Connecticut colonies entirely absorbed the trade of the Indians on Long Island Sound. To Salem and Gloucester had come Puritan emigrants, who promptly took possession of the fishing stage on Cape Ann, and drew to themselves as well the trade of the annual English fishing fleet.

Fortunately, the settlement of New England had also created an extremely brisk market for cattle and corn with such large profits that the leaders gave up the Indian trade and went to cattle raising.[1] In 1640 came a sudden fall in the prices of cattle which they were all at a loss to explain.[2] Truth was that the cessation of the Great Emigration, due to events in England, caused a fall in the hitherto unprecedented demand. Partly too the fall in prices was due to the sudden increase of supply at Plymouth and elsewhere, which had been stimulated by the abnormal prices of the past few years. Nevertheless, cattle continued throughout the history of the colony to be one of the chief sources of wealth. The economic structure never became highly developed and seems never during the period of the colony's independence to have achieved the basis of a money economy. John Cotton Junior's salary was paid him as late as 1677, one-third in wheat, butter, tar, or shingles; one-third in rye, peas, or malt; and one-third in Indian corn, each valued in money but not paid in money. "It is further agreed that if any will pay their Rates or part thereof in money they shall have liberty so to do."[3] They repaired the Minister's house at a cost of £60 and provided that one-half of the assessment should be paid in any kind of corn or in tar, provided the tar was salable and provided it could be accepted at twelve pence per barrel cheaper than

[1] Bradford, *History*, 436.
[2] *Ibid.*, 448, 458. See also on cattle values the notes in Goodwin, *Pilgrim Republic*, 296.
[3] *Records of the Town of Plymouth*, 154.

the market price in Boston. The other half was to be
paid in wheat, barley, peas, butter, or money.[1]

Industry in the modern sense of the word never developed at Plymouth at all.[2] As early as 1639, every house-
holder was compelled to sow one square rod of hemp
and flax. A supply of bog iron was discovered and worked
up at Taunton by the Brothers Leonard, which was during colonial days of some importance. Saw-mills, grist-
mills, brick-yards appear gradually during the century,
but beyond a very moderate manufacture of materials
immediately useful at Plymouth, industry as such did
not appear during the colony's independence. There
was indeed, except the limited supply of iron and tar,
no raw material which could have been manufactured.
It was simpler, easier, more profitable to raise cattle, to
sell dressed lumber and tar in Boston, than it was to
attempt to make articles which could be bought much
cheaper in Boston or in England. The colonies in general depended down to the American Revolution upon
the purchase of manufactured goods in England, and
Plymouth was no exception to the rule. There were of
course made at Plymouth, as in all parts of America,
rough cloth, candles, soap, woodenware, and simple
furniture, but such goods were commonly made to order
rather than for general sale in the open market at a profit.

The accumulation of wealth at Plymouth never approached that of the Bay Colony. The total was infinitely less and the proportion per capita was also

---

[1] *Records of the Town of Plymouth*, 58.

[2] There are a few notes in Weeden, *Economic History of New
England*, I; Goodwin, *Pilgrim Republic;* and the histories of the
town of Plymouth by Davis and Baylies. Something can be
gleaned from the colony and town records.

smaller. The tendency has therefore been to regard Plymouth as an economic failure. No error could be greater. Seven decades proved the colony an undoubted economic success, a real demonstration of what could be done in the wilderness with practically no capital at all. It must be remembered that the Pilgrims started heavily in debt, owing the merchants for everything except the clothes on their backs and the shoes on their feet. Whatever they created at Plymouth was wrung from a poor soil in an unfavorable situation by the labor of their own hands. Nor did the colony grow by great accessions of colonists who brought with them accumulated wealth from England. Plymouth in 1691 represented the labor of the Pilgrims themselves and of their descendants and certainly was an economic success. The wills of the first comers, who landed practically without anything, show that they had not only supported themselves at Plymouth during life, and paid their indebtedness, but had accumulated what would have ranked in England at the time as a comfortable property for farmers or artisans. Standish, for instance, had landed without property as a paid employee of the Merchants, and had migrated to Duxbury in 1631 with one cow and some little personalty. He died in 1656 worth £140 in land and buildings and £358 7s. in personalty. His one cow had become five horses and colts, four oxen, ten cows and calves, eleven sheep, and fourteen swine.[1] Howland, who had also come so far as we know without property, died possessed of £157 of personalty, including three horses, seventeen cows and oxen, thirteen swine, forty-five sheep, and

[1] Many Plymouth wills have been printed in full in the *Mayflower Descendant* and are a mine of economic and social information hitherto little worked. Standish's will is in vol. III, 155.

nearly *two whole pounds* in ready money.[1] The Browns, who arrived from England in 1634 with some property, died in 1662 worth £655 and £350 respectively.[2] The elder had ten oxen, four bulls, twenty cows, twenty young cattle, eighteen sheep, eleven pigs, and nine horses. His personalty included red leather chairs, a silver bowl, "Eight India table clothes," and a bed "in the Parlour," estimated at £24, but only six shillings in money. Even the poorer were able to bequeath in their wills from twenty-five to fifty pounds of personalty as early as 1633, and within five years after the enumeration and division of twelve cattle in 1627, most people had at least one cow or heifer, with a number of goats, swine in the tens, and great numbers of poultry.[3] The evidence of the Plymouth wills is absolutely conclusive: Plymouth was a decided economic success and the growth of wealth after 1627 was rapid and permanent. Each decade the wills bequeath decidedly more and after 1660 the amounts become really considerable and indicate real comfort and prosperity.

[1] *Mayflower Descendant*, II, 73.
[2] *Ibid.*, XVIII, 15–22.
[3] See the wills in the *Mayflower Descendant*, I, 29, 65, 79, 82, 83, 154, 157, 197, 203. Compare with these those of the later period, *ibid.*, II, 14, 25, 39; XI, 198; XVIII, 41. Steven Hopkins died in 1644, owner of the chief inn or hotel, and left in cash—six pence.

CHAPTER XVII

SOCIAL LIFE, 1627-1657

If there was one fact clearer to the Pilgrims than another, it was their duty to practice in daily life the truth as they felt God had revealed it to them. In the Bible were recorded, if only they could comprehend them, the infallible directions for individual conduct; they had but to read and obey. Were they so sunk in ignorance and indifference as not to know the unreality and falsity of this life as compared with the glory and splendor of the life to come? Had they not been assured that only he who loses his life shall find it, and that he who putteth his hand to the plow must not look back? Social life at Plymouth was an attempt to live literally in accordance with the teachings of the Scriptures. Because of their inability to create the sort of social atmosphere in which they wished their children to grow up, they had left Holland. Now that God had vouchsafed them success in their experiment, had assured them of the correctness of their interpretation of His intentions, they could proceed in confidence to live and act in accordance with His Word. As year followed year and found the colony growing in strength and prosperity, their joyous belief in the Divine approval grew into a certainty which no logic could strengthen nor argument shake. They were accordingly to use their authority in Church and State to live a serious purposeful life such as befitted God's elect, to aid those who had not yet seen the Light to comprehend it, and to assist them in keeping their feet from the paths of unconscious wrongdoing. Conscious evil none should do. The machinery of Church and State should repress the wicked and reclaim the wayward, whose trustees the leaders believed themselves to be.

The most difficult thing for us of the twentieth century to grasp about the Pilgrims is the literal domination of temporal life by the spiritual. Their history is much more nearly a study in the psychology of religion and its relation to the necessities of political and economic life than a political history in the ordinary sense of the word. We must become accustomed to looking through the temporal fact to the spiritual truth behind it, inherent in it. Of the many facts which must be spiritualized to be understood, none is more essential than that minute regulation of daily life, which seems to us as we read about it so intolerable and incomprehensible. It was to them a consecration and a God given opportunity never to return. They might indeed repent one day of the shortcomings of the day before, but never again in the whole of eternity would they have the opportunity to live that day as they should have. They attempted to apply an unflinching and uncompromising idealism to the problems of daily life, to the economic problems of existence, and to methods for administering the State. The system was an end in itself, not a means to an end, unless indeed that end be the future life. They lived it because they believed that in that way life should be lived. They urged others to live it because they believed it the method by which all must satisfy God. If we can almost certainly see in their political ordinances the evidence of ulterior purpose, if we feel that the economic life was consciously shaped to further the ecclesiastical and political, to make difficult the existence at Plymouth of those not deemed suitable Inhabitants, we must not bring to their social system, if such it may be called, any such feeling of ulterior purpose. It was in no sense intended simply for the repression of those who disagreed with them. It was an end in itself—life as they loved to live it, as they loved to think that others would want to live it.

While in many respects Plymouth was democratic, the social life in the colony moved along definite lines of caste, sharply outlined and rigidly observed. These reproduced no social status in the Old World, for none of them had possessed in England or Holland anything there recognized as social status. They had been simple tenant farmers, not even yeomen; or quite undistinguished artisans and tradesmen, not even in the seventeenth century sense, merchants. The new caste was rather a fact than a system, was seen to exist rather than was called into existence. In the first rank were the leaders, who arrogated to themselves social as well as civil and ecclesiastical leadership, and who assumed gradually titles with which they had been familiar in England, but which had in the main at Plymouth no such connotation as the English attached to them. In the list of Freemen of the colony entered in the records under the year 1636, there are one hundred and thirteen names. After fourteen of these we have the abbreviation "Gn," signifying, beyond a doubt, "gentleman." This first rank of the Pilgrim hierarchy was possessed by Bradford, Winslow, Prence, William Collier, John Alden, Timothy Hatherley, John Jenney, Steven Hopkins, John Browne, William Brewster, John Atwood, Ralph Smith, and Isaac Allerton. Standish is called Captain, but not Gentleman, and Howland simply by his name. One is indeed surprised to note how far down the list William Brewster is and how far up the list are Prence, Collier, and Alden. Twelve names bear the prefix "Mr.," the English equivalent for Master. Several of these were clergymen, among them Reynor. Smith, however, was called Gentleman.

These titles are repeated in the records with considerable fidelity wherever these names appear, although the lesser Gentlemen sometimes become Master. This is never the case with Bradford, Winslow, and Prence, who no doubt had much to do with the editing of the records. The rest of the Freemen had no titles in this list, but we find several of them elsewhere referred to as yeomen.[1] It is scarcely necessary to add that none of these men possessed any of the English qualifications for Gentleman or Master, and that the best of them scarcely possessed that financial competence and long freedom from anything resembling service in the feudal sense which distinguished the yeoman in England. Over the question whether or not the English term, Goodman, should become a third grade in the social hierarchy, there was considerable controversy between Williams, Smith, and the leaders. The latter were inclined to adopt it. The two clergymen objected to it vehemently, on the ground that it was sinful to call any man good, with the obvious inference that in their opinion the men to whom it was to be applied were quite the contrary. All of this shows us quite clearly that social distinctions were prized and valued at Plymouth far more than one would have supposed.[2]

[1] *Plymouth Colony Records*, I, 41, 64, 75, 106.
[2] For a case at Swansea, see Baylies, *Plymouth*, II, 245–246.

In accordance with the Calvinistic system, the interference of the leaders in the daily life of the majority was constant, searching, minute, and inquisitorial. It must not be supposed for a moment that they were less strict with themselves than with others or that they hesitated to accuse and punish each other on occasion. Bradford indeed expressed his amazement that any punishment or any regulation should be necessary in a group of people like the Pilgrims, that any misconduct of any sort should occur, to say nothing of the occasional commission of serious crime. But, he reflected quite sagely and truly, it did not portend a greater proportion of evil at Plymouth than elsewhere nor a more considerable degree of wrongdoing, but merely the fact that the inquisitorial system was so exceedingly stringent that every minute deviation from the strict rule set up by the Church was promptly discovered and incontinently punished.[1]

Indeed there was perhaps no single task to which the Pilgrim community set itself with greater diligence and enjoyment than that of watching each other, nor was there any phase of their manifold duties which they performed with greater assiduity than that of complaining about each other. The ecclesiastical and civil system sanctified and encouraged tale-bearing, spying, and accusations. In a small colony, where everyone lived very much together and could not get far apart, where everyone's affairs were conducted under everybody else's eyes, there was no possibility of escape. The whole community seem to have derived a grim satisfaction from thus investigating each other's affairs and punishing each other's peccadillos. Attendance at Church was

[1] *History*, 459–461.

compulsory for all, whether Church members or not, but was scarcely a hardship in a community where the rule against Sabbath breaking was enforced with the utmost severity by the civil authorities. Not many infringed it. One man persisted in working in his garden, another in the tar pits; one was punished for hunting deer on Sunday; another was "sharply reproved" for writing a letter on Sunday, "at least in the evening somewhat too soon." [1] Steven Hopkins was accused in 1637 of allowing men to drink in his inn "on the Lord's day, before the meeting be ended" and allowing servants and others, both before and after meetings, to drink "more than for ordinary refreshing." [2] But such cases were rare.

The Pilgrims observed no holidays. Christmas, Easter, and the ordinary Church festivals were an abomination to them because they smacked of Papacy. The King's birthday they naturally did not celebrate. There seems indeed to have been but one attempt at the celebration of a European holiday. The first Christmas the whole colony worked in entire harmony very hard all day. The second Christmas, some of those just come upon the *Fortune* were called by Bradford on Christmas morning to their work in the fields as usual, and "excused themselves and said it wente against their consciences to work on that day," an answer which nonplussed the leaders not a little. But they went away and left them. When they came home at noon to dinner, they found them in the street, pitching the bar, playing stool ball, and other good old English games. Bradford went

---

[1] *Plymouth Colony Records*, I, 86; II, 140, 156. The authorities admitted that drawing eel pots on Sunday might be necessary. *Ibid.*, II, 4.

[2] *Ibid.*, I, 68.

straight to them "and tooke away their implements, and tould them that was against his conscience that they should play and others worke. If they made the keeping of it mater of devotion let them kepe their houses but ther should be no gaming or revelling in the streets. Since which time nothing hath been atempted that way, at least openly." [1] Smoking the Pilgrims practiced. Tobacco was grown at Plymouth to some extent, more was bought from the Indians, and after the first decade was imported from Virginia. But the regulations for smoking were strict and men were fined again and again "for drinking tobacco in the heighway." [2] Apparently, a man might smoke in his own house or in the fields, but he might not smoke in Plymouth streets nor in the meeting house.

The most considerable body of regulations of a social character were those regulating marriage and the relation of the sexes. The Pilgrims never could understand why there should be any deviation from strict morality and invariably punished with almost brutal severity the slightest infraction. Dorothy Temple, dishonored by one of the undesirables of the colony and her crime revealed by the birth of her child, was publicly whipped until she fainted under the lash. Men honorable enough to marry the women they had ruined, were publicly whipped, often more than once, while the wife sat in the stocks. One Mr. Fels came to Plymouth in 1627 and had in his house a comely maidservant, about whose relations with him scandal was presently whispered. Although the Pilgrims were unable to prove anything, they so frightened him and his whole family that, when after-

[1] Bradford, *History*, 134–135.
[2] *Records*, I, 106; IV, 47.

wards it appeared that the maid was with child, they all decamped in a small boat, panic-stricken. They nearly lost their lives in the attempted flight and were forced to return to Plymouth, where they were dealt with with the greatest severity.[1] There were in the whole history of Plymouth until 1691, only six divorces and not many cases of any sort, type, or variety of immoral conduct.[2]

The regulation of individual conduct further provided that no man should strike his wife, and that no woman should beat her husband under the penalty of the fine of £10. One woman indeed was presented "for beating and reviling her husband and egging her children to healp her, biding them knock him in the head and wishing his victials might coake him." The significant entry in the margin follows—"Punished att home."[3] One Thomas Williams, a bond-servant, fell into a dispute with his mistress, apparently because he was unwilling to perform some task or had failed to do so to her satisfaction. She tried to clinch the matter by exhorting him to fear God and to do his duty. He answered that he neither feared God "nor the diuell." For this horrible blasphemy he was brought into court, witnesses collected, and an infinity of trouble taken. Bradford would have had him soundly whipped, but the majority disagreed and he was simply reprimanded.[4]

How to regulate the relation of the sexes in courtship puzzled the Pilgrim fathers considerably. Finally in 1638 a law was passed that no man should propose to a girl without first getting the consent of her parents or of

---

[1] Bradford, *History*, 265.
[2] Goodwin, *Pilgrim Republic*, 596–597, 599–600.
[3] *Records*, III, 75, 1654–1655.
[4] *Ibid.*, I, 35, 1635.

her master, in case she were a bond servant. There were a good many cases of men punished for making offers of marriage "irregularly" and of girls similarly punished for accepting them.[1] The most celebrated is that of Arthur Howland, Jr., who found the daughter of Governor Prence pleasant to look upon, and apparently quite willing to receive his advances. There can be no doubt whatever that he courted her in an eminently respectable and sober way, and, like a good American, finally asked her to marry him. The father was furious with rage, brought the swain before the Court of Assistants, and accused him with having "disorderly and unrighteously endeavored to obtain the affections" of his daughter Elizabeth. Howland was compelled to pay a fine of £5, to produce sureties for good behavior, and to deposit a bond of £50 that he would not again propose to the girl in that same fashion. Some months later he felt it wise "solemnly and seriously" to engage himself never to approach her in any way again. No doubt this was the result of the fact that the young people were not quite able to take their eyes off of each other, nor to keep entirely apart in so small a colony. In the end Prence relented and the couple were married.[2]

The general impression which we have been given of Pilgrim life as dire, sad, and forbidding, is certainly wrong. Proper conduct was expected of everyone, and the social machinery, as well as that of Church and State, was devised to aid the individual to keep his feet in the narrow path of rectitude, but it is by no means true that life at Plymouth was so exceedingly unpleasant as we have been taught to believe. At the same time

[1] *Records*, I, 97; III, 5.
[2] *Ibid.*, IV, 140–141, March 5, 1666–1667; July 2, 1667.

neither the letters nor the records give us even a glimpse
of anything resembling society or anything mildly approaching dinners, parties, or entertainments, serious or
otherwise. For the upper ranks of the social hierarchy,
a quiet evening of conversation on serious and suitable
themes, enlivened with a studiously moderate portion of
beer, ale, or wine, seems to have been all they allowed
themselves. This too in the privacy of their homes, with
none present but the Elect. Candles, too, were expensive; the hours of work long for everybody, certainly
until 1640; and only in the long winter afternoons and
evenings can the leaders have permitted themselves such
relaxation. Such intercourse must be what Bradford
had in mind when he wrote that Brewster was of "a
very cherfull spirite, very sociable and pleasante amongst
his freinds." [1] But among the lower ranks of the social
hierarchy, for the Inhabitants and the unprivileged, es-
pecially for the servants, there was an abundance of
simple amusement, such as they had been accustomed
to have in England.[2] This the leaders tolerated and
condoned as harmless for those not possessed of sufficient intelligence and mentality to devote themselves
entirely to spiritual contemplation. Out-of-door games
like bowls and pitch bar seem to have been commonly
played. Inns and taverns were licensed by the authorities,[3] at which beer, wine, and strong waters were to
be had, and in these a good many really hilarious scenes

---

[1] Bradford, *History*, 492.

[2] The most cursory reading of the *Records* will leave no doubt on
this point.

[3] James Leonard, innkeeper of Taunton, lost his wife by death,
and was straightway deprived of his license on the ground that he
was now unfitted to keep an inn!

were enacted by servants and apprentices. Cards are not infrequently mentioned in the court records and the fact that one man was fined for playing cards on Sunday raises the presumption that he might have played on a week day without breaking the ordinance.[1] Dancing [2] seems not to have been countenanced.

In fact, it is one thing to realize that Plymouth was a place where literal idealism was attempted and a very real conformity to the ordinances expected in letter and spirit, and quite another to make out of it an impossible abode for human beings. The sins against which the leaders legislate point to a fairly normal English social life for all except Church members,[3] and both legislation, and the punishment meted out to enforce it, were in the nature of regulation rather than of repression or prohibition. They must not amuse themselves on Sunday and they must come to Church. They must drink only for "refreshing" and not to bestiality. There seem indeed to have been numerous grades of offence with liquor, leading all the way from excess "upon refreshing" to plain drunkenness, beastly drunkenness, filthy drunkenness, and a drunkenness of so extreme a degree that the details were necessarily related to the court. In 1636 a definition was made of the proper consumption of liquor, which provided that wine or strong water should

---

[1] *Records*, IV, 42, 1663.

[2] Mercy Tubbs was to answer for "mixed dancing." Was there another variety which was permissible? *Records*, III, 5, 1651–1652.

[3] It is interesting to note that the Widow Ring possessed in 1631 these works: "1 bible 1 dod. 1 plea for Infants 1 ruine of Rome 1 Troubler of the Church of Amsterdam 1 Garland of vertuous dames." This last seems not thoroughly ecclesiastical in tone. *Mayflower Descendant*, I, 34.

not be sold or drunk except at a licensed inn. There the innkeeper should not sell the townsmen any strong liquor at all and only one Winchester quart of beer, which retailed at two pence. To strangers at their first coming, he might sell strong water to the extent of two pence worth.[1] Here is very evidently the definition of drinking for "refreshing" only. This strict control and this inquisitorial system proved very distasteful to a good many who came to Plymouth beside Oldham and Morton of Merrimount. The strictness of regulation was far greater than in Massachusetts and Connecticut, and the colony was so much smaller that its enforcement was simple and punishment for infractions certain. The social atmosphere was one reason why people did not like Plymouth, but it was after all merely a corollary of a dislike founded, like the system itself, on a lack of agreement with the Church and a desire for civil and economic privilege without fulfilling the ecclesiastical prerequisites. There is no reason to believe that the social ordinances at Plymouth were disagreeable to the overwhelming majority or that it was necessary at any time to enforce them, by means of civil authority, upon more than an insignificant minority.

Seventeenth century Calvinism was unquestionably hostile to the æsthetic in life, to the beautiful in music, in art, in furniture, or in clothing. Its influence on social life and social environment was almost as great at Plymouth as in Scotland and at Geneva. At the same time the very real simplicity at Plymouth was not wholly the result of choice. Poverty is a powerful dictator of frugality, though the Pilgrims did not, when they could, purchase luxurious clothes or furniture, or

[1] *Records*, I, 38.

MADAME PADISHAL

attempt the cultivation of music or the fine arts. But Plymouth was by no means made intentionally ugly, nor did they attempt to make themselves unbecoming in appearance or uncomfortable. The hostility to the æsthetic was a tendency rather than a literal fact. Probably no Puritans or Pilgrims ever wore at any time such garb as modern artists have placed upon them. There is no evidence that the early Puritans at the time of Elizabeth and James I wore any distinctive clothes. The Pilgrims themselves were poor country people and certainly never wore "stylish" clothes in England or Holland. A simple smock and trousers of coarse cloth, a simple gown of ample folds for the women, heavy shoes, and either no hats at all or caps of skins must have been the rule in the first years. Close cut hair the men wore as in England and Holland, where it was the rule for the lower classes, long hair being the mark of the gentleman only and indicating not only wealth, but social status. There is no reason to suppose that the Pilgrims and Massachusetts Puritans before 1650 wore the sort of clothes common in England after the Civil Wars had produced a distinctive dress for the Parliamentarians different from that worn by the Cavaliers.

Nor was Plymouth clad in black and gray, with tall, ugly hats for the men and hoods for the women of unattractive design, void of ribbons or laces. On Sunday indeed the dignitaries wore black gowns, as was the rule in the Calvinist Churches abroad. But Elder Brewster's wardrobe contained a violet-colored cloth coat, a pair of black silk stockings, a doublet, and various other garments such as a fairly well-to-do Englishman of no particular rank might have worn. Since there were tailors and their apprentices at Plymouth, there can be little doubt that they made clothes. We also hear of red silk stockings obtained in Boston [1] and find in the inventories of the effects of persons deceased all sorts of garments of silk, satin, woolen, cotton, and linen, of a variety of shades and hues which we by no means would consider "sad" or sombre. Red, blue, purple, violet, and green were common, besides the expected grays, browns, whites, and blacks. We should not have expected to see, however, any such number of people possessed of laces, ruffs, and petticoats, of napkins, tablecloths, sheets, and handkerchiefs. [2]

The wills published in the last ten years have altered very much our conception of dress and household luxury at Plymouth. A very poor woman owned a looking glass, [3] for which, if tradition were dependable, the Pilgrim mothers had no uses. But looking glasses were common and presume articles of dress to be adjusted with their aid and some degree of attention to appearances. One Mistress Ann Atwoods left a total estate worth £24 and nevertheless had a "turky Mohear petty-

---

[1] *Records*, I, 93. Bradford speaks of Brewster's dislike of those who became haughty "being rise from nothing and haveing litle els in them to comend them but a few fine cloaths." *History*, 492.

[2] One poor man died in 1633, possessed of a "satten sute," two ruffs, an embroidered silk garter, and a "cap with silver lace on it." *Mayflower Descendant*, I, 83. Another, who was so poor that he owned only three-quarters of a cow, had in 1633 a feather bed, bolster, blankets, a green rug, sheets, tablecloths, napkins, "pillowbeeres," cushions, a chair bed, and sundry pots and kettles. The whole was valued at £71. *Ibid.*, I, 157. A woman, whose whole property was worth in 1633 only £20, had aprons, napkins, a tablecloth, and towels. *Ibid.*, I, 82.

[3] Godbert Godbertson and wife, 1633. *Mayflower Descendant*, I, 154–155.

coat," "a silke Mohear petticoat," a "green phillip and Chyna petticoat"; "one old silk grogrum (GroGrain?) gowne," with red broadcloth, French serge, and green aprons. There were also four lace handkerchiefs, four pairs of lace cuffs, a whole dozen of stomachers, six "head clothes," a lace scarf, a "velvet muffe," a riding suit, with much linen, napkins, tablecloths, many sheets and pillow cases. There were as well silver bowls and spoons, glass bottles, much pewter, brass, and iron, with cushioned chairs and stools.[1]

The houses were simple, plain, substantial, but by no means poverty stricken. They were built of hewn plank and those erected after 1628 had plank roofs instead of thatch. The first chimneys seem to have been of sticks plastered with clay, but, proving inflammable, they were forbidden, and the later chimneys were probably of rough stone, laid in clay, as the majority of New England chimneys have been since. Some were of brick, for there was in Plymouth as early as 1639 a bricklayer with an apprentice. The furniture probably did not come from England, but was made up by carpenters in Plymouth. It was comfortable, substantial, and plentiful after 1630. For the first decade nothing beyond the indispensable was probably to be had, although some of the leaders may have imported from England some pieces of oak furniture. Earthenware was not common until the eighteenth century and there was certainly no Delftware on the *Mayflower.* Pewter dishes and spoons, wooden bowls and iron knives with some glass of poor quality probably completed the table equipment of most Pilgrims. There were some silver bowls and

[1] *Mayflower Descendant*, XI, 200–206. See also effects of Widow Ring in 1631, *ibid.*, I, 29. She owned a "mingled petticoat!"

spoons. Forks they certainly did not use in the seventeenth century.

While the influence of the wilderness was not very clear in the clothes, the houses, or utensils, its effect upon the food was striking. Corn bread instead of wheat bread was practically universal, beef, mutton, and veal were not to be had for many decades because the animals were too valuable for other purposes to be killed for meat. After 1630, milk, butter, and cheese seem to have been plentiful and within the reach of nearly everyone. Fish and game from the first had been always obtainable although not much eaten. Oysters, clams, and mussels the Pilgrims disliked and even in the years of the starvation they had to be hungry indeed before they would resort to them. Beans and pumpkins were common staples from the garden, where also were grown peas, squash, turnips, parsnips, and onions. Apple and pear trees were brought from England and the former were cultivated with some success, though the latter did not do well. The wild fruits, grapes, huckleberries, and strawberries, were used freely. Cranberries, the typical product of Cape Cod and the Plymouth district today, were not known. Beer was brewed from barley and rye and its use was universal. Cider was soon made from apples and a homemade wine from wild grapes. After 1640, however, French and Spanish wines, Dutch and English "strong waters" were common, although sold under strict rules. There can be also no doubt that they were used with extreme temperance. Tea, coffee, cocoa, and potatoes, seem not to have been known at Plymouth before 1691. Pie, the traditional New England dish in the minds of the ignorant, was certainly not made in the seventeenth century. On the other hand, hasty pudding, made of corn meal boiled in water or milk, was the almost universal breakfast dish. Beans baked with pork was also a Pilgrim staple. Puddings or bread made of rye meal (perhaps a forerunner of New England brown bread) were common. So were soups made of peas and beans. Boiled peas, squash, and other vegetables were common adjuncts of Pilgrim meals, in which fresh meat appeared less frequently than we should have supposed. Wild game within easy hunting range of Plymouth seems to have been killed off comparatively early. Fishing the Pilgrims never enjoyed, but after a while fresh fish became one of the staples of diet.

On the whole, there is no reason to doubt that life at Plymouth, while never in one sense luxurious, was vastly more comfortable than the life these same people had led in England. They had more to eat and wear and of better quality. They lived in better houses than at Scrooby, and had more land, more cattle, and a future better assured. There is no hint that they were not well satisfied with the results. They deemed their social life adequate, pleasant, and far above their deserts or station, as the laws of God might define the one or the social code of England the other.

CHAPTER XVIII

TENDENCY AFTER THE DEATH OF BRADFORD

The political history of Plymouth from the death of Bradford until its absorption into Massachusetts Bay in 1691 is if anything more quiet than the decades immediately preceding. For two or three years some little trouble was experienced with Quakers who attempted to migrate to the colony or to pass through its jurisdiction. In 1663 Governor Prence, who had succeeded Bradford, moved his residence from Eastham to Plymouth, an event of real importance for the rehabilitation of the influence of Plymouth proper. In 1664 came the visit of Royal Commissioners to investigate the colony. A certain rephrasing of political privilege immediately preceded and followed that visit. In 1667 the reorganization of the Church in the town of Plymouth was undertaken by John Cotton, Jr. In 1676 came King Philip's War. Eight years later the New England Confederation held its last session; 1686 saw the beginning of the jurisdiction of Andros and a general government over all New England, which was presently overturned by the Glorious Revolution of 1689 and the new Charter of 1691. Such is a fairly inclusive list of events of importance in Pilgrim history for this period.

The death of Bradford marked the end of an epoch. The old leaders had passed away. Brewster had died in 1644 and from his loss the Church never entirely recovered. Winslow had left in 1646 for England on a mission for the Massachusetts Bay colony, despite the

EDWARD WINSLOW

Painted in London in 1651

opposition of Bradford and others. There he had been well received and had found a régime thoroughly congenial. Cromwell seems to have regarded him as a useful man, for he was made in 1652 chairman of a joint commission to award damages for vessels destroyed by the Dutch in neutral Denmark. In 1655 he was made the chief of three commissioners, his associates being none other than Admiral Venable and Admiral Penn, father of the noted Quaker, who were to lead an expedition to the West Indies. There Winslow died of fever May, 1655. In the next year Standish died. He had left Plymouth proper in 1631 and had lived at Duxbury ever since. He had not only been the military leader of the Pilgrims, their very best scholar in the Indian languages, the man best able to deal with the Indians on their behalf, but he had also been an exceedingly useful man in government, thoroughly trusted and respected. In the spring of 1657 Bradford died and then indeed was the older generation gone. There were left of the original group of leaders only Howland, who lived till 1673, and Alden, who died in 1687, neither of whom, despite their long and continued usefulness in administration, had ever shown capacity for leadership. They did not at this time possess the confidence of the little colony. William Bradford, Jr., who seems to have been a man of some ability, became Assistant the year after his father's death and was reëlected for twenty-four years. He was also for several years Deputy-Governor but was not able to fill the place that his father left.

The mantle of Bradford fell upon Thomas Prence, who became autocrat of Plymouth accordingly and held the reins until his death in 1673. He had come to Plymouth in 1621 on the *Fortune* and had early become one of the leaders. In 1634 he had married the daughter of William Collier, the richest man in the colony. In 1657, he had already been Assistant for many years, Governor twice, and had held many of the lesser offices. The records of the First Church describe him as "excellently qualified for the office of Governor. He had a countenance full of majesty and therein as well as otherwise was a terror to evil doers." "God made him a repairer of breaches and a meanes to setle those shakings that were then threatening." [1] Prence was succeeded as Governor, after a few years' interim, by Thomas Hinckley, who had been, like Prence himself during Bradford's long reign, Assistant from 1658 to 1680. Hinckley ruled from 1680 until the end of the political independence of Plymouth.

The first problem with which the new régime had to deal was that of the Quakers. In March, 1657, one of this brotherhood entered the jurisdiction from Rhode Island and was promptly ejected. Several weeks later another appeared and was also ejected, both without violence or penalty. In the following year, two others appeared and seem to have received some kind of trial before the General Court. One of them constantly interrupted Governor Prence,—the majesty of whose appearance we may well remember in this connection for the Quaker seems not to have been terrified by it,— with a constant flow of such remarks as "thou liest," "Thomas, thou art a malicious man," "thy clamorous tongue I regard no more than the dust beneath my feet." The pair declined to take the oath of fidelity to England, but seem to have alleged no scruple about the oath itself, and, having defied the Court to do its worst, were ac-

---

[1] *Mayflower Descendant*, IV, 216. He was also declared "amiable and pleasant in his whole conversation."

cordingly whipped and sent on their way, writing from Rhode Island a letter prophesying for Prence all sorts of calamities. Another they wrote to Alden, upbraiding him for having renounced his former tolerance; a hint interesting to us. They also begged Alden not to be a "self conceited fool" because called magistrate. In 1658 several other Quakers appeared, some of whom were whipped. In 1659 the famous Mary Dyer visited Plymouth, but was promptly sent to Rhode Island and the cost of her deportation, with true Yankee shrewdness, was collected. In all, some ten were deported and some five were whipped. No Quaker suffered death at Plymouth or extended ill-treatment. There is, however, no evidence that the more characteristic of Quaker demonstrations took place at Plymouth.

It is perhaps advisable to mention here that the witchcraft delusion, which swept through the colony of Massachusetts Bay somewhat later, never secured credence at Plymouth. There seem to have been only two cases. In 1651 Dinah, the wife of one Sylvester of Scituate, claimed to have seen a neighbor, the wife of a man named Holmes, in conversation with the devil, who had for this colloquy assumed the form of a bear. Holmes brought suit for slander. The lady was convicted and ordered to confess and to pay £5 damages. The fact that she chose to do so seems to have considerably discouraged witch hunting. The second case was in 1677 and resembles somewhat the famous cases at Salem. An elderly lady was charged with bewitching a young girl and with causing her to fall on the ground in violent fits. She was tried by a jury, Governor Josiah Winslow presiding as Judge, and to their everlasting honor the verdict was brought in of "not guilty."

The tendency of the political development at Plymouth was revealed immediately after the death of Bradford by a prompt attempt to reduce the autocratic power of the Governor and to provide some sort of formula, by which freemen might be more easily and frequently admitted to the privilege.[1] The change indeed was less one in the structure of government than of emphasis. It was not less essential than before to be a Church member, but it was easier to become one. The ecclesiastical line was less rigid and had great effect in extending political privilege. No doubt too the fact that the new leaders (until 1663) did not reside at Plymouth emphasized the growth of other towns in jurisdiction, led to an increase in the power of the town authorities and to a more considerable freedom of the towns from the colonial dictation, as well as a considerable weakening of the political leadership of Plymouth itself. The discretionary power of the Governor and Assistants seems to have been less freely used than by Bradford and their administration followed more closely certain stereotyped and routine lines. The autocratic power, which had been retained by the General Court to combat the Assembly, in order to preserve and enhance the influence of Plymouth, indeed in order to preserve a degree of influence in the colony to which the physical size of Plymouth no longer entitled it, now had precisely the opposite effect from that originally intended. The overwhelming majority of the freemen had migrated to the

[1] These conclusions are unavoidably deductions and inferences from the formal records, for there seems to be no direct evidence as to the policy or intentions of the leaders. The majority of explicit facts and laws referred to can be readily found under the date in the *Records*.

other towns and the very power of the General Court militated now against Plymouth. In general, however, the tendency was, so far as we can make out from the fragmentary records, for the General Court to become more and more a Court of Elections, for the Assembly of Deputies to arrogate supremacy in legislation, and for the Governor and Assistants to secure in practice control of the judicial machinery. The increase in the colony's population to over 7000 in 1690 made the representative system, for which the Assembly of Deputies stood, more important, more logical, and more useful. Taxation, hitherto hardly systematic at Plymouth, was reorganized after 1657. In 1646, excise taxes had been levied on wines, beer, and strong waters, and were soon extended to tobacco and oil. After 1662, the principal revenue came from export taxes on exports of boards, plank, staves, and headings, tar, oysters, and iron. Some revenue came from the lease of the trading rights on the Kennebec [1] and from a lease of the mackerel fishery off Cape Cod, which the colony attempted to monopolize as early as 1646. A barrel of oil from each drift whale was also demanded. Exactly how the revenue was collected and for what it was spent we cannot be sure, for salaries as such seem not to have been paid before 1690, though presents and expense accounts were authorized, and grants of land were made to officials.

The people remained divided as before into Freemen,

[1] An attempt was made during the Commonwealth to secure the grant of the whole of the Kennebec, which was finally agreed to for seven years. There was of course in 1660 no disposition on their part to call attention to it. Interregnum Entry Book, XCIV, pp. 425-526; CLXI, pp. 10-11. The entries relating to the Pilgrims in the English manuscript archives for the period subsequent to 1620 are few and unimportant.

Inhabitants, Sojourners, and the non-privileged, but it became decidedly easier to become a Sojourner and reside in the jurisdiction, to secure a grant of land, and therefore to become an Inhabitant. Some attempt now was made to provide a less rigid statement of the requirements for political privilege. In 1656 it was voted that the freemen of the towns should be permitted to "propound" new candidates to the General Court for admittance. Two years later it was amended to read that the man should be accepted by the Court "upon satisfying testimony from freemen of his town." He should then "stand propounded" for a year, and then be considered a freeman "if the Court shall not see cause to the contrary." Knowing as we do the powerful forces at work to break down the rigid lines of the older privilege, we shall perhaps not be far wrong if we see in these provisions an attempt to admit men to political privilege who were vouched for by men from their own town, and against whom within a year nothing serious should be alleged. It seems almost as if a vote by the General Court as to whether they should be accepted was precluded. In 1658 an oath of fidelity was required of all citizens and certain classes of men were defined who should not be admitted freemen, among whom were enumerated Quakers, "opposers of the good and wholesome laws of this colony," or "manifest opposers of the true worship of God, or such as refused to do the country service being called thereunto." All existing freemen who were Quakers or encouragers of Quakers were to lose their privilege, and all likewise who were adjudged "gravely scandalous," as "liers, drunkards, swearers, etc." It may be that the new régime was less strict than the old, but it seems nevertheless to have possessed a certain stringency of its own. At the same time it is very clear that the importance of these provisions lay in the spirit in which they were interpreted.

In 1664 Plymouth received a visit from the Royal Commissioners, who came thither from Boston after what must have been for them a sorely trying experience. The suavity and cordiality of their welcome at Plymouth made therefore a great impression upon them. Prence indeed thoroughly appreciated the fact that, as against the King, the little colony possessed no rights of government. There had been considerable doubt whether the Council for New England had been able to convey any rights of government by the patent of 1630, and now that the Council had surrendered its powers to the King, those doubts were very certainly ended so far as the royal authority was concerned. The Commissioners invited complaints against the jurisdiction and received but one, from a man who had attempted to purchase land from the Indians on his own authority.

They seem to have been entirely satisfied with what they saw and heard, and made indeed only four recommendations: that all householders should swear allegiance and the courts act in the King's name; that all men of competent estate and civil conversation be admitted as freemen to vote and to hold office; that all of orthodox opinions and civil lives be admitted to the Lord's Supper and their children to Baptism, either in the existing congregations or in such as they might form; that any laws or legal phrases disrespectful to the King should be changed. The General Court replied that the first two points represented the colony's constant practice, while for the last, there were none. To the third they replied at great length, alleging in substance that all of orthodox opinion were already welcome in their churches, that they forbade none the right to pursue such worship as they preferred, and merely required that, pending the institution of some regular worship of their own, they should support and attend the Churches in existence. The Commissioners were well satisfied with the reply, and the letter, which the King later sent to Plymouth, seemed to the Pilgrims to augur well for their future cordial relations with the Crown. In 1671 they adopted the suggestion of the Commissioners and provided that all should be freemen, who were twenty-one years old, possessed of £20 of ratable property, and were as well "of sober and peaceable conversation," and "orthodox in religion." There was still ample warrant in these phrases to withhold privilege from anyone whom they disliked, but the tendency seems to have been to increase the number of freemen rather than to restrict it.

The trend of economic development at Plymouth emphasized those interests complementary to Massachusetts Bay. An economic structure closely related to the larger colony had been developing for some time, and gradually independent trade with England and the other American colonies ceased and Plymouth bought from the Bay and sold to it. This was naturally enough the result of the founding of towns in the western part of the Plymouth patent by settlers from the Bay colony itself, in locations better suited to agriculture than Plymouth proper. This district became gradually the predominant economic section of the little state, and naturally, being upon the high road from Boston to Rhode Island and in closer proximity indeed to Boston than to Plymouth, grew more and more nearly a part of the economic structure of which Boston was the centre, and tended more and more to sever its connections with Plymouth itself. Indeed, the Plymouth area did not form an independent economic unit nor did it occupy a natural geographical subdivision of Massachusetts Bay. On the contrary, it was itself economically a part of a larger unit whose natural centre was Boston. More and more the economic and social influence of the Bay Colony transformed the greater number of Plymouth towns. The old system of rigid seclusion gradually broke down. The old scrutiny of newcomers was less and less maintained. While this assisted in a way the breakdown of the older ecclesiastical lines, it was itself in turn assisted by the general failure of the Plymouth Church to maintain its old-time ascendency. While it was perhaps never easy for a stranger to secure a grant of land and economic privilege in the Old Colony or in Massachusetts, the two ceased, certainly after 1660, to regard each other with the old suspicion. A man of good standing in the one could without great difficulty transport himself to some part of the other's jurisdiction and there secure privilege.

The economic and ecclesiastical results of King Philip's War give it now practically its only title to a place in Plymouth annals. Time was when Philip occupied a romantic and prominent place in Pilgrim history, but the more recent students have united to strip this war of its glamor and of its importance.[1] They point out to us

---

[1] Palfrey and Goodwin are particularly emphatic. It should perhaps be said that the more romantic idea of Philip involves the very decided guilt of the Pilgrims for ill-treatment, undue encroachments, selfishness, and cruelty. Everything else we know about Plymouth leads us to reject such an idea as inconsistent with Pilgrim character and ideals as well as with their professions, and with the evidence in their Records of their previous treatment of Indians.

that Philip was no king and was not even an intelligent Indian; that he lived in squalor and possessed no particular property of which the white man could deprive him. As a figure typifying the downfall of a proud race, protesting against the loss of its independence before the ever encroaching white man, Philip was a name with which to conjure. As a dirty, quarrelsome, treacherous, degenerate Indian, bent upon making trouble for the Pilgrims, who had done their best to protect his land and property, he ceases to occupy in history a position of importance. The later students have put the blame for the war squarely upon the Indians, have denied continued and unfair encroachments by the whites, and have reduced the war to a series of Indian raids, destructive of life and property, chiefly because of the carelessness of the whites and of the failure of Massachusetts and Plymouth to coöperate promptly.

So far as Plymouth was concerned, the influence of the war was indirect and lay in its economic and ecclesiastical results rather than in its inception or its happenings. The latter are not particularly interesting nor instructive and a detailed narrative seems out of proportion here in so brief an account of the Pilgrim story. The economic loss, which the war entailed, nevertheless was for so weak a colony a serious matter. No exact estimate is available, but certainly several towns were burned and several hundred houses, while several hundred people were killed and a good many thousand pounds' worth of property was destroyed, including some thousands of cattle. The public debt which the colony incurred in putting down the rising amounted to twenty-seven thousand pounds, a staggering sum considering their resources, but one which was eventually paid to the

penny. The existence of this debt and the comparative
lack of means for paying it, was apparently one of the
reasons which led Hinckley to favor secretly the inclusion
of Plymouth within the Massachusetts patent.

The outbreak of the war caused a "searching of consciences" at Plymouth and a renewal of the Covenant of
the Church with God. They felt that in one way or
another it indicated the wrath of God upon them for
their shortcomings, and that the weakness of the Church
at Plymouth was due to their own lack of spiritual
strength. A great day of fasting and humiliation was
held and, as the Church records add, "within a month
after our solemne day," Philip was slain. Thus prompt
was the indication of divine approval of their repentance.
The leadership of the Church at Plymouth had been disturbed by the foundation of various towns after 1630
and by the removal of Elder Brewster from Plymouth as
early as 1633. The difficulty was increased by the fact
that the newer towns in the majority of cases possessed
a minister abler than the incumbent at Plymouth itself,
and was doubly accentuated by the death of Bradford
and by the lack of any minister at all at Plymouth from
1654 to 1667. During those years all pretence of leadership was lost by the Plymouth Church. The calling of
John Cotton, Jr., son of the famous Boston minister,
trained at Harvard College, and a man of real ability
and energy was an important event in the history of
the colony. This was in 1667, but it was not until 1676
and 1677 that the real reorganization of the Church was
begun and an active spirit of coöperation engendered
among the people themselves.

The mere presence of Cotton at Plymouth was definitive proof that the old line between the Plymouth

and Massachusetts Churches had disappeared. Truth
to tell, the Bay Churches had accepted the Pilgrims'
standpoint. They no longer maintained the rightness
of the Church of England nor the desirability of connection with it. They no longer claimed as they had in
the first decade the right to attend its communion on
their visits to England. The Pilgrims themselves were
not more assured of its inadequacy than the Massachusetts ministers in 1667. An entire generation had passed
away since they had first come to the New World, during
which they had been separated from the Mother Church
not only in distance but in time. A new generation had
risen in New England, born on the soil, which knew
neither Joseph nor Pharoah, and had long been accustomed to formulate its own policy in ecclesiastical affairs. For nearly two decades, moreover, Episcopacy
had been abolished in England, and the renunciation of
Bishops and canons in the mother land had made illogical
any attachment to them by the Puritans of New England. The change was probably in no sense a conscious
adoption by the Bay Colony of the Pilgrim Separatist
belief, but the work of circumstances over which neither
of the colonies in New England had any control.

Nor must it be forgotten that the negative character
of Pilgrim theology, its insistence on the observances of
the transitional period, made difficult its maintenance
against the more positive theology of later years. The
presence in the Bay Colony, too, of so many abler ministers and of so many laymen, intellectually more capable
than the majority at Plymouth, insensibly in the course
of decades produced an impression. New colonists had
begun in 1631 to drift into the Pilgrim jurisdiction by
twos and threes from the Bay Colony and remained

naturally more favorable to its traditions than to the original Pilgrim ideals. Gradually, as the leaders at Plymouth and the older generation had died, the newer generation had grown up in other towns than Plymouth, in close connection with immigrants from Massachusetts, and in most cases outnumbered by them. It cannot be said that the Pilgrim Church was absorbed into the Massachusetts system, nor yet perhaps that the Massachusetts system transformed itself in accordance with the Pilgrim example. The two Churches seem to have grown toward each other and away from what they had both originally been, and merged into a product different from either and better than both.[1]

As in the State so in the Church, the reorganization under Cotton was actuated by a desire to strengthen the Church by a broader and more tolerant policy, by a lessening of the rigidity of the older ecclesiastical requirements. Something of the precise changes we know.[2] Cotton and the deacons had undertaken in 1667 a house to house visitation of the whole town and had inquired "into the state of souls." A change was made at once in the method of admission to the Church. It had hitherto been essential, not only for the individual to satisfy the authorities of his orthodoxy, but for him also to state orally before the Church as a whole the grounds of his faith and to answer such questions as were put to him, a terrifying ordeal which had no doubt

[1] The issue was somewhat debated at the time. John Cotton Senior and Bradford both disclaim any conscious attempt to model the Bay Churches on the Pilgrim idea. See a discussion of this point in C. Burrage, *Early English Dissenters*, I, 357–368.

[2] The Records of Plymouth First Church tell us much of interest. They have been printed in full in the *Mayflower Descendant*, IV, V, VIII, etc.

kept many from Church membership. This was now no longer required. The authorities were to satisfy themselves by private conversation with the candidate of his orthodoxy and fitness. Undoubtedly this was responsible for the admission of so many new members at this time and for the continued accessions in the years after 1676. There had been forty-seven members in 1669; twenty-seven more had been admitted in that year; fourteen in 1670; seventeen in 1671; and six in 1672. This will give some idea of the previous stringency. The members also solemnly renewed their covenant in 1676 and entered into a further definite agreement to revive the active life of the old Church.

The service too had been calculated to make participation difficult rather than easy for those unable to read or not possessed of a ready memory. Books no doubt were scarce, but the psalms had been sung straight through, without any such assistance, as was already common in Massachusetts, as giving out the line before it was sung. This practice was introduced at Plymouth in 1681, and was then changed to the reading of the psalm by the Pastor with an exposition of it, before the Deacon proceeded to give it out, line by line, for singing. Ainsworth's *Psalms*, hitherto used at Plymouth, was after a time abandoned for the *Bay Psalm Book*. Thus was new life introduced into the Plymouth Church.

At this time, too, education at Plymouth received serious attention. From the first they had been solicitous about it, and, even in the earliest years, the children had received some instruction. As early as 1624, Bradford hints at something like a school, and after 1630 there were certainly several schools in the colony. It was not until 1662, however, that a law was passed by the

General Court charging each town to employ a school-master, and not until 1677 that schools were made compulsory. Laws were passed holding masters and parents responsible in case the children were not trained in reading, writing, and arithmetic. Some inducement was offered after 1670 for the establishment of a classical school, and probably in 1674 the first free school established in New England by law was opened at Plymouth. There had long been free schools in Massachusetts Bay, but they had not the sanction of law or were not supported by taxes. For anything beyond the elements, however, it was essential to resort to the schools of the Bay Colony and to Harvard College.

Secular education, indeed, the Pilgrims did not entirely approve of. University learning seemed to them unnecessary beyond the rudiments, for the true enlightenment of the mind was to be derived from the study of the Bible and not from the classics as taught by colleges. There was to this opposition a certain ecclesiastical tinge. The Established Church made much of college degrees and exacted from clergymen for ordination requirements which could be fulfilled only in colleges. For the ordination of that Church, the Pilgrims had the most supreme contempt and any requirements which it made they placed in the same category.[1] They were unwilling to accept the contention that a man might not be entirely learned without having "saluted a University" or peered between the covers of a Greek Grammar. To admit that college education was essential would have been to condemn their own opinions and

[1] An amusing commentary on this attitude by Morton in his *New English Canaan*, Prince Soc. ed., 282, is our chief direct evidence of its existence.

accept those of the college professors and college-trained Clergy whom they had left behind in England, and whose learning they had rejected as unavailing for salvation. The true Light had come to them without education. The educated of their own day seemed not to see the Light. They were therefore not anxious to teach their children anything beyond the rudiments of that education, which seemed so powerless to confer upon its possessor spiritual guidance and insight.

It is quite clear that after 1660 a great change came over social conditions at Plymouth; not that the main outlines of the social structure were seriously changed nor its main purpose altered, but the spirit and tendency of life were freer.[1] The individual was less subject to scrutiny and greater latitude was allowed him. With this later Plymouth we are less interested, though we know about it comparatively more than about the earlier Plymouth of the forefathers. It is interesting chiefly as the first stage in the breaking down of a system which time was to prove incompatible with its own chief tenets. The Pilgrims preached the responsibility of the individual to God for his own salvation, and his paramount responsibility for informing himself of religious

[1] The members of the First Church agreed in 1676 that they had been "listlesse and sluggish" in attendance at Church; had not kept the Sabbath strictly; had "set our hearts upon the world and creature comforts and vanities and have too much conformed to the world." "Wee have bin a proud generation—haughty in spirit, in countenance, in garbe and fashion, and have too much delighted to follow the vaine and sinfull customs of an evil world." The Elders told the Church that "some of the brethren walked disorderly, in sitting too long together in publick houses and with vaine company and drinking." *Mayflower Descendant*, V, 216; VIII, 215, 217. We must certainly not interpret such utterances too literally.

truth. They taught without deviation or compromise that none but he could save his soul, that priests, churches, ministers, and friends were unavailing to do more than offer him some little assistance and enlightenment.

In Europe, they had preached freedom to act, freedom to think, freedom to read, with the full comprehension that it meant freedom to disobey statutes, to renounce the Pope, to absent themselves from the service of the Established Church, and, so long as they had remained in Europe, this new freedom of the individual which they preached had remained merely freedom to disregard certain former requirements of the old order, so conspicuously thrust into the foreground by Church and State as to conceal the fact that real freedom to think and act was equally withheld from the Pilgrims by their own system. At Plymouth, far removed from Europe and its Churches and kings, the Pope become already a dim myth, and Bishops and canons unrealities, the system involved a control of the individual by society and the church which was entirely incompatible with its own primal tenet, his freedom to think and act in accordance with his own information and not in accordance with that of others. Theoretically, the Church members accorded to each other the right to investigate and conclude, but they never even in theory extended that right to their wives, their children, their servants, and their apprentices. A minority of the community attempted to coerce the majority on the basis of an intellectual pretension to dictate their conduct as well as their beliefs, to dictate their civil, economic, and social status as well as the road to salvation. It was a system inconsistent with itself, which denied its own tenet, which crushed the individual instead of freeing him, which subjected him to a yoke far heavier than any Bishops or Pope had laid upon him, and manyfold more stringently enforced.

Time could not fail to reveal the inconsistency. Men began to see that they had freedom only to agree with the strictest Calvinists and to act in social affairs in accord with Bradford's and Brewster's consciences. They might, it was true, leave the colony; but they came in the end to realize that the fundamental tenets of the system itself endowed them with the right to follow their own consciences, and with the same right to resist dictation from the leaders as from the Pope. Dimly, unconsciously, something of this seems to have been appreciated toward the close of Pilgrim history. This was unquestionably the leaven at work at Plymouth, as at Boston, in England, and elsewhere. The process of evolution was to be long. Real toleration was still many decades distant, and the freedom of social life from ecclesiastical direction was not to come within the span of Plymouth's political independence.

The Plymouth of 1691 would scarcely have pleased the original settlers. Long before Bradford died, he began to suspect something of the real trend of events. To him the gradual disappearance of the sharp ecclesiastical antagonism between Plymouth and the other colonies, the growth in population, the founding of new towns, the increase in the number of churches were proof that the end for which he had striven throughout his life would not be achieved. Had he but known it, the diffusion of population, the apparent breaking down of the barriers surrounding Plymouth, were but the signs that the influence of the Pilgrims was extending, was leavening a larger lump than Plymouth, and was about to become the heritage, not of a Church but of a nation.

CHAPTER XIX

THE LOSS OF POLITICAL INDEPENDENCE

It was not until January, 1687, some little time after the establishment of a General Governor for the New England colonies at New York and Boston, that Sir Edmund Andros found time to take the necessary legal steps for the abolition of the old government at Plymouth and the institution of his own.[1] The last session of the old General Court occurred October 5, 1686, and the new Government lasted until April 22, 1689, though the next entry in the Plymouth records is October 8, 1689. There is not much to tell about the Andros régime at Plymouth. It seems to have been rather an interim than a radical change of any sort. The ecclesiastical, social, and economic life of the colony seems to have gone on as before; local government in the hands of the towns continued, even though an intention to change it had been expressed; only the central authority was suspended, and, inasmuch as no very considerable activity of any of its parts was common, it betokened no great change of significance that for three years neither the Governor and Assistants, the General Court, nor the Assembly held their accustomed sessions.

[1] Sewall duly noticed that on December 30, 1686, "the gentlemen from Plymouth and Rhode Island" came to Boston to take oaths to the new government. Diary, *Mass. Hist. Soc. Coll.*, 5th *Series*, V, 163. This famous source is disappointing, for it contains only a very few perfunctory notices about Plymouth. Nor does the considerable volume of contemporary material on the Andros régime much better reward perusal.

Indeed, nothing of importance seems to have been attempted by Andros at Plymouth. The same polity he tried to apply in the other colonies was outlined; the land titles in particular were declared invalid, and announcement was made that new and thoroughly legal titles and documents were to be had upon payment of fee. Clark's Island, which had long been rented out by the colony for the benefit of the poor, was granted by the new Government to Nathaniel Clark, a Plymouth man, and one of Plymouth's seven members in the new Governor's Council. He seems to have been the only Plymouth citizen to whom Andros listened, and the only one who in any whole hearted way gave his allegiance to the new régime. He could however accomplish little in so short a time, whatever his intentions, and there is some doubt whether he ever secured possession of the island. Andros and his henchmen were too busy with the other colonies to give much time to the affairs of the smallest and least troublesome part of his jurisdiction, particularly as no open or avowed opposition was attempted, and where even expressions of disapproval seem to have been relatively guarded. There was, too, the obvious question whether the owners of Plymouth estates were able to pay the new fees. Hinckley, ex-Governor, declared them incapable. This no doubt gave Andros pause.

Hinckley, the old Governor, Nathaniel Clark, the old Secretary, who had been educated and trained by Morton, himself for so many years Secretary of the colony, became members of Andros's council, Clark, in all probability to further his own nefarious endeavors, Hinckley to perform the public service of thwarting Andros's schemes regarding Plymouth in the Council itself before they should mature.[1] At any rate he could surely discover what was intended, and, being forewarned, might in some way or other frustrate the execution of the measure, if not its inception. He could certainly give the men at Plymouth plenty of time in which to make their preparations for resistance, in case such should seem expedient. Some protest to the King against the new measures Hinckley made, but with so little opposition possible in the Council, with nothing better than half-hearted support from the other members, he felt it inexpedient to organize any resistance at Plymouth. It is perhaps due to his efforts that nothing of importance was executed at Plymouth. When Andros was imprisoned at Boston and the régime fell with a crash on the receipt of the news of the Glorious Revolution in England, Hinckley and the officers who had been in power at Plymouth in 1686 quietly resumed office, without comment or official action. Clark to be sure they imprisoned. The whole incident produced no effect now traceable on Plymouth life or institutions; no important event happened at Plymouth during these years worth chronicling; and what is still more surprising no vital change in the rights or privileges of Plymouth, in the attitude of the colony to the Crown, or of the Crown to the colony can be discovered.

The policy of submission which Hinckley represented and for which at the time he was criticised somewhat sharply was really a continuation of what the Pilgrims in the earliest times had determined was their only expedient attitude toward the Crown, and indeed, toward

[1] The Hinckley Papers contain a considerable amount of information on Plymouth from about 1675 to 1692. *Mass. Hist. Soc. Coll., 4th Series*, V.

any in England or America possessed of unquestioned authority. They themselves never possessed by patent or otherwise any political authority which was not seriously open to question, and they therefore from the first deemed it wiser not to have that question raised, or, if it were, it should not be pushed by them to an open issue or a trial of strength. The loss of the political independence of Plymouth is intelligible only when studied in the light of its previous economic and ecclesiastical development, and in the light of its previous relations to the English Government and to the other New England colonies.

When they landed, they were without authorization of any kind, but nevertheless in the Compact of 1620 utilized phrases, which have since seemed to many to betoken an intention of downright independence.[1] They bound themselves "into a civill body politik" "to enacte, constitute, and frame such just and equall lawes, ordinances, actes, constitutions and offices, from time to time as shall be thought most meete and convenient for the general good of the Colonie, unto which we promise all due submission and obedience." This Bradford declared was as valid and useful a document, so far as they were concerned, as the patent they brought with them from the Virginia Company, and no doubt he considered it as valuable as the one which their associates got from the Council for New England. They themselves certainly possessed no title to land and surely no rights of government until the Warwick Patent issued to Bradford in 1630. In the meantime West had

[1] Professor Channing emphatically declares the Compact only a temporary arrangement without the "slightest thought of independence." *History of the United States*, I, 309.

arrived as Admiral of New England and Gorges as Governor of New England, both with commissions from the Council for New England, and both of them seem to have assumed the inferiority of the Plymouth jurisdiction. Gorges in particular issued definite orders to them and demanded that they execute warrants for the arrest of Weston, which implied very definitely their subordinate political authority. While aware of the implication, they judged it best to yield, when they saw that he also appreciated it. From these apprehensions however they were soon free.

Scarcely had the new patent to Bradford been issued, and the first murder occurred at Plymouth by Billington than a very active discussion took place as to the possession by the colony of the power to execute him, indeed as to the possession by the colony of any governmental authority at all. There were not a few who seemed to feel that the patent conferred nothing but titles to land, and so the majority of the Pilgrims seem to have thought. They consulted Winthrop and Dudley, newly come to Boston and better acquainted with English law, and received from them advice to assume that they possessed such powers of government, and to exercise them accordingly, a decision based no doubt upon expediency rather than law. They executed Billington and proceeded to act otherwise in matters of government as if full authority were theirs. To this presently by Sir Christopher Gardiner, Gorges, and others objection was raised in 1631 and 1632, and formal complaint made to the Privy Council in London. Winslow however successfully explained matters to the Privy Council in January, 1633, and a formal statement under seal was issued to approve all of their previous practices. It also spoke in a very encouraging way of the importance of the venture and the desire of the royal Government to further it. They now began to write in the records [1] of the "Freemen of this society of New Plymouth" and later write of "this government" and of "the Commonweale"; 1636 found them enacting a law which might have been interpreted to imply a disregard of the royal authority. "No imposition, law, or ordinance be made or imposed upon or by ourselves or others, at present or to come, but such as shall be made or imposed by consent, according to the free liberties of the state and kingdom of England, and no otherwise."

Not long after news must have come of the surrender in 1635 to the Crown of the patent and rights of the Council for New England, the grantor of their own patent, and which made the King at once paramount over them. This seems to have caused somewhat greater circumspection at Plymouth for we find the records promptly began to run in the name of the King. In 1639 an entry begins "Whereas our soueraigne lord the King is pleased to betrust us, T. P., W. B., E. W., etc. with the gouernment of so many of his subjectes as doe or shal be permitted to liue within this gouernment of New Plymouth." [2] They were careful moreover that everything should hereafter be done, even coroners' inquiries and other minor judicial matters, "on the behalf of our sovereign lord the King," for all which in due time they had reason to be thankful. In 1642, at the out-

[1] *Plymouth Colony Records*, I, 5, 22, 52, etc.

[2] *Plymouth Colony Records*, I, 113. The use of the King's name begins as early as the winter of 1636 in a case of coroner's jury, to inquire into the death of ——, "in the behalfe of our soveraigne Lord the King." *Ibid.*, I, 39. See also pp. 48, 49, 91, 105, 107, etc., etc.

break of the Civil War, the success of the Long Parliament was not as reassuring to the men at Plymouth as it was to those at Boston, and the downfall and capture of Charles in 1646 was still more puzzling. In June, 1649, they voted that "whereas things are mutch unseteled in our natiue cuntry in regard of the affairs of the state (so much for poor Charles I's head!) whereby the Court cannot so clearly prosseed in election as formerly," all officers and magistrates were to continue for a year as before and Bradford and John Brown were requested to act as Commissioners, "who condescended thereto." [1]

No further action seems to have been taken and when the Royal authority was restored in 1660, the colony still continued its administration as before, with circumspect and loyal expressions of their reasonable satisfaction at His Majesty's restoration to his kingdom. They discreetly neglected to call attention to their previous days of prayer and thanksgiving for the Parliament and the Commonwealth of England after the news of Dunbar and Worcester. When the Royal Commissioners arrived in 1664, they had reason to congratulate themselves upon this circumspection. Their writs had run in the name of the King and the records proved it. They had not excluded men from political privilege on the score of loyalty to the Crown in the past two decades, nor were there any laws on the books hostile to the King. This attitude pleased the Crown and so apparently matters continued during the reign of Charles II.

This policy of deference and submission to whatever took place in England, this caution and fear of raising the awkward question, whether or not they possessed

[1] *Plymouth Colony Records*, II, 139.

authority, was precisely the policy which led Hinckley to accept the rule of Andros, to take a seat upon his Council, and, after the Glorious Revolution, to attempt no very strenuous opposition to the inclusion of Plymouth in the Massachusetts Charter of 1691. He saw that it was idle for them to expect consideration from William III, on the score of such past legal rights as the Massachusetts colonists unquestionably had. It was entirely within the law for the King's officials to claim that the Plymouth colonists had never possessed authority. Nor was the choice before them apparently that of continued independence or annexation to Massachusetts. Rhode Island, Connecticut, and New York were all apparently anxious to absorb them and had been for some considerable time. These pretensions to superior authority over Plymouth on the part of the other colonies, these claims that the Plymouth territory was included in the patents already granted to others, were old and not infrequently asserted in the past. In 1634 an attempt was made by an Englishman to proceed above the Plymouth grant on the Kennebec, and there establish an Indian trading post which would intercept the trade before it reached the Pilgrim territory. The Pilgrims forbade him to go but he was determined to proceed, and in an endeavor to prevent him perhaps by some little hustling and pushing, a musket was discharged and a man killed. Some little excitement was caused in Boston by the news, and, when one of the Plymouth ships put in to Boston Harbor somewhat later, the authorities imprisoned Alden, although they allowed the ship to proceed. This was an evident claim of jurisdiction over the Plymouth men, who were nonplussed to know what to do. After deliberation, they sent Standish to Boston with letters demanding Alden's release, and explaining their rights on the Kennebec. Alden was indeed allowed to go free but was required to give bond for further appearance, and Standish as well was bound to appear at the next session of the Massachusetts Court, and was ordered to produce a copy of the patent and testify in regard to the affair. There could have been no conceivably clearer claim of jurisdiction and superiority than this. After some correspondence and visiting, a great deal of explaining and insisting, the Massachusetts Colony was gotten to accept the Pilgrim's explanation, although no definite withdrawal of their assumed rights seems to have been made.[1]

Two years later Hooker's colonists appeared on the Connecticut and proceeded to occupy as waste land a considerable tract which the Pilgrims had bought from the Indians. It was furthermore entirely outside the Massachusetts boundaries, though this fact was probably not known at the time. Despite the protestations of Jonathan Brewster, the Pilgrim agent on the spot, the Connecticut men settled the land and had no primary intention to leave the Pilgrims any of it. After much ado, with protests and visits, they were finally gotten to recognize the Pilgrim title, on condition that the Pilgrims should immediately transfer it to them, reserving only a small portion as a basis for their trade. However satisfactory this technical endorsement of the Pilgrim jurisdiction may have been, it was certainly disconcerting to find colonists of their own race and religious persuasion, entirely unwilling to recognize their legal position in the new country. Considerable bitterness long remained at Plymouth over this, as Bradford is forced to

[1] Bradford relates the affair at some length. *History*, 377–379, 382.

admit. And so, too, the Pilgrims felt that the Massachusetts men ought to have aided them in the expulsion of the French from the trading post on the Penobscot, seized by the latter in 1635, and which the Pilgrims failed to retake.[1] In 1638 an incident occurred which was more reassuring.[2] Four indented servants ran away from Plymouth and murdered an Indian in the western part of the jurisdiction, and, when they landed in Rhode Island, were detained for the deed upon the complaint of the Indians, who demanded justice. Williams, much to the disgust of the Plymouth people, for the deed had been committed not only by Plymouth servants but in Plymouth territory, referred the cause to the authorities in Boston, who, mindful perhaps of the late dispute in the case of Alden, referred it back to Plymouth. Thither the men were eventually brought, tried for their crime, and executed.

The following year an active dispute arose with Massachusetts as to the boundaries of the colony. Bradford declared that the Pilgrims held their land by right of purchase from the Indians, confirmed by the King, to which Winthrop replied, "it was the first I heard of it and it would be hard to make their title good and as hard to proue their grant to them." [3]   Indeed not only were the exact limits of the Warwick patent debated, but, as Winthrop hints, its validity to confer anything upon them was questioned. Rhode Island similarly raised a number of questions as to the ownership of particu-

---

[1] Bradford, *History*, 420–422.

[2] *Ibid.*, 432.

[3] *Mass. Hist. Soc. Coll.*, *4th Series*, VI, 156.   There are in this same volume many letters upon this aspect of Pilgrim relations. Bradford's account in the *History*, 439–443, is very full.

lar districts. The Plymouth men retorted by claiming Providence. They also laid claim to Shawomet (now Warwick, R. I.); Massachusetts men were sent to occupy it; and blows were very nearly exchanged, but the Plymouth title was finally admitted. It was at this time, in 1639 and 1640 that the Plymouth men first became conscious of the desire of Massachusetts and Rhode Island to annex the whole of their territory.

This knowledge made them hesitate somewhat to enter into the New England Confederation which was at this time suggested. In the first meetings of the men at Boston, who thought it useful for the settling of such disputes as have just been mentioned, consideration was also given to the attaining for Massachusetts of "some preëminence." This was in 1638, and no doubt the fact and the disposition of Massachusetts to lord it somewhat over the others was thoroughly well known and appreciated. It probably explains in particular the arrival of the Plymouth delegates in 1643 for the final act of organization without power to sign. No adequate investigation of the history of the New England Confederation seems as yet to have been made, but it would be out of place in this book to detail at length the experience of Plymouth in the Confederation or attempt the story of the Confederation itself. The events in its history were not closely associated with the affairs of Plymouth nor was Plymouth able to play any very considerable part in their decision. Together with Connecticut and New Haven, the Plymouth men pretty commonly stood out solidly against the attempts of Massachusetts to dominate and direct. Frequently they were able to succeed, but, on questions of real importance, upon which the Massachusetts men were thoroughly determined, the latter were unfortunately able to compel the acceptance of action by the others or to nullify the action which the others wished to undertake. So far as Plymouth is concerned, the colony seems to have entered the Confederation with the expectation that New Haven and Connecticut would assist her in the preservation of her independence and in thwarting the ambitious claims of Massachusetts. Certainly those of Rhode Island could thus be forestalled.[1] The four New England colonies thoroughly agreed in their dislike and distrust of the "Islanders."

Constant attempts were made by the Massachusetts Commissioners to emphasize in one way or another their superiority over Plymouth, which were generally received quietly by the Plymouth men and pushed to one side. The question was never entirely settled but no open quarrel took place. Plymouth was never quite sure that Massachusetts accepted the legality of her authority, the reality of her independence, or the correctness of the boundaries assigned her.[2] In 1660 the Restoration caused all the colonies to feel that greater circumspection was essential, and the New England Confederation, an extra-legal association, they thought likely to meet criticism in England and accordingly

[1] "Concerning the Islanders," wrote Bradford to Winthrop, "we have no conversing with them, nor desire to have, furder then necessitie or humanity may require." May 17, 1642. *History*, 463.

[2] The General Court at Boston issued an order on March 7, 1644, for the release of Randal Holden, and the New Plymouth *agents*, and their banishment from Massachusetts on pain of death. *State Papers Colonial*, XI, No. 1. See also the case of the Schism in the Church at Rehobah in 1649 in which the Massachusetts General Court also interfered—Goodwin, *Pilgrim Republic*, 515.

they allowed it to fall somewhat into disuse. Certainly it became less active. The absorption of New Haven into Connecticut in 1667 left only three colonies, and still further weakened the position of Plymouth, though no doubt it roused its apprehensions. There was no surprise therefore in Plymouth when they learned in 1690 that the Massachusetts men were ambitious to extend the limits of their boundary on the south so as to include the Plymouth jurisdiction, and that the Rhode Island men were also anxious to secure a new patent, which would beyond doubt give them possession of Plymouth. We cannot be entirely sure, but it is probable that the authorities at Plymouth allowed it to be known in London that they preferred annexation to Massachusetts.

Truth to tell the two colonies had long been practically one in many ways. Very early the economic centre of New England had shifted to Boston and the fact that Plymouth was merely a part of its economic area was soon thrust upon them. As early as 1640, Plymouth had practically ceased to trade direct with England and bought from and sold to Boston. The western towns of the jurisdiction had for the most part been settled from the Bay Colony and had their economic affiliations with it from the first rather than with Plymouth itself. There was no wrenching or tearing therefore of natural associations in 1691. Politically Plymouth was absorbed with ease into the Massachusetts Town System and merely sent its deputies to Boston instead of to Plymouth. Indeed the Massachusetts representative system had grown up inside the older Pilgrim system and had by 1691 taken control of it. The reality of local independence was not disturbed, and was rather better assured under the Massachusetts system than under the previous rule of Plymouth, where the General Court had always technically possessed a paramount authority over the towns which the latter had then found it difficult to endure. So far as political leadership was concerned, too, there had been little in Plymouth Colony for some decades. Certainly the town of Plymouth had itself been incapable of the direction of affairs and the other towns were unwilling to concede it to each other. There was indeed no intellectual group of men in the jurisdiction capable of that degree of administrative direction needed to offset the influence of so large and admirably organized a community as the Bay Colony was.

Nor was political independence any longer essential to insure the perpetuation of the prime fact of the Pilgrim creed which they had sacrificed so much to establish. Separation from the Established Church of England and the rejection of its Ordination as insufficient was already a fact in Massachusetts, and the inclusion of Plymouth within the larger jurisdiction perpetuated and strengthened the Pilgrim ecclesiastical position. Indeed it was more than possible that the continued independence of Plymouth might have given color to an interference from the Established Church in England, which the inclusion within Massachusetts made less probable. The doctrinal differences between the Puritan and Pilgrim Churches had been from the first slight and had not been considered important by Brewster and Bradford. They had been thoroughly minimized and had indeed chiefly disappeared by the foundation from Massachusetts of the newer towns in Plymouth jurisdiction and by the fact that the great majority of ministers outside of the town of Plymouth itself came from Massachusetts.

The truth seems to be that Massachusetts did not in any literal sense absorb Plymouth or Plymouth leaven Massachusetts. They had grown together in the course of a century, had not merely developed side by side, and emerged in 1700 a new political, economic, ecclesiastical, and social entity, different from either at the beginning, certainly different from the plans originally projected by the leaders of both, and on the whole more satisfactory to the people in each than the Government of either had been before. The political independence of Plymouth had indeed become an anomaly which ignored the real fact that its towns were now an integral part of a new entity and as such shared in a new type of political life and activity. In this new state the control of the Church was immeasurably less. The real reason for the dominance over the State by the Church at Plymouth and of the social and economic life by both combined had now disappeared. The ecclesiastical position, which they had come to New England to establish, and which they had felt needed such protection from the State, was assured beyond a possibility of doubt. It was now obvious that civil affairs might be conducted upon the basis of temporal needs and expedient policy, that economic and social questions might now be handled without primary relation to the stability of State or Church and might hence be decided on their merits. The influx of population they no longer feared and there was not the same necessity of scrutinizing so carefully the newcomers or of a restriction of their acquisition of political, economic, and social privilege. The reason therefore for political independence had disappeared. Nor was there justifiability for the economic and political inconvenience of different boundaries and for additional machinery for administrative, legislative, and judicial work. Nothing in fact seems to have been lost in 1691. Nothing was destroyed.

The ideal of the Pilgrim fathers was perpetuated by a larger and stronger state. It was retained not merely at Plymouth, but was spread by the outgoing of Plymouth and Massachusetts men throughout the length and breadth of a great continent. Their example to posterity was preserved, not as they had hoped as a tiny candle burning in seclusion, but as a beacon light for the nations to see throughout the ages, taken from under the bushel and set upon a hill. Bradford quoted Second Corinthians: "As unknowen yet knowen; as dead, and behold we live." The loss of political independence deprived the Pilgrim tradition of localism and made it a heritage of the nation as a whole. In the days of the Revolution, when the colonists came to look back into their own past and study somewhat their own origin, they all regarded Plymouth as a general possession, not merely as the tradition of one state. The extinction of formal political life at Plymouth also tended to scatter the Pilgrims throughout the United States. It diffused the blood throughout the whole and leavened the lump with the example of Plymouth. Not at Plymouth itself has been the true influence of the Pilgrims, but outside Plymouth in Massachusetts, in New England as a whole, and in those far parts beyond the mountains to which in the coming centuries so many valiant sons of the old colony were to migrate, and where so many thousands of their lineal descendants are now to be found. There are now more sons of the Pilgrims in the Mississippi Valley than in Massachusetts, more on the Pacific Coast than in Plymouth. The failure of the Pilgrims to per-

petuate the political independence of the colony is perhaps not the least important of their successes. They
became not merely the progenitors of a tiny state, but
the ancestors of a nation. "Verily, a little one has become
a thousand; yea, a little one, a great nation."

APPENDIX

The most considerable expenditure of time and effort ever yet devoted to Pilgrim history is the attempt of Dr. Dexter and his son to ascertain the number and personnel of Robinson's Church and Congregation at Leyden. The histories of the Pilgrims at Leyden and in America, written during the last forty years, have been based upon the assumption that the estimate of the total Congregation by the Dexters at a figure of about five hundred was reliable and authoritative. The relation of the Church to the Congregation was of course a much more difficult matter and for that the Dexters did not venture to give a definite figure. Upon the assumption that Robinson's Congregation was large, Dexter's *England and Holland of the Pilgrims* was based and all the calculations and figures in it regarding births, deaths, marriages, residence, business transactions are dependent upon the belief that the four hundred and seventy-three names given in the Appendix were the Congregation. Whether or not the people to whom these facts relate were or were not members of Robinson's Church is therefore the vital issue in dealing with the history of the Pilgrims at Leyden. Both Dr. Dexter and his son realized the extraordinary difficulties in which this calculation involved them, but it seems still worth while to discuss these critical problems. So large a figure seems not entirely consistent with the direct testimony of the Pilgrims and with other known facts. Indeed, it is possible to quote Mr. Morton Dexter against himself. In the *Mass. Hist. Soc. Proc.*, 2nd Series, *XVII*, 167–184, he gave the names of 117 persons of whose membership we were positive and of 91 persons almost certainly associated with them. He stated further that the Congregation probably did not exceed in 1620 two hundred people and was in all probability between one hundred and one hundred and fifty. When he came later, however, to publish the book in 1905, he printed in the Appendix a first category of 473 names who were "certainly or presumably" members of Robinson's Congregation and stated also his opinion that the total membership from 1609–1620 cannot have fallen short of five hundred. Upon the assumption that the whole four hundred seventy-three were members, he then bases his statistics. Is it not surprising that he should have thus abandoned his first category of those whose connection with the Church could be positively demonstrated and have based his volume upon those who were only "presumably" members? The "presumably" entirely deprives the whole list of finality.

It is perhaps worth while to call attention to the fact that Dr. Dexter's results, considerable as they may seem, are dependent in the first place literally upon the possibility of accurately transliterating English names from the phonetic spelling used by the Dutch recorders. The significant thing to demonstrate is the reliability of the process of transliteration, the extent to which pure conjecture and guess work can be excluded from it. The difficulty of the work was appalling and required unlimited patience, great ingenuity, the utmost caution, to say nothing of a knowledge of both Dutch and English phonetics in the seventeenth century, neither of them subjects beyond dispute. For instance, is "Ament" Hammond; "Chinheur" Singer; "Ians" Jones? Do "Sodert," "Sodwoot" and "Houthward" all equal "Southworth" or do they stand for different individuals? The Dexters could not entirely rid themselves of the fear that some proportion of these transliterations represented their own eagerness to discover at Leyden some trace of people known to have been at Plymouth. Those who have followed the Dexters will not find this difficulty insurmountable. There is every reason to suppose that the list of four hundred and seventy-three names is the maximum which science and diligence can recover.

The more considerable difficulty is after all the truly significant point: the connection with Robinson's Church of English people known to have been at Leyden between 1609–1620. Direct evidence furnishes us with relatively few identifications and for the rest we must erect an elaborate structure of presumptions and probabilities. For the number whose membership direct evidence substantiates are very clearly only a very small portion of the Church, and as we can perhaps be quite sure that any membership list will not include all members, certain assumptions become necessary. Dr. Dexter concluded that the wives and children of the men of the Congregation must be treated also as members; that Englishmen known to have had business or legal associations with known members of the Congregation were probably also members; and lastly, that those who could be shown to be members immediately after 1620 were in all probability members immediately before the emigration of the Pilgrims. The justice of these assumptions is obvious and the difficulties which they might involve in an attempt not to assume too much were also clear to those who have subsequently utilized this book. The Dexters' list, however, includes one hundred and twenty children, many of whom died in infancy, the majority of whom were under ten years of age in 1620, and who were therefore babes in arms for the greater part of the Leyden period. Only a relatively few of the children were old enough to be counted as active members of the Congregation, and in an attempt to reach some notion of the real size of that body in practical affairs, we must subtract at least one hundred children.

We know also from Bradford that a considerable number of the boys and girls, who attained anything resembling an age of discretion, left the Congregation, and for them too some allowance must be made. A considerable number of the adult men on this list were married more than once at Leyden, and in many cases two and in some three wives are counted in the total on the strength of their relationship to one man. Here again is a necessary deduction, if we are to reach from a total figure of members from 1609–1620 any approximate notion of the strength of the Congregation at any one time. It will also be clear that if the membership of a man is at all doubtful, by the time we have counted his wife and children we have multiplied our error several fold. If we accept John Jennings, we also count both of his wives, six children, the wives of his children, and his grandchildren. The son of Thomas Willet, born in 1610, reached Plymouth in 1631. On the score of that fact Thomas Willet himself, his wife, five children, and his sister are added to the Congregation.

The assumption in regard to the men who had business relations with members of the Congregation is a more fruitful source of difficulty. If we accept a man or a woman who is a witness at betrothals or who guarantees for citizenship or other purposes known Pilgrims, shall we also count the other English people for whom he witnesses, and if not all of them, how many of them? If we accept those men for whom the Pilgrims themselves certify, shall we accept those for whom they in turn certify? Nor must we forget that in each case we add to the list the wives, children, brothers, sisters, and in some cases mothers and fathers of men whose sole identification is the fact that they become guarantors for a man, who is assumed on other grounds to have had business relations with one of the lesser known Pilgrims. It seemed worth while to compute from Dr. Dexter's list the number of individuals whose membership depended solely on legal relations with men or women of whose membership we were not positive. This computation therefore will not include those who vouch for Brewster, Carver, Cushman, and the like, the partners in the purchase of the Great House, or the men and women for whom they directly vouched. We can perhaps afford to assume that any clear business relationship involving a certification of good character, either by the leaders or for them, raises a satisfactory presumption of membership. But what of those men and women whose mutual testimony seems to be the principal basis for considering them members at all? Fifty-four men and twelve women were witnesses of legal documents and on the strength of their membership thirty-six wives and twelve children were also included in the list, making one hundred and nineteen in all. There are also in Dr. Dexter's list seventy-five men for whose membership the evidence is subsequent to 1620, and with them were counted fifty-nine wives and twelve children. There were therefore in all two hundred and sixty-five out of four hundred and seventy-three whose membership is doubtful.

How can we now raise a presumption as to what proportion of the doubtful cases were members? According to the first computation of Mr. Morton Dexter, only one hundred and seventy names, including children, could be established with certainty, leaving three hundred and fifty-six more or less doubtful. According to the computation just made, two hundred and sixty-five names are really dubious. There are certain facts which will be of assistance in the raising of a more definite presumption as to the total number of the Congregation and as to its probable figure in 1620.

1. Bradford and Winslow tell us that when the vote was taken on the question of migration to America, the number who decided to go was only a trifle less than those who voted to stay. Thirty-five only sailed from Leyden for Plymouth. We know also that some who had originally intended to go changed their minds in March or April, 1620, after the rejection by the merchants in London of the terms which Weston had signed. Eighteen also returned to London on the *Speedwell*, some of whom certainly came from Leyden, most of whom certainly did not. If we count the entire eighteen, however, those who started number only fifty-five, and we must then assume a very considerable defection in April, if we are to predicate the original number who voted to emigrate at more than sixty-five or seventy, or believe the total Congregation at that time was over one hundred and fifty, all of these figures of course including children. We also know that the number of people of the Leyden Congregation who eventually reached Plymouth was eighty-two. Surely a first party of thirty-five and a subsequent migration of forty-seven is a very small figure for a Congregation of several hundred. If we assume that five hundred were members from 1609–1620 and that only one hundred and fifty were actually members in 1620, the personnel of the Congregation must have changed with a rapidity and to an extent which the Pilgrim accounts do not suggest.

2. It seems probable from Bradford that the first idea was that the whole Congregation should go; that they might all embark upon one ship and might finance the venture themselves without recourse to capitalists. The first charter they attempted to procure assumed that they would finance their own venture, which seems to have been urged in their favor to the Virginia Company. But is this not totally inconsistent with a Congregation of three hundred let us say, in 1620,

which would surely not be an unfair figure if the total membership for ten years was five hundred? Is it probable again that the first computation contemplated taking between two hundred and three hundred people without assistance from capitalists and that they eventually with very considerable assistance were able to provide for no more than thirty-five from Leyden and one hundred and two in all?

3. We know also from Bradford and Winslow that the Congregation failed to grow in Leyden as they felt it should. Now all calculations based upon adequate growth are dependent upon some definite knowledge of the number who first reached Leyden. This we lack. But a reasonable presumption can be raised that not more than one hundred to one hundred and twenty-five came, because a larger number would be inconsistent with the sort of flight from England they attempted. The movement of a more considerable number of people on boats down the river or walking over land would have attracted attention a good deal quicker than it did. If, then, about one hundred came and the total membership within ten years reached five hundred, and the probable residuum in 1620 was perhaps not less than two hundred and fifty or three hundred, it would seem that either their expectations of growth were unreasonable or our calculation is somewhere in error. To have doubled the actual number in ten years would seem satisfactory for a people in exile. On the other hand, if about one hundred and twenty people had come and the actual Congregation in 1620 was between one hundred and fifty and two hundred, their complaint of the failure of people to resort to them would have more foundation. It is a positive fact that they felt the growth of the Congregation highly unsatisfactory and with it somehow or other our estimate of the Congregation's number must agree.

4. We also know that at Leyden the whole Congregation met throughout its history in one house, which they bought in 1610. If they then estimated that so large a house was required and had during the next decade at least five times as many members at one time or another, is it not surprising that a larger meeting place was not required? We know also something about the house. The lot, as measured by Dexter, after inspection of the old plans, measured twenty-five feet wide on the street by one hundred and twenty-five feet deep. Behind this lot was another very much larger lot on which was eventually built twenty-one small houses. In Dr. Dexter's opinion only about half of the first lot was occupied by the "great house," which could not therefore have been larger than about twenty-five feet by seventy-five. If now we suppose that the entire house down-stairs was thrown into one room, we shall not get in more than three hundred people, and we can only conceivably get in between four hundred and fifty and five hundred if we assume that they sat upon benches and stools as close to one another as possible. From what we know, however, of Dutch domestic architecture, it seems not likely that the house was so constructed that the whole lower story could be made into a single room, without thoroughly re-building the house. So far as we know, this was not done. The presumption is that the size of the Congregation at any one time was not very much greater than the first Congregation that arrived, and that the fifty or seventy-five additional members at any one time easily found room in the same house.

5. We also get a distinct idea from the various accounts that Robinson's Congregation was not as large at any time as that of the other English Churches in Holland. While we have no very definite figures about them, the various estimates do not run to five hundred for any of them and the

Ancient Church, which seems to have been the largest, was estimated by Bradford himself as possessing "at some times" three hundred members, *i. e.*, was usually less.

6. It seemed interesting to attempt a computation, based upon Dr. Dexter's list, which should estimate the positive and probable numbers with somewhat less rigidity than his first account published in the *Mass. Hist. Soc. Proc.* and with somewhat more rigidity than his second computation, which seems rather too inclusive.

The lists which follow contain the results.

The following members seem to be certain beyond a reasonable doubt: 37 men, 48 women, 67 children, total, 152.

The following seem probable beyond a reasonable doubt: 24 men, 24 women, 24 children; 72 in all.

Combining the two lists we have: 61 men, 72 women, 91 children, total, 224.

We have to be sure counted in these figures minor children and wives who died during the decade, but the adult men, sixty-one in all, were pretty certainly alive in 1620, and, if we assume about sixty women were also alive, we shall have one hundred and twenty-one as the adult Congregation. The proportion of children is interesting and remarkable. A reasonable allowance for lack of evidence now would seem to make two hundred the probable outside figure of the actual Congregation in 1620, and perhaps three hundred and fifty as the total probable membership during the ten years.

ROBINSON'S LEYDEN CONGREGATION

Membership positively demonstrated

Allerton, Isaac, wife, five children, one grandchild.
Bassett, William, three wives.
Blossom, Thomas, wife, three children.
Bradford, William, wife, one child.
Brewer, Thomas, two wives, eight children.
Brewster, William, wife, six children, son's wife, and grandchild.
Butler, Mary.
Carver, John, wife, two children.
Crackstone, John, (widower?) two children.
Cushman, Robert, two wives, three children.
Cuthbertson, Cuthbert, two wives, one child.
Fletcher, Moses, two wives.
Fuller, Samuel, three wives, one child.
Goodman, John, two wives.
Jenkins, ———,
Jenny, John, wife, one child.
Jepson, William, wife, three children.
Lee, Bridget, sister of Samuel.
Lee, Josephine, mother of Samuel.
Lee, Samuel, three wives, one child.
Morton, George, wife, four children.
Morton, Thomas, brother of George, and one child.
Nash, Thomas, two wives.
Neal, Elizabeth, from Scrooby, married William Buckram.
Peck, Ann, ward of William Brewster.
Pickering, Edward, and wife.
Pontus, William, wife and child.
Priest, Degory, wife, and two children.
Ring, William, and wife.

Robinson, John, wife, and nine children.
Rogers, Thomas, one child.
Southworth, Edward, wife, two children.
Southworth, Thomas, brother of Edward.
Thickins, Randall, wife, one child.
Tinker, Thomas, wife and child.
Tracy, Stephen, wife and child.
Turner, John, and two children.
White, William, wife, (Susanna Fuller), three children.
Williams, Thomas.
Wilson, Roger, and wife.
Winslow, Edward, and wife.
Wood, Henry, and wife.

Membership probably demonstrated

Buckram, William.
Butterfield, Stephen, wife, and child.
Carpenter, Alexander, (two children elsewhere counted).
Carpenter, Priscilla.
Ellis, John, two wives, one child.
Ellis, Christopher, wife, three children.
England, Thomas, (English of the *Mayflower?*)
Fairfield, Daniel, wife, three children.
Gray, Abraham.
Jennings, John, two wives, three children, son's wife.
Jepson, Henry, wife.
Jessop, Edmond, two wives, one child.
Jessop, Francis.
Keble, John, wife, four children.
Lisle, William, (children elsewhere counted).
Masterson, Richard, and wife.
Pettinger, Dorothy.

Peck, Robert, two wives, two children.
Reynolds, John, and wife.
Simmons, Roger, and wife.
Smith, Thomas.
Terry, Samuel, and wife.
White, Nicholas.
Wilkins, Roger, two wives, one child.
Willett, Thomas, wife and five children.
Wilson, Henry, and wife.

INDEX

Abbot, George, Archbishop of Canterbury, 54, 55

Administration, character of at Plymouth, 169, 202–219, 260–264; 275–277

Ainsworth, Henry, leader of Separatist congregation at Amsterdam, 33, 34, 42, 43, 185

Alden, John, 69, 88, 92, 108, 126, 153, 172, 181, 205, 241, 242, 257, 282, 283

Allerton, Isaac, 36, 68, 69, 88, 90, 92, 108, 152, 191, 212, 230–234, 241

Ames, A., notice of his *Log of the Mayflower*, 50, 56, 58

Amsterdam, Pilgrims at, 32–33

Andros régime at Plymouth, 256, 275–277

Anne, the ship, 94, 97, 105, 106, 107, 145, 146

Arber, Edward, notice of his *Pilgrim Fathers*, 50, 56

Assistants, functions of, 212, 215, 221, 223, 260–261, 275

Bancroft, Richard, Archbishop of Canterbury, 20, 24–26.

Billington, John, 68, 92, 131, 279

Bishops, hatred of Pilgrims for, 3–4, 22–24, 47, 186, 189; attitude of toward the Pilgrims, 1, 18–26; attitude of Pilgrims toward, 184–185; fears of interference from in America, 47–48, 51–54, 66, 72

Blackwell, Francis, 54–55, 57, 64

Boston, Mass., 92, 171, 174, 259, 264, 265, 287, 288

Bradford, William, in England, 12–13, 18; part in emigration to Holland, 28–30; personal history at Leyden, 36, 41; argument in favor of emigration to America, 146; his share in the exodus, 68, 69, 71, 77, 78; first months in America, 80, 81, 83, 86, 88; elected governor, 90, 91, 92; functions as governor, 203–216; patent to, 142, 153, 155, 156; activities of at Plymouth, 120, 130–137, 146, 147, 166, 167, 169, 174, 181, 193, 198, 199, 205, 228, 241, 242, 256; estimate of, 91, 108, 193, 203–206; mentioned or quoted *passim*.

Bradford, William, *History of Plymouth Plantation*, notes on, 14, 16, 33; quoted *passim*.

Brewster, Jonathan, son of Elder Brewster, 10, 36, 283

Brewster, William, father of Elder Brewster, 7, 8

Brewster, William, Elder of Pilgrim Church, early life in England, 7–12, 17–27, 108; exodus to Holland, 28–30; life as a printer at Leyden, 36–38; chosen Elder, 40; share in preparations for emigration to America, 50–52, 56, 58, 61, 68, 69; religious ideas of, 189–190, 193–194; at Plymouth, 81, 86, 87, 88, 92, 131, 153, 169, 172, 181, 191, 205, 231, 241, 247, 256, 267

305

Printed in the United States of America